M000204034

Preaching Hebrews

Preaching Hebrews

The End of Religion and Faithfulness to the End

DOUGLAS D. WEBSTER

CASCADE *Books* · Eugene, Oregon

PREACHING HEBREWS
The End of Religion and Faithfulness to the End

Copyright © 2017 Douglas D. Webster. All rights reserved. Except for brief quotations in critical publications or reviews, no part of this book may be reproduced in any manner without prior written permission from the publisher. Write: Permissions, Wipf and Stock Publishers, 199 W. 8th Ave., Suite 3, Eugene, OR 97401.

Cascade Books
An Imprint of Wipf and Stock Publishers
199 W. 8th Ave., Suite 3
Eugene, OR 97401

www.wipfandstock.com

PAPERBACK ISBN: 978-1-5326-0806-3
HARDCOVER ISBN: 978-1-5326-0808-7
EBOOK ISBN: 978-1-5326-0807-0

Cataloguing-in-Publication data:

Names: Webster, Douglas D.

Title: Preaching Hebrews : the end of religion and faithfulness to the end / Douglas D. Webster.

Description: Eugene, OR: Cascade Books, 2017 | Includes bibliographical references.

Identifiers: ISBN 978-1-5326-0806-3 (paperback) | ISBN 978-1-5326-0808-7 (hardcover) | ISBN 978-1-5326-0807-0 (ebook)

Subjects: LCSH: Bible/N.T./Hebrews Commentaries. | Preaching. | Title.

Classification: BS2775 .W35 2017 (print) | BS2775 (ebook)

Manufactured in the U.S.A.   AUGUST 23, 2017

In memory of a good friend and a resilient saint,

Dan Deaton

Contents

Acknowledgments

I am grateful to editor Rodney Clapp for his wisdom and skill in guiding this work to publication. Stimulating interaction with students at Beeson Divinity School and in the Beeson Lay Academy gave shape to the pastoral and preaching impact of Hebrews. Jim Meals and Mike Denham offered valuable insight and encouragement along the way. I am especially thankful for Virginia, who has been my chief advisor and soulmate for more than forty years.

A Preaching Challenge

"Cause my mind to fear whether my heart means what I say."

MARTIN KÄHLER'S PULPIT PRAYER[1]

BEFORE HEBREWS WAS A letter it was a sermon. The early church grasped this well-crafted sixty-minute sermon in a single worship service. Believers, probably living in Rome, understood then what we recognize today. Hebrews is unique. It has been described as "the most extensively developed and logically sustained piece of theological argumentation in the whole of the New Testament."[2] Hebrews is a powerful proclamation of the gospel. The finality of Christ's revelation, the efficacy of his atoning sacrifice, and the everlasting encouragement of his faithfulness energizes the sermon's spiraling intensity of exposition and exhortation.

Hebrews weans us away from our preoccupation with the start of the Christian life and focuses our attention on the perseverance of faith. Life is not a sprint; it's a marathon. Faithfulness to the end affirms faith from the beginning. "Today we emphasize the New Birth," writes Peter Gillquist, "the ancients emphasized being faithful to the end. We moderns talk of wholeness and purposeful living; they spoke of the glories of

---

1. Quoted in Thielicke, *The Trouble with the Church*, 14.
2. Hughes, *Hebrews*, 35.

the eternal kingdom . . . the emphasis in our attention has shifted from the completing of the Christian life to the beginning of it."[3]

Hebrews is a *tour de force* for the person and work of Christ and a manifesto against respectable, self-justifying religious habits. The sermon counters those who seek, under the guise of tradition, to smuggle back into Christianity the ceremonies and practices that stand fulfilled in Christ. Religion is transcended by the finished work of Christ. There is no hiding behind ancient traditions and cherished rituals. The invisible truths of the gospel take on an altogether new visibility. Hebrews calls for the end of all religion—the very best religion—even as it calls for a living faith and faithfulness to the end. If we let the Word of God have its way with us, Hebrews will deepen our faith in Christ and strengthen our faithfulness.

Overcoming a Bias

On the subject of Hebrews some scholars open their commentaries with the intellectual equivalent of a cold shower. Hebrews is cast as an "enigma" that "poses more problems than any other New Testament book."[4] The work has "baffled" commentators through the centuries.[5] If you like puzzles, one writer claims, you will like Hebrews.[6] Another commentator warned that those who study this "strange and fascinating" epistle will quickly find "themselves lost in its serpentine passages and elaborate theological arguments."[7] To explore Hebrews is to trek "through beautiful but imposing theological and homiletical terrain."[8] The great Reformer Martin Luther had some high praise for Hebrews but he also called it "a disorderly mixture of wood and stubble, gold and silver, not representing apostolic levels of thought."[9] Another biblical scholar warned that if you "descend into the murky cave of Hebrews," be ready to experience the frustrating secrets of authorship, destination, date, and audience.[10]

3. Gillquist, "A Marathon We Are Meant to Win," 22.

4. G. Guthrie, *Hebrews*, 15.

5. Ibid., 27.

6. Lane, *Hebrews 1–8*, xlvii.

7. Long, *Hebrews*, 1.

8. G. Guthrie, *Hebrews*, 386.

9. Evans Jr., *Hebrews*, 30.

10. Ibid., 1.

But what if the problem is not Hebrews, but our bias against the unfamiliar terrain of this powerful sermon? "We live in a 'googlized' world," warns Missiologist Timothy Tennent, "which is inundated with information, but most of it trivial. We live in a day which resists serious, long-term, reflection. We live in a time when Coptic Christians are being beheaded and the next morning's headlines are still about the Kardashi-ans. The trivialization of information, the reductionism of all things sa-cred, and the shockingly short attention span, all confront you as bearers of the sacred gospel in the 21st century."[11]

Hebrews challenges our retreat from the Word of God. Sadly, we have acquired over time and with remarkable ingenuity a calculated incapacity to think and communicate about anything other than the shallow level of small talk, sound-bite snippets, and instant messaging. "Our capacity for reflection and understanding has retracted, as our ability to sort through the data has expanded," asserts Nicholas Carr. "I'm not thinking the way I used to think. . . . The deep reading that used to come naturally has become a struggle."[12] The impact of retreating from the word, scanning over reading, cobbling together a customized worldview, and preferring images over words, has not only changed the way we communicate, but the way we think.

Preaching Hebrews is our opportunity "to go forth and inhabit a robust, muscular, deeply rooted apostolic gospel."[13] Our aim is to inter-pret and preach Hebrews with such confidence and clarity that people's common misperceptions about the Bible are proven wrong. We may be conditioned to think that "the Bible is an opaque book whose truths are hidden in an endless maze of difficult words, unfamiliar history, unpro-nounceable names, and impenetrable mysticism."[14] For some readers Hebrews is exhibit A. To the unsuspecting believer Hebrews can come across as a bewildering array of Old Testament references, heroes, ritu-als, and traditions, all jumbled up together. This is where the challenge comes in. "The best preachers . . . guide in such a way that their listen-ers discover that the labyrinth is a myth. There are no dark passageways through twisted mazes of logic. . . . Only a well-worn path that anyone can follow if a preacher sheds some ordinary light along the way."[15]

11. Tennent, "I Came, I Saw, I Loved."
12. Carr, "Is Google Making Us Stupid?"
13. Tennent, "I Came, I Saw, I Loved."
14. Chapell, *Christ-Centered Preaching*, 103.
15. Ibid., 103.

What some find baffling about Hebrews was designed by its author to be compelling. When we find ourselves in the Spirit, mentally and spiritually alert, with ears to hear, Hebrews becomes a powerful meditation on the gospel. The flow of reasoned argument for Christ and against religion, along with the pulsating emotional intensity of ultimate issues laid bare, and the heartfelt warnings against complacency and unbelief, strike a responsive chord in us. We "feel" the message as much as we "think" it. The extraordinary well-crafted use of the Old Testament is heard more like a well-played symphony than a lecture. The momentum of the sermon is impressive. The running comparison between Christ and angels, Christ and Moses, Christ and Joshua, Christ and Abraham, Christ and the Old Testament sacrificial system, continues to build to a climax. The thrust of the message is straightforward: Christ is the final word, superior to everyone and everything. He is the better way, the better covenant, the better sacrifice, and the better word. Hebrews is an ancient model of good preaching and a modern guide to preaching today. Harold Attridge calls Hebrews "a masterpiece of early Christian homiletics, weaving creative scriptural exegesis with effective exhortation."[16] The pastor is a "masterful homilist," a preacher whose "handling of structure, choice of vocabulary, wordplay, illustrative materials, and application strategies can teach us much about the importance of form and focus in making sermon content clear, forceful, and engaging."[17]

A Passion for the Truth

> "The witness borne to Christ by Hebrews is still clearer, stronger, better than that of all the commentaries written about or against it taken together." MARKUS BARTH[18]

The challenge begins when we delve into the biblical text. Read the entire text in one sitting. Read and reread, and then keep on reading. Country singer Johnny Cash reportedly said, "I read the Bible to understand the commentaries." That's good advice. Over several days read the text through again and again. Imagine yourself in a first-century household of faith hearing it for the first time. If you have studied Greek in seminary, open up your Greek New Testament and study the text along with your

16. Quoted in Cole, *The God Who Became Human*, 104.

17. Massey, *Preaching from Hebrews*, 105–6.

18. M. Barth, "The Old Testament in Hebrews," 78.

English version. If you know another language, like Spanish or Chinese or Russian, read it in your second language. If you are monolingual, like me, don't despair. Embrace your mother tongue. Meditate on Hebrews. Mull it over in your mind. Memorize it. Pray out the meaning of the text. Read it more for formation than information—read it for both. Take special note of the weave between exposition and exhortation.

Pastor Eugene Peterson reminds us that "exegesis is not in the first place a specialist activity of scholars." Yes, we need the help of scholars, but exegesis is mainly about paying attention, "simply noticing and responding adequately (which is not simple!) to the demand that words make on us."[19] Peterson continues: "Too many Bible readers assume that exegesis is what you do after you have learned Greek and Hebrew. That's simply not true. Exegesis is nothing more than a careful and loving reading of the text in our mother tongue. Greek and Hebrew are worth learning, but if you haven't had the privilege, settle for English. Once we learn to love this text and bring a disciplined intelligence to it, we won't be far behind the very best Greek and Hebrew scholars. Appreciate the learned Scripture scholars, but don't be intimidated by them."[20]

The exegete is on a quest for the truth. When Agatha Christie's fictional detective Hecule Poirot, played by David Suchet, was asked if he was an artist, he said, "No, no, my friend, I'm not an artist. I have known crimes that were artistic, supreme exercises of the imagination. But the solving of them, no, not the artist, the creative power is not what is needed. What is required is a passion for the truth."[21] Explanation and understanding are not as elusive as they are made out to be. Through the careful work of meditating on the text, asking basic questions, and hearing the text, we can grasp the biblical message. Bryan Chapell reminds us, "Excellent preaching makes people confident that biblical truth lies within their reach, not beyond their grasp."[22]

You may not be surprised to learn that many pastors don't keep up with Greek and Hebrew. But what is surprising is how many pastors give up on reading altogether. They claim to be too busy with the day-to-day business of the church to read much of anything, let alone commentaries and theology. One pastor explained that he quit reading commentaries years ago. He judged them too dull and boring for his busy pastorate.

19. Peterson, *Eat This Book*, 51.
20. Ibid., 55.
21. From the PBS series, *The Hollows*.
22. Chapell, *Christ-Centered Preaching*, 110.

Whenever he was in search of new sermon ideas he visited the self-help section of his local Barnes and Noble.

Meanwhile, pastors in developing nations are desperate for good resources. We are blessed in our Western culture with an abundance of excellent commentaries. Pastors in resource-deprived regions see these helpful works advertised on the Internet, but they do not have the money or the means to acquire them. As the Internet improves, hopefully many of these biblical resources will become available online. Ironically, what we have in abundance and sadly take for granted, third-world pastors long for. They would love to get their hands on our commentaries to strengthen their preaching, yet these are the commentaries that are arranged neatly on our bookshelves that go unread.

If we are inclined to write commentaries off as dull and boring, it might be wise for us to reconsider. Commentaries help us poke around in the text. They challenge our preconceived notions and our easy familiarity with the text. If we expect to preach Hebrews faithfully and accurately we need to read through a few good commentaries. F. F. Bruce's commentary on Hebrews is excellent. Gareth Cockerill has spent more than thirty years studying Hebrews from every conceivable angle. It seems wise for pastors to avail themselves of his hard work. Peter O'Brien's commentary is helpful, along with works by Raymond Brown, N. T. Wright, and Thomas Schreiner. George Guthrie's commentary is particularly accessible and insightful. These commentaries represent various levels scholarship and pastoral concerns from technical to popular. We have a wealth of resources to choose from. A careful study of these commentaries will answer basic questions, stimulate fresh insights, and lead us deeper into the text.

Instead of using commentaries the way we use a dictionary or an encyclopedia, it would be beneficial to read commentaries cover to cover. "I recommend reading commentaries in the same way we read novels, from beginning to end, skipping nothing," writes Eugene Peterson. "They are, admittedly weak in plot and character development, but their devout attention to words and syntax is sufficient. Plot and character—the plot of salvation, the character of the Messiah—are everywhere implicit in a commentary and persistently assert their presence even when unmentioned through scores, even hundreds of pages."[23] Before we feel at home in the biblical text, a fair amount of reading, prayer, study, and reflection is required. Coming to terms with a biblical text is a long, slow process

23. Peterson, *Eat This Book*, 54.

that requires patience and perseverance. We also want to pay attention to what the biblical text is saying to our culture. Simply explaining what the Bible says does not proclaim the impact of God's Word for Christians today. We have to find ways to bridge the Word of God and contemporary culture.

The Apostle Paul compared preaching to manual labor. "Admonishing and teaching everyone with all wisdom" meant hard work (Col 1:28–29). The apostle chose to describe this work in blue-collar terms as manual labor. He compared it to exhausting physical work, commonly associated with farming and construction. But good preachers always make preaching look easier that it actually is. What is hidden is all the hard work and prayer. The listener benefits from the fruit of the skilled preacher's labor without being constantly reminded of the effort behind the finished message. Preachers are like musicians in this regard. We don't listen to hours upon hours of practice time. Much of the preacher's work is unseen by the congregation and that's how it should be. Our sermon is not meant to impress people with our hard work, but with how wonderful the gospel is.

Preachers can be like Dr. Cuticle in Herman Melville's novel *White Jacket*. A sailor fell ill with sharp abdominal pain. Dr. Cuticle, the ship's surgeon, diagnosed an acute appendicitis attack. With assistance from the crew, Dr. Cuticle performed an emergency appendectomy on the poor sailor. Not accustomed to very many surgical opportunities, Dr. Cuticle took his time extracting the diseased organ. He was careful to make precise incisions and point out interesting anatomical details to the sailors assisting him. At first the sailors were amazed at the doctor's skill and knowledge, but their awe quickly turned to dismay. Dr. Cuticle was so lost in his work and absorbed in the fine art of surgery that he failed to notice that his patient had died—and none of the sailors had the nerve to tell him!

My father was a mathematician, but his avocation was woodworking. His tools and workbench were in the basement of our home. When he was running his power saw or turning wood on a lathe, he produced a lot of sawdust, but he made sure that the sawdust never made it upstairs. Only his finely finished hutch or hand-crafted desk made it upstairs. Good preachers make a point of not tracking their exegetical sawdust into the sanctuary. Their hard work remains hidden and their finished work speaks for itself.

Sermon preparation is a community effort. The idea that the pastor prepares a sermon in secret and springs it on an unsuspecting congregation is a prescription for failure. The idea that the solitary pastor emerges from his study with an authoritative word from the Lord may sound more spiritual than it really is. The truth of God's word belongs to the body of Christ and is shared, nurtured, proclaimed, preached, mentored, modeled, and discussed in the matrix of the household of faith. The church has been entrusted with the authoritative word of God. Reading good commentaries factors into this dialogue, but so also does discussing Hebrews with brothers and sisters in Christ. I can't imagine preaching without gaining the perspective of "many advisors" (Prov 15:22), including men and women, older people (like myself), college students, and young people. Often when there are multiple Sunday morning services I will go for coffee between services with one or two people who were in the early service to discuss the sermon. We need conversational partners that will stimulate our thinking, inform our perspectives, deepen our discernment, correct our grammar, hold us accountable, and pray for us.

The Textual Weave

Text is an old Latin word with roots in the textile industry. It comes from the root word *tex-ere,* to weave. *Texture* literally means the process or art of weaving. The idea of weaving a garment and weaving a sermon are linked linguistically. There is a connection between weaving strands of yarn together and weaving a message out of verbs, nouns, prepositions, and adjectives. The word *text* in today's vernacular is associated with text messaging, the speedy transmission of binary information over the Internet. This new form of communication replaces the slow art of weaving a sermon. The relational power of speech and story is reduced to sound bites. Communication is more often than not a matter making of a connection rather than experiencing communion. A technician parses the text down into its component parts. A textuary discovers the meaning of the text. Textuaries eat and digest the Word of God so that it metabolizes in them. Instead of sitting in judgment on the text, textuaries enter into the message of salvation.

Hebrews is a tight weave of Old Testament testimonies and New Testament truths. The author of Hebrews preaches Christ from the Old Testament in order to make resilient New Testament disciples. His message is empowered by a spiraling intensity of *exposition* and *exhortation*.

The sermons within the sermon are propelled forward by exhortations that climax one sermon and catapult the hearer into the next sermon. The so-called warning passages are not parenthetical or a break in the action. Instead of interrupting the expository flow these exhortations focus the author's post-Emmaus interpretation of the Old Testament and bring the message home. They climax one sermon and introduce the next. One reason we find Hebrews difficult to preach is because the weave of the text is so tight, the truths so well integrated, and the transitions so carefully crafted, that it is difficult to know how to rightly divide up Hebrews into "preach-able portions." There are many sermons in Hebrews, but we must remember that in all probability it was originally preached as one tight-knit sermon. The momentum of the message is constantly building a case for resilient saints who are faithful to the end of their lives or to Christ's second coming.

Every truth is applied pastorally in the context of the worshiping Body of Christ. The individual is always perceived to be a body-and-soul-in-community. The hearers are never consumers, passive recipients of information or entertainment. Throughout Hebrews believers are the people of God and pastoral application never focuses on the lone individual. Preachers who want to focus on culturally induced felt needs have to ignore the text and do their own eisegesis. The following verses indicate that we are being addressed along with our brothers and sisters in Christ:

"We must pay the most careful attention . . ." (2:1);

"Therefore, holy brothers and sisters, who share in the heavenly calling, fix your thoughts on Jesus . . ." (3:1);

"Let us hold firmly to the faith we profess . . ." (4:14);

"Let us then approach God's throne of grace with confidence . . ." (4:16);

"Therefore let us move beyond the elementary teachings about Christ and be taken forward to maturity . . ." (6:1);

"Let us draw near to God with a sincere heart . . ." (10:22);

"Let us hold unswervingly to the hope we profess . . ." (10:23);

"Let us consider how we may spur one another on toward love and good deeds . . ." (10:24);

"Let us run with perseverance the race marked out for us . . ." (12:1);

"Keep on loving one another as brothers and sisters" (13:1).

The author's exegesis of the Old Testament weaves the various themes of the sermon together. "No NT book, with perhaps the exception of Revelation, presents a discourse so permeated, so crafted, both at the macro- and micro-levels, by the various uses to which the older covenant texts are part . . . ." George Guthrie counts "roughly thirty-seven quotations, forty allusions, nineteen cases where Old Testament material is summarized, and thirteen where an Old Testament name or topic is referred to without reference to a specific context."[24] The author of Hebrews understands the rich tapestry of the Old Testament. He depends heavily on the Psalms, the Pentateuch, and the Prophets, especially Isaiah, followed by Jeremiah, Habakkuk, and Haggai. He also makes use of Proverbs and 2 Samuel.[25] Like the careful theologian that he is, the preacher uses each quote and allusion in a way that is true to the larger biblical context and overarching history of God's people. Instead of isolating texts, pulling them out of context, and proof-texting, the author poetically integrates each line of Scripture within the matrix of meaning provided by a serious and comprehensive understanding of the Old Testament. Hebrews is an excellent example of biblical theology.[26] Guthrie writes, "More than any other New Testament book, Hebrews, from beginning to end, preaches the Old Testament."[27] Graham Cole concludes, "The Old Testament testimonies and the fact of the Christ's coming are creatively brought together in a way that no Old Testament writer appears to have imagined."[28]

The expository momentum of the sermon uses the Old Testament like a fast-paced sixty-minute movie trailer. The preacher does not intend his hearers to stop and camp out on an Old Testament quote or allusion. The power of Hebrews is found in its persistent and pervasive call for perseverance. To hinder that thrust by dwelling on a single quote from Exodus or an allusion to Leviticus would miss the mark. Hebrews is not a sermonic invitation for the preacher to go back and review Leviticus chapter by chapter for a month of Sundays. Whoever uses Hebrews to belabor Old Testament details does not understand its true nature and

24. G. Guthrie, *Hebrews*, 919.

25. Ibid., 921.

26. Rosner, "Biblical Theology," 10: "Biblical theology may be defined as theological interpretation of Scripture in and for the church. It proceeds with historical and literary sensitivity and seeks to analyze and synthesize the Bible's teaching about God and his relations with the world on its own terms, maintaining sight of the Bible's overarching narrative and Christocentric focus."

27. G. Guthrie, *Hebrews*, 923.

28. Cole, *The God Who Became Human*, 104.

purpose. We should keep in mind what the preacher said about the furniture of the tabernacle, "But we cannot discuss these things in detail
now" (Heb 9:5).

The gospel according to Hebrews is woven from the narrative of
God's people. Gentiles as well as Jews hear the gospel out of this Old
Testament revelation. Every history, myth, and ideology; every religion,
philosophy, and existential quest, is renegotiated out of the revelatory impact of the Old Testament. Sadly, we cling to our cherished histories and
ethnic heroes. For proud Mongolians it is the triumphs of Genghis Khan;
for African Americans it is Martin Luther King, Jr. and the civil rights
movement; for middle-class Americans it may be Ronald Reagan or Steve
Jobs; for many Asians it may be Confucius or Alibaba co-founder Jack
Ma; for American teens it may be Taylor Swift or the Kardashians. We
live with competing narratives that must be renegotiated in the light of
the better story—the gospel. We are attached to the stories and heroes
that inspire and energize our sense of self, our ethnic pride and our nationalistic identities, but all of these are eclipsed by the one story that
fundamentally changes everything. "God's redemptive history is of one
piece. For the connections between promise and fulfillment, between
type and antitype, and the continuity of themes in the Bible are possible
only because of God's covenant faithfulness in redemptive history. In
other words, a single, God-guided, redemptive history is the basis, the
foundation, of the unity of the Old and New Testaments."[29]

The Pastor

The familiar background questions, the who-when-where-and-to-whom
questions, remain unanswered when it comes to Hebrews. The upside
of the mystery is that the message of Hebrews is simply thrust upon us.
We embrace this first-century sermon and preach it today the way it was
preached to the early church. The sermon's internal evidence shapes our
understanding of the preacher, the congregation, and the purpose of the
message.[30]

29. Greidanus, *Preaching Christ from the Old Testament*, 48.

30. Jobes, *Letters to the Church*, 53. "This elegant piece of Greek rhetorical prose
from the first century comes to us with many unanswered questions about its author,
about the original audience, and about the events that surrounded its writing. As interesting as these questions may be, the lack of certain answers does not impede an
understanding of the book's timeless message. As Scripture, it was meant to be read by
people in all places and ages."

We don't know who the author was. Most agree that the Apostle Paul was not the author due to the remarkably different literary and linguistic style of Hebrews. Possible authors include Apollos, Barnabas, Luke, Silas, Aquila, and Priscilla; maybe even someone we have never heard of. But we do know that "another remarkable mind and heart besides Paul's was at work in interpreting the significance of the crucified and raised Messiah Jesus . . . ."[31] We know that he was "a creative theologian who adopted traditional Christian teaching to the urgent issues facing his community."[32]

What began as a sermon and became a letter yields ample evidence that the author was trained in rhetoric, well-versed in philosophy, and saturated in the Old Testament Scriptures.[33] This makes Apollos our most likely author for this beautifully crafted sermon that was designed to be heard. Its literary features, alliteration, chiasm, inclusions, transitions, dramatic momentum, and symmetrical arrangements, point to a gifted poet-pastor. Nevertheless Hebrews does not fit "the template of the classical Hellenistic structure."[34] It is a blend of Old Testament prophetic insight, linguistic skill, christological passion, and pastoral concern. One of the notable Puritan preachers, Edward Deering, wrote, "Who wrote this Epistle, I cannot tell, nor do I see a reason to seek it. For when the Spirit of God has left it out, can I think it better if I should add it?" God knows the author's name, Deering concluded, and "we will leave him as we find him, a faithful witness of Jesus Christ."[35]

Nor do we know the date for Hebrews. It may have been early or late in the first century. But we know that its timing was critical. The letter conveys a palpable sense of urgency. From beginning to end this exhortation expresses deep concern that the believing community is vulnerable to drifting away. Professing Christians are tempted to ignore a great salvation (2:1–3). The author warns his brothers and sisters of the dangers of "a sinful, unbelieving heart that turns away from the living God" (3:12). He laments that some have given up trying to understand the truth (5:11). The author's concern was intense, even passionate, but always inclusive of the author himself. The preacher's repeated use of the

31. Johnson, *Hebrews*, 9.

32. O'Brien, *Hebrews*, 8.

33. Ibid., 8.

34. Ibid., 26.

35. Deering, "The Reflections of Edward Deering on Hebrews," First Lecture, 4.

first person plural intentionally placed himself under the admonition of his pastoral charge. "If we deliberately keep on sinning after we have received the knowledge of truth, no sacrifice for sins is left, but only a fearful expectation of judgment and of raging fire that will consume the enemies of God" (10:27).

Various recipients have been proposed for Hebrews, including Jewish Christians, Gentile Christians, a group of former priests, and even disciples from Qumran. A narrow profile of Hebrew's original hearers is eclipsed by the universal recognition and timely impact of Hebrews throughout the church. The congregation that received this message faced the rising pluralism of the Mediterranean world. There were plenty of religious, political, and social pressures that threatened to sabotage their commitment to Christ and their faithfulness to the end.

Some interpreters have argued that the recipients can be divided into three types: sincere believers who were secure in their salvation, nominal believers who lacked true commitment, and a third group who were openly non-Christian. Expositor John MacArthur believes that the expository flow of the sermon is directed to genuine believers who are in danger of losing confidence and clinging to their old religious habits. The strongly worded warning passages that challenge apostasy are directed to the second group of nominal Christians who have not yet made a true commitment to Christ. Finally, the judgment passages are directed against the third group, unbelievers, who are neither intellectually convinced that Jesus is the Messiah nor inclined to make any personal commitment.

Dividing the preacher's hearers into these three definable groups is entirely speculative and driven by the concern that Hebrews could not possibly be exhorting real Christians with the kind of dire warning against apostasy that punctuates his sermon throughout.[36] The simple fact, however, is that the pastor is doing exactly that: boldly addressing the confessing church. There is no internal evidence to suggest otherwise. The message was preached to the whole church. The recipients of this pastoral sermon are in danger of drifting away (2:4), turning against the living God (3:12), rejecting the gospel (6:4), growing weary (12:3), and giving up because of persecution (12:4).

36. John MacArthur in his Hebrews sermon series (http://www.gty.org/resources/sermons/scripture/hebrews) warns that the reader who does not recognize and identify which particular type of person is being addressed in any given text will face "monstrous problems."

We don't know the letter's destination. It may have been Rome or Jerusalem. But we know that the message was targeted for real Christians like us, who were in danger of drifting away from the gospel.[37] Hebrews' canonical status as Spirit-inspired Scripture underscores the gospel's impact then as now. Our task is not to make Hebrews relevant. It is already relevant. The pastor who wrote Hebrews drew his ancient readers into the text even as the Holy Spirit draws us into the drama of the gospel message in Hebrews.

In dedicating his commentary John Calvin expressed the hope and humility that all pastors feel as they endeavor to preach Hebrews faithfully: "I do not say that I have succeeded in the exposition which I have undertaken, but I feel confident that when you have read it you will at least approve my fidelity and diligence. As I do not claim the praise of great knowledge or of erudition, so I am not ashamed to profess what has been given to me by the Lord for the purpose of understanding the Scripture (since this is simply to glory in him). If I have any talents for assisting the church of Christ in this direction, I have endeavored to give clear proof for it in this study of mine."[38]

O Splendor of God's Glory Bright[39]

O splendor of God's glory bright, from light eternal bringing light;
Light of Light, light's living spring, true Day, all days illumining:

O Lord, with each returning morn, your image to our hearts is born;
O may we ever clearly view our Savior and our God in you.

AMBROSE OF MILAN, C. 374

---

37. Bruce, *Hebrews*, 268—Bruce observes that on the basis of 12:4 "it is reasonable to conclude that the people addressed in this Sermon had not yet experienced brutal persecution and martyrdom. This would rule out the church of Jerusalem because they had "suffered death in the persecution that broke out immediately after Stephen's execution about AD 33 (Acts 8:1–3; 26:10), as also in AD 43, under Herod Agrippa I, when James the son of Zebedee was beheaded (Acts 12:2), and in AD 62, when James the Just was stoned at the instance of the high priest Annas II."

38. Calvin, *Hebrews*, x.

39. McKim, ed., *The Presbyterian Hymnal*, 474.

2

Overture
(Hebrews 1:1–4)

"All the parts of preaching can be taught: exegesis, language, metaphor, development, delivery. What is hard to teach is how to put them all together, so that what is true is also beautiful, and evocative, and alive."

BARBARA BROWN TAYLOR[1]

THE FIRST FOUR SENTENCES in our English version are just one single well-crafted sentence in the Greek text. This sentence serves as a powerful overture to the entire sermon. A veteran pastor once warned, "Don't flatter the text, preach it." He was concerned that a stream of superlatives might substitute for the hard work of understanding the text. Excessive praise covers up lazy exegesis. But with that said, words like *magnificent, majestic, evocative,* and *eloquent* are often used by scholars to describe the first four verses of Hebrews. This beautifully orchestrated overture to the entire sermon impresses the hearer not only of the pastor's linguistic skill, but more importantly, of the depth of the gospel.

Luther characterized Hebrews as "a strong, forcible, noble epistle, preeminently and emphatically teaching the great article of faith concerning the Godhead, or divinity of Christ."[2] Commenting on the intro-

1. Taylor, *The Preaching Life*, 83.
2. Luther, "Third Christmas Sermon," 167.

duction, Luther wrote, "These words are more easily understood by the heart than explained by tongue or pen. They are themselves clearer than a commentary renders them, and in proportion as they are explained are they obscure."[3] His commendation applies the famous first rule of medicine to preaching: "First, cause no harm."

The truth of Jesus Christ deserves to be communicated with all the thought, skill, passion, and ability that we can summon. Pastors who take after the author of Hebrews care too deeply for the truth of God's revelation to trivialize the text with a hastily thrown together sermon that relies on the personality of the preacher rather than the passion of God's truth. My sense is that the pastor who wrote Hebrews did not take himself half as seriously as he did the revelation of Jesus Christ.

Introductions reveal what we think of our listeners. Our respect for the people to whom we are preaching is reflected in our opening remarks. Are we addressing an audience or a congregation? Do we feel the need to be the light-hearted performer or can we be the thoughtful pastor we want be? Are we under pressure to entertain a restless crowd of consumers or are we prepared to feed a hungry family of faith? Is the introduction part of our act or a continuation of genuine worship?

If we see our hearers as restless consumers, holding a mental stopwatch counting down the first thirty seconds to see whether they are interested in what we have to say, we will cater to their felt needs. But if we see them as the people of God or genuine seekers, we will feed them from the Bible. Good preachers gather people around the Word of God, rather than around their charisma. Instead of crafting amusing anecdotes designed to humanize the speaker, they seek to point people to Christ. They set aside any hint of artificiality or put-on persona and in their own voice and personality invite their congregation of saints and seekers to think deeply about the gospel. They set aside excuses about their busy week or poor health or favorite sports team and they focus on their congregation's desire to be moved by God's Word. Preachers who convey an attitude of "Come, let us reason together, though your sins are as scarlet, they shall be as white as snow" (Isa 1:18) will gain the respect of their congregation. They will come to know that their pastor truly values their time and their ability to think.

---

3. Ibid., 175.

Expository Worship

The introduction to the sermon is not the beginning of the worship service. All that has gone before—the call to worship, the hymns and songs of praise, the prayer of confession and the prayers of the people, the gifts of offerings and anthems—is critical to preaching. Every aspect of the worship sets the tone for the message from God's Word. Expository worship is a corollary of expository preaching, the art of letting the Bible make its own point. True Word-centered doxology expresses and evokes meanings which are at once intellectual, emotional, volitional, and spiritual. Expository worship is tethered to the text and seeks to convey through every aspect of the liturgy the lived meaning of the text.[4]

Richard Baxter, the seventeenth-century Puritan pastor, called for a reverence in preaching that was consistent with the very presence of God. From time to time I reread his perspective on humor in the pulpit as a reminder to shun the frivolous and embrace true meaning: "I hate that preaching which tends to make the hearers laugh, or to move their minds with tickling levity and affect them as stage-plays used to do, instead of affecting them with a holy reverence of the name of God."[5]

Led by gifted musicians and liturgists, prayer and praise create a holy momentum in worship that propels the preacher and prepares the congregation for the preached Word. True worship is a gift to both the congregation and the pastor. The people are prepared to receive the Word of God. The preacher is standing on holy ground. Word and worship energize the congregation. In some ways, the sermon has already been preached in the hymns, in the confession, and in the prayers. Good worship creates a palpable sense of reverence and affection. I experienced this kind of worship at Central Presbyterian Church in New York City. The credit belongs to the Holy Spirit working in and through Seth Ward, who selected and arranged hymns and songs of praise in light of the biblical text, creating a momentum to the worship that was vital and reverential. Expository preaching is best served by expository worship. The household of faith is the place for good preaching. Prayers and praise set the table for biblical proclamation. It is like the family meal at Thanksgiving. The meal is special and the food tastes better because of the table

4. Denham, *Reverberating Word*, 6.

5. Baxter, *The Reformed Pastor*, 149. Baxter has some choice quotes along this line, such as, "You cannot break men's hearts by jesting with them, or telling them a smooth tale, or pronouncing a gaudy oration" (ibid.).

fellowship. Good preaching is never self-consciously contrived for effect. It is not art for art's sake. Stylistic rhetoric invariably calls attention to itself, but Spirit-inspired proclamation lifts up Jesus Christ.

Communicators who stress that preachers only have thirty seconds to grab the attention of their congregation discredit their hearers. They sell the listener short and place on preachers an unreasonable burden. Authentic communication is not a contest that requires a captivating performance. If people turn off a preacher in thirty seconds, it may be because they are tired of hearing trite platitudes and religious jargon. I have heard preachers blame their boring sermons on their biblically illiterate congregation. They claim they can't go "deep" because "their people" can't handle it. But I suspect that in these same congregations there are many earnest believers who long for the whole counsel of God to be preached with passion and depth.

There is a scene from the movie *Air Force One* that captures an aspect of authentic communication. Harrison Ford plays the President of the United States delivering a speech at a state dinner at the Kremlin. His speech writers have carefully crafted his political speech on the topic of terrorism. Their intention is for the President to say something diplomatic without say anything significant or controversial. But it becomes immediately apparent to the dismay of his advisors that the President has put their prepared speech aside and is speaking without notes. Instead of the typical political rhetoric, the entire assembly can sense that the President is owning his own words and saying what he believes. Congregations can tell the difference between preachers who have a message from the Lord to deliver and preachers who are giving a cliché sermon.

Like the DNA code of a living cell, the Hebrews' overture contains the themes for the entire sermon. The pastor will go on to develop at length how God's revelation in the past "through the prophets at many times and in various ways" is fulfilled in the Son of God. He will preach the Psalms and tell the story of Moses and Joshua and the Israelites in the wilderness. He will explore the significance of Abraham, Melchizedek, Aaron's priesthood, and the new covenant. He will draw out the significance of the Tabernacle, the priestly order, and the sacrificial system. He will do all of this to underscore the finality and fulfillment of Jesus Christ, the mediator of the new covenant, who "was sacrificed once to take away the sins of many" (9:28).

Hebrews begins boldly, but without bravado. "Preaching that lacks authority leaves a congregation longing for the divine voice," writes Bryan

Chapell. "Lives sickened by sin, seduced by evil, and crushed by tragedy, desire no 'uncertain sound.' Still, we need to understand that real authority resides in the truth of the Word rather than in our tone or delivery. We need to distinguish carefully between preaching with authority and merely sounding authoritarian."[6]

I remember the night that John Stott preached to our southern California congregation as being very special. His gifted exposition of Scripture was so clear and compelling that he could have preached through an entire biblical book that night as far as I was concerned. His straightforward manner focused on the text without regard for himself. He finished by applying the text in a way that was both practical and pastoral. I thought the understated beauty of his powerful biblical exposition was evident to all. But I was mistaken. Not everyone was impressed. One angry young man came to me after the service and complained. "Who does this old man think he is? He acts like he is the sole authority on the truth. He acts like a know-it-all." What I had received as genuine biblical authority the young man had equated with authoritarianism. I explained that the sermon we had just heard was a testimony to John Stott's humility before God. His task was not to voice his own opinions and feelings, nor was it his job to entertain us with anecdotes and human interest stories. John Stott's responsibility was to preach the Word of God. He was submissive to the truth as stated in the Bible and he proclaimed it with compassion and conviction.

From the start, Hebrews plunges its hearers into truth too deep for humanistic consumption. The ocean of God's truth can be overwhelming apart from the grace of God. But ocean depth has always characterized God's Spirit-filled pastors and theologians. Whether or not one of the named apostles actually wrote Hebrews, we know the church came to agree that it was conceived, written, and delivered under apostolic authority. The nameless author making no claim to genius hides behind the authority of Christ and the inspiration of the Spirit.

The nineteenth-century Danish Christian thinker Søren Kierkegaard made an important distinction in his memorable essay, "On the Difference Between a Genius and an Apostle." Kierkegaard complained that many of the preachers in his day were "affected." Their intensity was artificial. "It is bad enough," Kierkegaard wrote, "the way they talk in a sugary voice and roll their R's like foreigners, and wrinkle their brow and

6. Chapell, *Christ-Centered Preaching*, 94.

use violent gestures and ridiculous poses. But even more pernicious is that their whole way of thinking is affected. Preachers have become like foolish parents who have to beg, plead, and promise to get their children to obey them."[7]

Kierkegaard believed that the power of the Word of God was not enhanced, but obscured, by the eloquence or brilliance of a genius. He maintained a qualitative difference between a genius and an apostle. A genius is respected for his brilliance, the command of his intellect, the inventiveness of his mind, and his quick assimilation of facts. A genius is an innovator whose abilities are clearly superior to others'. Apostolic authority, on the other hand, resides not in human abilities but in the call of God. We do not listen to the author of Hebrews because he was clever or eloquent, but because he was wise — wise with the wisdom of God. We respond to the sermon because it is true.

The purpose of the sermon "is to declare, to disclose, to reveal something."[8] The language of the marketplace aims to make a sale. Political language is after your vote. Religious language invokes a sense of obligation and moral effort. But biblical language is largely in the indicative mood. It tends to be straightforward, declarative, and forthright. "Thus saith the Lord" anticipates surrender and obedience. There is power in biblical affirmations.[9]

The eloquence found in Hebrews flows naturally from the wisdom of God. The overture sets the decisive and authoritative tone for the entire sermon. Whatever skill and style the pastor uses to communicate is dictated by the message he is led to deliver by the Holy Spirit. Augustine held that the sacred writers communicated with a kind of eloquence suitable to those "who justly claim the highest authority, and who are evidently inspired by God."[10] To what extent the author of Hebrews was constrained by the rules of classical rhetoric, we cannot say, but we can say that the message is anchored in divine wisdom and conveyed with confident authority. To borrow a line from Augustine, Hebrews can be described as "wisdom not aiming at eloquence, yet eloquence not shrinking from wisdom."[11]

7. Kierkegaard, *The Present Age, and Of the Difference Between a Genius and an Apostle*, 103.

8. Stott, *Between Two Worlds*, 57.

9. Ibid.

10. Augustine, "On Christian Doctrine," 577.

11. Ibid., 581.

This is the eloquence that emphatically denies all forms of artificiality, manipulation, and deception, yet artfully embraces every literary skill or linguistic technique or theological angle that commends the truth. Those who have a truly high view of Christ will also have a high view of his people. Pastors who look up to Christ, look up to their congregations. Instead of talking down to the people, they will respect them enough to work hard on the content and delivery of their sermons. People are quick to realize the difference between those who are committed to inhabiting the biblical text afresh, "and those bent on just dispatching it with efficiency and technical skill."[12]

Vision over Visibility

The opening sentence of Hebrews provokes a crisis of authority. This bold beginning stands out all the more in the late modern culture of unbelief. The preacher confronts doubt with a confident, worshipful confession of faith. His declarative tone and forthright manner show little sympathy for skepticism. He begins calmly but emphatically for the truth, without apology and without regard for the hearer's internal spiritual struggle or crisis of faith. Doubt is not so much ignored or explained away as vanquished. The sermon is an unabashed proclamation of the gospel.

When the first sentence of Hebrews is read aloud in Greek it literally pops out. Five words are alliterated with a "p" sound, beginning with *polymerōs* ("in many parts") and *polytropōs* ("in many ways"), followed by *palay* ("of old"), *patér* (patriarchs), and *prophétes* (prophets). The rhetorical effect gives "aural cohesion" to the opening line, causing the listener to pay attention.[13] The flow of the sentence goes like this: "At various times and in various ways, in the past, God spoke in and through the patriarchs and the prophets, but at the end of these days he has spoken to us by one who is Son."

By design the climax of the opening sentence is reached in the Son. The absence of the definite article before "Son" does not suggest that Jesus is one son among many, but "emphasizes the exalted status of the final messenger and may be rendered 'one who is Son.'"[14] This is not one son

---

12. Gardiner, *Bach*, 10. I have transposed Gardiner's insight from music to preaching.

13. Cockerill, *Hebrews*, 89; O'Brien, *Hebrews*, 49.

14. O'Brien, *Hebrews*, 50.

among many sons, but the one and only one who relates to the Father as Son. There were many prophets but only one Son.

Hebrews is more interested in proclaiming the gospel boldly than in appealing to culture apologetically. Hebrews begins with God, not culture. The preacher confronts us with the supernatural drama of the gospel. Hebrews delivers a bold declaration that God has spoken definitely in Christ.[15]

Hebrews runs against the grain of our late modern culture. It is not addressed to people "who might be feeling a little lost," or "who just want to be part of something bigger than themselves." Hebrews challenges the notion that what I think of myself is more important than what God thinks of me. The sermon ranks my felt need for affirmation below my deep need for salvation. Theology trumps therapy. The temporal surrenders to the eternal; the soul transcends the self. Pastor Eugene Peterson writes: "We set out to risk our lives in a venture of faith. We committed ourselves to a life of holiness. At some point we realized the immensity of God and of the great invisibles that socket into our arms and legs, into bread and wine, into our brains and our tools, into mountains and rivers, giving them meaning, destiny, value, joy, beauty, salvation. We responded to a call to convey these realities in Word and sacrament."[16]

Writer David Brooks is insightful and irenic. He began his 2015 Commencement Address at Dartmouth by cutting out, as he said, "the usual garbage advice" of commencement speakers, like "Listen to your inner voice. Be true to yourself. Follow your passion. Your future is

---

15. The progression from patriarchs and prophets to the Son leads us to Jesus' parable of the vineyard and the tenants. He describes the landowner sending his servants to collect the fruit, but each time the servants are sent the tenants reject them. "Last of all, he sent his son to them. 'They will respect my son,' he said" (Matt 21:37). The positive progression from servants to Son is reflected in this opening line. In the past, the revelation of God was piecemeal and partial, but now in these final days—these last days—God has spoken definitively in the Son. The revelation fulfills all that has gone before. The Son's revelation is final, not fragmentary; complete, not partial; and decisive, not diverse. To deny the revelatory authority of the Son is to reason like the wicked tenants. They recognized the son's identity, but refused to accept him. "This is the heir," they said. "Come, let's kill him and take his inheritance." What they did next was tragically consistent with their fallen human nature. They killed the son. Against all logic and good sense they sought the son's inheritance without the son. What were they thinking? Jesus asked, "Therefore, when the owner of the vineyard comes, what will he do to those tenants?" His listeners replied, "He will bring those wretches to a wretched end."

16. Peterson, "Lashed to the mast," 56.

limitless. Don't be afraid to fail." Entitling his address, "The Ultimate Spoiler Alert," Brooks gave the graduates a picture of their life to come. He talked about the long hard search for a job. He promised that their twenties would be one of the happiest phases of life, but that there would be long periods of loneliness and heartbreak. Through trial and error, Brooks encouraged, you'll discover your true loves and you'll come up with your own criteria for success.

"By the time you hit your thirties, you will realize that your primary mission in life is to be really good at making commitments. Making a commitment," Brooks says, "simply means falling in love with something and then building a structure of behavior around it that will carry you through when your love falters." He outlined four key commitments: to your spouse and family; to your career and vocation; to your faith or philosophy; to your community and village.

Real love operates on two levels, "the level of gritty reality and the level of transcendent magic." Love takes you out of yourself. It casts off cost-benefit analysis. Love demands that you enter into a different and inverse logic. It is self-sacrificing; it is self-denying for the sake of the other. Love defies normal utilitarian logic. Love calls for moral logic. You have to conquer your desire to get what you crave. You have to make commitments. "Adulthood is about closing around commitments. Dartmouth has opened your mind. The purpose of an open mind is to close around certain beliefs. The highest joy is found in sending down roots." Brooks hoped the grads would eventually look back over the totality of their lives and experience a sense of gratitude for a life filled with joy, "a joy beyond anything they could possibly have earned."[17]

Brooks's commencement address is beautiful, filled with uncommon common grace. He is winsome and witty, a gracious, hopeful advocate for the moral order. He is all for taming the self-centered, selfish self, and he is all for living into lifelong commitments. But I can't shake the nagging thought that sensible types like David Brooks pose the greatest threat to the Christian faith. Hostile atheists and jihadist terrorists don't undermine the gospel nearly as much as the preeminently reasonable "almost Christians," who dismiss the beliefs and doctrines of the Christian faith as weird. Listening to Brooks makes you feel he's got the totality of life covered.

17. Brooks, "The Ultimate Spoiler Alert."

T. S. Eliot observed in the 1930s: "The World is trying the experiment of attempting to form a civilized but non-Christian mentality. The experiment will fail; but we must be very patient in awaiting its collapse; meanwhile redeeming the time: so that the Faith may be preserved alive through the dark ages before us; to renew and rebuild civilization, and save the World from suicide."[18]

Brooks believes in everything reasonable, everything that is, but the stuff our culture calls weird. He avoids all the absurdities, like the virgin birth, the incarnation, the atoning sacrifice of Christ on the cross, the bodily resurrection and the ascension. Life minus God's one and only Son. The Son who is "appointed heir of all things, and through whom he made the universe."

Brooks never identifies the source for his uncommon common grace. His wisdom is like a beautiful state-of-the-art hospital that has no need of doctors or surgeons. Everyone who comes to the hospital comes only to visit. There are no patients. No one needs healing. No one needs surgery. This is wisdom without sin and salvation; without God in Christ reconciling the world unto himself. This is the wisdom of transparency over repentance, self-acceptance over forgiveness, and affirmation over atonement. This is wisdom without the love of the Father, the grace of the Son, and the fellowship of the Holy Spirit.

This is the sensible, modern wisdom that caused the Danish Christian thinker Søren Kierkegaard to identify the great invisibles as absurd: "Christianity has declared itself to be the eternal essential truth which has come into being in time. . . . It has required of the individual the inwardness of faith in relation to that which is an offense to the Jews and folly to the Greeks—and an absurdity to understanding."[19] This is why the world thinks Christians are weird, and who can blame them? Of course the world thinks the followers of the Son of God are strange. The gospel of Christ speaks of truths the world finds utterly inexplicable.

God Has Spoken

God is there and he is not silent. God has spoken "through the prophets at many times and in various ways . . . ." God is the ultimate polyglot, speaking all the languages, all 7,000 of them, plus the more than 500

18. Quoted in Webster, *Paradise in The Waste Land*, 11.
19. Bretall, ed., *A Kierkegaard Anthology*, 222.

extinct languages. God is not limited to phonology, but deploys every conceivable language to communicate. The "voices" of molecular biology, mathematics, and music, to name only three, *declare*, in their own special way, "the glory of God." As the psalmist says, "Day after day they pour forth speech; night after night they display knowledge." C. S. Lewis warned us not to mistake the medium for the message. Like an infatuated lover, who has fallen in love with the feeling of love rather than with the true object of his devotion, we are in danger of falling in love with molecules or math or music or markets and missing the message! "The books or the music in which we thought the beauty was located will betray us if we trust in them; it was not *in* them, it only came *through* them, and what came through them was longing. . . . For they are not the thing itself; they are only the scent of a flower we have not found, the echo of a tune we have not heard, news from a country we have not yet visited."[20]

God has spoken "at many times and in various ways, but in these last days he has spoken to us by his Son." The well-known proverb, "Where there is no vision the people perish," is often confused with capital campaigns to build bigger buildings. But its true biblical meaning in a good translation is clear enough: "Where there is no revelation, people cast off restraint" (Prov 29:18).

Divine revelation is the determinative factor for human destiny, whether personal or global, whether ancient or modern. God has spoken and is speaking and this makes all the difference in the world. God breaks in with his compelling, convicting truth and we yield. We may be like C. S. Lewis on the night of his conversion, the most dejected convert in all of England. We may be like Saul on the road to Damascus blinded by the light. Or, our conversion may be strikingly ordinary, like the one U2 sang about in "Moment of Surrender": "I was punching in the numbers at the ATM machine / I could see in the reflection / A face staring back at me / At the moment of surrender / Of vision over visibility / I did not notice the passers-by / And they didn't notice me."

God has spoken. This is what Christians believe. Our culture is fixated on the physical as the antidote for what ails us spiritually. Late modernity believes in a material world, a world that is all about the visual, visceral, tangible, and tactile—the literal, physical world. This is the world of sex, statistics, cells, microbes, salaries, stocks, sports, apps, markets, workouts, and weapons. Visibility conquers vision in the late

20. Lewis, *The Weight of Glory*, 7.

modern mind. "We have quite literally flipped our priorities, and now privilege the temporal over the transcendent."[21]

SoulCycle is a fitness chain that has developed a cult-like following among young affluent urban professionals. Julie Creswell of the *New York Times* writes, "Early on a summer morning in Manhattan's Upper East Side, dozens of mostly young svelte women file into a candle-lit studio where they mount gleaming stationary bikes. . . . This is SoulCycle. A sort of spinning, self-help therapy session with dim lighting and primal dance beat." As one investor said, "SoulCycle and its brand have tapped into the notion of exercise as food for your mind as well as your body. What's happening in those cycling classes involves spirituality, psychotherapy and some self-help."[22] The temporal trumps the transcendent. Visibility over vision. Spirituality is what we make it out to be. Brené Brown, best-selling author and professor of social work, defines spirituality as "a deeply held belief that we are inextricably connected to one another by something bigger than us, and something that is grounded in love. Some people call that God, and some people call that fishing."[23]

Pastor Mark Buchanan paints a portrait of an idyllic wedding on the Sunshine Coast of British Columbia. He describes the setting, a rustic Anglican chapel built into the cliff, the scent of wild flowers and cedar pews filling the air, a perfect sanctuary for worship, ideal for hosting the simple elegance and the quiet dignity of the bride and groom. "The service had a beautiful simplicity to it," Mark wrote, "like something hand-carved." The reception was held on a promontory overlooking the harbor. Sailboats were off in the distance. A gentle breeze caressed the guests gathered on the lawn. "Laughter. The ping of crystal. The smell of Cajun shrimp frying over hickory coals. The couple, Edenic in their joy, moving among us, speaking and receiving benediction. The day was perfect."

"In the midst of this," Mark describes a conversation he had with a young philosophy student. He asked Mark if he really believed "all that religious stuff" that Mark "had spouted back at the church." Mark said he did. The young man smirked. Mark asked him what he believed: "I tried your religion for a while," he said, "and I found it's just a burden to carry. You know what I figured out? Life justifies living. Life is its own reward and explanation. I don't need some pie-in-the-sky mirage to keep

21. Jeremiah Webster, personal correspondence, August 2015.
22. Creswell, "Investors Hope to Ride Swell of SoulCycle Fever in Coming I.P.O."
23. Brown, "8 Questions," 88.

me going. This life has enough pleasure and mystery and adventure in it not to need anything else to account for it. Life justifies living."

"Good," Mark replied. "Very good. And I believe you. Today, here, now—feel the warmth of that breeze, listen to the laughter of those people, smell the spiciness of that shrimp cooking, look at the blueness of the sky—yes, today I believe you. What a superb philosophy. Life justifies living! Bravo!"[24] Then Mark went on to describe two friends that he had on his mind, one dying hard from AIDS, the other in his mid-forties distraught over his children and his health. Mark's point was simple: life is not idyllic, it's broken. "Life does not justify living. Eternity does."[25]

Visible perfection lasts only for the moment and it's gone. Hebrews reveals a vision of Christ that lasts forever. Vision over visibility is the key. We live by faith, not sight, but faith is the earnest expectation of sight. The temporal tangible, tactile world of ours is authored by the one true and living God in whose image we are made. The myth of the autonomous individual self spreads the lie. We are neither known nor loved. The myth contends that we are cosmic orphans adrift in a meaningless universe without identity and security.

Vision over visibility calls the question. Are we the holy possession of God in Christ, personally chosen by God, predestined for communion with God, adopted into the community of God's people, recipients of God's grace, redeemed by his personal sacrifice on our behalf, and signed, sealed, and delivered by the promised Holy Spirit, or are we the accidental product of an impersonal universe, subject to blind chance and random forces, existing in a sphere of energy devoid of promise, plan, purpose, and fulfillment?

"How can you cope with the end of the world and the beginning of another one?" asks N. T. Wright. "How can you put an earthquake into a test-tube, or the sea into a bottle? How can you live with the terrifying thought that the hurricane has become human, that fire has become flesh, that life itself came to life and walked in our midst? . . . Christianity either means that, or it means nothing," declares Wright. "It is either the most devastating disclosure of the deepest reality in the world, or it's a sham, a nonsense, a bit of deceitful play-acting."[26]

24. Buchanan, *Things Unseen*, 59–61.

25. Ibid., 62.

26. Wright, *For All God's Worth*, 1.

Many sincere people say they believe in God but do they believe in the God who has spoken, the God who has spoken by his Son? It appears that many people are trying to live in a no-man's land, halfway between a real relationship with God in Christ and surviving as a cosmic accident. They can't bring themselves to say there is no God but they can't bring themselves to accept the God who has spoken by his Son, "whom he appointed heir of all things, and through whom also he made the universe. The Son who is the radiance of God's glory and exact representation of his being, sustaining all things by his powerful word."

The sixteenth-century Swiss Reformer of Zürich, Ulrich Zwingli, preached on the clarity and certainty of the Word of God in 1522. His sermon begins with God's out loud self-deliberation in Genesis, "let us make mankind in our image" (Gen 1:26). Zwingli proceeds to argue that we were created with the innate ability and the intellectual capacity to receive and resonate with the Word of God. The "universal desire for eternal blessedness" is everywhere because it is "native to us."[27] He admits that this desire for salvation does not belong to our sinful self with all of its perverted desires, but it does belong to our true nature—who we are made in God's image.

Zwingli recounts the many ways that God has spoken. God told Noah to build an ark, Abraham to sacrifice his son, Moses to lead his people out of Israel. They received God's clear and certain word and acted upon it. Looking back, we marvel that Noah and Abraham and Moses took God at his word. They did not allow themselves to be "deflected" by "acute questioning and extremity."[28] They believed God had spoken, even though God spoke into a vast vacuum of pagan thought. The patriarchs had little to go on, as did the prophets, but they believed. The salvation story line persisted. Then there is God's shocking word to Mary, delivered out of the blue with only the faintest prophetic hints: "You will conceive and give birth to a Son, and you are to call him Jesus. He will be great and will be called the Son of the Most High" (Luke 1:31–33). Surely it was more difficult for Mary to believe that God had spoken than it is for us to believe in the Word made flesh. In the past, God spoke through the patriarchs and the prophets. He declared his revelation in precepts and pronouncements, commands, and statutes. God painted his revelation in poetry and parable, metaphor and symbol, figures and types. But now,

27. Zwingli, " Clarity and Certainty of the Word of God," 62.

28. Ibid., 76.

at long last, he has spoken to us in person through his Son. "God makes his voice heard and his identity and person known, through the two-testament voice of Christian Scripture."[29]

If they believed the Word of God, why can't we? Zwingli contended that it was not a matter of human interpreters and human persuasion. "Even if you hear the gospel of Jesus Christ from an apostle, you cannot act upon it unless the heavenly Father teaches and draws you by the Spirit. The words are clear; enlightenment, instruction, and assurance are by divine teaching without any intervention on the part of that which is human."[30] Zwingli placed his confidence in Jesus' reliance upon the Father: "No one can come to me unless the Father who sent me draws them . . . ." (John 6:44). The disciples confirmed that faith did not rest on human teachers, but on the Lord Jesus: "Lord, to whom shall we go? You have the words of eternal life. We have come to believe and to know that you are the Holy One of God" (John 6:68-69).

One Truth / Seven Assertions

Seven assertions declare the beauty and power of the Son's messianic identity. Each assertion invites deeper biblical study and theological understanding, but the author of Hebrews intended his hearers to take in the totality of this seven-fold description as it was spoken out loud. Perhaps, the best way to preach this text is not to dissect its finer points, cross reference its phrases, and exhaust the text linguistically. We are better off meditating on this sentence (1:1-4), committing it to memory, and declaring it with passion. The final, climactic revelation of God has come. ". . . But in these last days he has spoken to us by his Son . . ."

> whom he established as heir of all things,
>
> through whom he also made the worlds,
>
> who being the radiance of his glory and the exact representation of his very being,
>
> and bearing all by the word of his power,
>
> having made purification for sins,
>
> sat down at the right hand of the Majesty on high,
>
> becoming as much superior to the angels as the name he has inherited is superior to theirs.

29. Seitz, *The Character of Christian Scripture*, 190.
30. Zwingli, "Clarity and Certainty of the Word of God," 80.

These colorful poetic phrases arch like a rainbow over the Son. Who he is and what he has done are inextricably bound together; his essential being is one with the achievement of his becoming. Each biographical assertion opens up the Son's resume that encompasses everything from the creation of the world to the exclusive means of redemption. The penetrating light of this description shines on the full spectrum of human concerns, including politics, science, art, history, and philosophy. The pastor does not stop here and elaborate on the specifics of this illumination. His purpose is to establish the vision over visibility for the sake of the visible, created world.

These seven assertions stand in bold contrast to the prevailing affirmations of the narcissistic age. The Son's radiant glory outshines the collage of bright images and the competing glories of money, sex, power. His word creates a large salvation shaped universe that dwarfs the modern self's small, small world of self-realization and self-discovery. His sacrifice for our sins redeems us and frees us from our futile coping strategies. The Son sits at the right hand of the Majesty in heaven eclipsing the self's quest for success.

These opening lines in Hebrews critique any form of spirituality or religion that depends on anything other than Christ. Faith in self or faith in religion is a dead end. Faith is not about inspiration or will power or optimism. Faith is the God-empowered grasp of the objective reality of the Son, the heir of all things, the creator of the world, the radiance of God's glory, the exact representation of his being, who after he had provided purification for sins, sat down at the right hand of the Majesty in heaven. Faith is the earnest expectation of sight. In Christ and his church, vision takes on visibility. The Word was made flesh and dwelt among us (John 1:14). He became our "merciful and faithful high priest in service to God" so that "he might make atonement for the sins of the people" (Heb 2:17). He was appointed "to offer gifts and sacrifices for sins" on our behalf (Heb 5:1). He sacrificed for our sins "once for all when he offered himself" (7:27), "and by his wounds we are healed" (Isa 53:5).

Of the Father's Love Begotten[31]

Of the Father's love begotten, ere the worlds began to be,
He is Alpha and Omega; he the source, the ending he,
Of the things that are, that have been, and that future years shall see,
Evermore and evermore!

This is he whom seers in old time chanted of with one accord,
Whom the voices of the prophets promised in their faithful word.
Now he shines, the long-expected. Let creation praise its Lord,
Evermore and evermore!

O ye heights of heav'n adore him. Angel hosts, his praises sing.
Pow'rs, dominions, bow before him, and extol our God and King.
Let no tongue on earth be silent; every voice in concert ring,
Evermore and evermore!

Christ, to thee with God the Father, and, O Holy Ghost, to thee,
Hymn and chant and high thanksgiving and unwearied praises be.
Honor, glory, and dominion, and eternal victory, Evermore and evermore!

AURELIUS CLEMENS PRUDENTIUS, fifth century
(trans. John Mason Neale and Henry Williams Baker)

31. McKim, ed., *The Presbyterian Hymnal*, 309.

3

The Radiance of God's Glory
(Hebrews 1:3–4)

"Immortal, invisible, God only wise,
In light in accessible hid from our eyes.
Most blessed, most glorious, the Ancient of Days,
Almighty, victorious Thy great name we praise."

WALTER CHALMERS SMITH[1]

FAITH IN ONE'S OWN faith journey is the dominant theme of modern spirituality. The "modern believer" conceives of faith as free of any "intellectualized understanding." It is "mutable and messy," it does not rest on "any fixed, mental product."[2] The "modern believer" alleges that Christ is at the point of our unknowing, when life makes no sense and is filled with pain. In one sense, the pastor of Hebrews agrees. Christ is indeed there in our suffering, but not as the "modern believer" conceives him, as "a failure of both words and intellect." On the contrary the pastor proclaims Christ, the revelation of God.[3]

1. Smith, "Immortal, Invisible, God Only Wise," 33.
2. Wiman, *My Bright Abyss*, 18.
3. Ibid., 43.

Hebrews and the Modern Faith Journey

"Modern spiritual consciousness is predicated upon the fact that God is gone," writes poet Christian Wiman, "and spiritual experience, for many of us, amounts mostly to an essential, deeply felt and necessary, but ultimately inchoate and transitory feeling of oneness or unity with existence. It is mystical and valuable, but distant." Wiman reasons that this distance is overcome by Christ who is anything but vague. He is "a shard of glass in your gut. Christ is God crying *I am here*, and here not only in what exalts and completes and uplifts you, but here in what appalls, offends, and degrades you . . . ."[4] Christ is present in the midst of everyday life and at the poignant point of pain and tragedy, but to know him, Wiman insists, "is to 'know' absolutely nothing."

Wiman calls himself an "atheist Christian," because it is better to "lay claim to the God that you believe in rather than forever drawing a line at the doctrine you don't."[5] Wiman wants Christ but not his atoning sacrifices. "I don't know what it means to say that Christ 'died for my sins' (who wants that? who invented that perverse calculus?), but I do understand—or intuit, rather—the notion of God not above or beyond or immune to human suffering, but in the very midst of it, intimately with us in our sorrow, our sense of abandonment, our hellish astonishment at finding ourselves utterly alone, utterly helpless."[6] Beyond that intuition, according to Wiman, there is nothing but godtalk.

Hebrews rejects godtalk as well, but the winsome skeptic's disdain for empty religious jargon meets in Hebrews the power of God's personal revelation. This revelation is alive and active and penetrating to the core. Write off the language of systematic theology as "mulishly orthodox" if you must, but listen to the language of Hebrews before you claim that there is a disconnect between language and life.[7] If you are tempted to "do a little linguistic dance around Christianity," it's time to grapple with the fact that God "has spoken to us by his Son," and this is not godtalk—this is revelation.[8] God has spoken.

4. Ibid.,
5. Ibid., 123.
6. Ibid., 134.
7. Ibid., 26, 142.
8. Ibid., 142.

Theological Vision

Churches are encouraged to develop a theological vision: "a faithful restatement of the gospel with rich implications for life, ministry, and mission in a type of culture at a moment in history."[9] Hebrews offers a powerful theological vision to the twenty-first–century church. Its inspired, precedent-setting originality models how we can think and act faithfully. Its canonical status means that its impact is not limited to the first-century Jewish/Gentile cultures. Hebrews proclaims the gospel in a way that penetrates and transforms the values, commitments, and longings that are fundamental to the human condition. Even in a culture that prefers to talk about extraterrestrial beings rather than angels, Hebrews projects a powerful theological vision. All cultures wrestle with the spiritual and religious issues that Hebrews addresses in-depth.

The primary purpose of Hebrews remains today what it was from the beginning: to remove the religious fog that threatens to rob the gospel of its meaning and significance. The singular argument of Hebrews is that religion, even the very best divinely designed religion, is inadequate to save and satisfy the human soul. Only what Christ has done for us and in us is sufficient to save, redeem, and sanctify. Hebrews is a powerful weapon against religiosity and Christless Christianity.

"The Son is the radiance of God's glory . . . ." The word "radiance" (*apaugasma*) points to the poet in our preacher. It is the only time the word is used in the New Testament. Those who struggle to find the right word to communicate gospel truth are in the company of this faithful pastor. In a word, "radiance" covers the full range of God's glory from our comprehension to the limits of our imagination. Creedal confession gives way to doxology and doxology is rooted in creedal confession. The pastor's theological reflection on the Son's glory calls for worship. "Just as the radiance of the sun reaches this earth, so in Christ the glorious light of God shines into the hearts of men and women."[10] "We believe that the sun is in the sky at midday in summer not because we can clearly see the sun (in fact, we cannot) but because we can see everything else."[11] The word triggers New Testament descriptions of the splendor and intense brightness of the incarnate One, such as John's description in his prologue, "The Word became flesh and made his dwelling among us. We

9. Keller, *Center Church*, 19.

10. Bruce, *Hebrews*, 48.

11. Lewis, *Miracles*, 114.

have seen his glory, the glory of the one and only Son, who came from the Father, full of grace and truth" (John 1:14). Little by little, Jesus "revealed his glory" (John 2:11), as if we needed the truth to dazzle gradually. Emily Dickinson's poem captures this sense: "Tell all the Truth but tell it slant— / Success in Circuit lies / Too bright for our infirm Delight / The Truth's superb surprise / As Lightening to the Children eased / With explanation kind / The Truth must dazzle gradually / Or every man be blind."[12]

There is only one time during Jesus' earthly ministry that his appearance is described in any other way than ordinary. At the transfiguration, when "Jesus was transfigured before them," two phrases describe the metamorphosis: "His face shone like the sun, and his clothes became as white as the light." At his birth, the angelic host appeared to the shepherds and the glory of the Lord shone around them, but the normal looking Christ child was laid in an unadorned manger. At his resurrection, the angel of the Lord blazed like lightning, his clothes shimmered snow-white, but the risen Jesus was mistaken for an ordinary gardener. In the Gospels, virtually nothing is said about the outward appearance of Jesus. The transfiguration was a rare instance when the glory of the incarnate One broke through *visibly*. Just this once, what Jesus was *within* is made visible *without*. The transfiguration reveals Jesus "inside out." John alludes to this experience when he speaks of "the true light that gives light to everyone was coming into the world." Years later the Apostle Peter described the transfiguration this way: "For we did not follow cleverly devised stories when we told you about the coming of our Lord Jesus Christ in power, but we were eyewitnesses of his majesty. For he received honor and glory from God the Father when the voice came to him from the Majestic Glory, saying, 'This is my Son, whom I love; with him I am well pleased.' We ourselves heard this voice that came from heaven when we were with him on the sacred mountain" (2 Pet 1:16–18).

Light is a popular metaphor for meaning, even in a world that has given up on a kind of meaning that is universal and lasting. In their book, *All Things Shining*, UC Berkeley professor Hubert Dreyfus and Harvard philosopher Sean Kelly claim that there are no universal truths—no sacred revelation. They admit we may very well be cosmic orphans. Humanity's choice, they claim, is between the moods that inspire meaning or the abyss of nihilistic despair. Dreyfus and Kelly challenge moderns to rediscover Homer and the Greek gods as a solution to the human feeling of

12. Dickinson, *Complete Poems*, 507.

lostness. Salvation is found in life's "truly extraordinary moments," when "something overwhelming occurs. It wells up and carries you along as on a powerful wave." This sacred shining moment may be an overwhelming sexual experience, a great moment in contemporary sport, the Thanksgiving family meal, the birth of a baby, or being accepted at your number one school. For Dreyfus and Kelly true bliss can come from watching a great athlete perform on the sacred grass of Wimbledon, revealing a fully embodied, worldly kind of sacred.[13] All things shining describes the euphoria that comes over you in that moment of exultation, when you sense that you are participating in something that transcends you.[14]

This form of spirituality is popular among those who strive to live between despair and doxology. The raw belief that there is nothing besides chance and fate in this vast unknowing universe is too nihilistic for daily living, but to believe that God has spoken definitively in his Son is too fantastic to accept. Consequently, late modern spirituality finds comfort in an intellectual fog and in vague notions about life. C. S. Lewis observed: "Speak about beauty, truth and goodness, or about a God who is simply the indwelling principle of these three, speak about a great spiritual force pervading all things, a common mind of which we are all parts, a pool of generalized spirituality to which we can all flow, and you will command friendly interest. But the temperature drops as soon as you mention a God who has purposes and performs particular actions, who does one thing and not another, a concrete, choosing, commanding, prohibiting God with a determinate character. People become embarrassed or angry. Such a conception seems primitive and crude and even irreverent."[15]

Missiologist Timothy Tennent writes, "When you walk into a vibrant church, you can immediately sense the difference. At every point, you meet gospel clarity. The church exudes confidence in the unique work of Jesus Christ. They understand the power and authority of God's Word. They feel the lostness of the world and the urgency to bring the

---

13. Dreyfus and Kelly, *All Things Shining*, 197.

14. Lewis, *Miracles*, 160. Lewis writes, "We feel quite sure that the first step beyond the world of our present experience must lead either nowhere at all or else into the blinding abyss of undifferentiated spirituality, the unconditioned, the absolute. That is why many believe in God who cannot believe in angels and an angelic world. That is why many believe in immortality who cannot believe in the resurrection of the body. That is why Pantheism is more popular than Christianity" (ibid.).

15. Ibid., 83–84.

good news to everyone. At every point, you observe gospel clarity. . . . The clarity is palatable. It is infectious. You can actually sense the presence of Christ in your midst. . . . In contrast, when you walk into the churches in decline you are immediately brought into 'the Fog.' What is the fog? It is the inability to be clear about anything. There is no clarity about who Jesus Christ is and what He has done. There is no clarity about the Scriptures as the authoritative Word of God. There is no clarity about the urgency to reach the lost. . . . In the 'fog,' Jesus Christ is just one of many noble teachers in the world."[16]

This may be why we try to form our image of Christ around our subjective experiences and according to our imagination rather than on the basis of God's revelation. In lieu of biblical revelation belief is a matter of skeptical probability or spiritual intensity. In the modern imagination there is little correspondence between "believing" and "beholding." We are tempted to substitute a vague notion of "our" custom-made Jesus in place of the "Word made flesh." The late modern "believer" is comfortable saying, "To every age Christ dies anew and is resurrected within the imagination of man."[17] The preacher sees Christ differently: "Jesus Christ is the same yesterday and today and forever" (Heb 13:8).

Hebrews begins by declaring that true spirituality is not found in vague, undefined feelings that stir the self. True spirituality is not to be confused with soul-inspiring music or incredible sports plays or altruistic acts of human kindness. These are all wonderful, but true spirituality is found in the revelation of God. The influential nineteenth-century German theologian, Friedrich Schleiermacher, found in the Christmas story a source of inspiration for maternal love and the triumph of human nature. Schleiermacher believed Christmas evoked strong sentiments of joy and wonder, which elevated humanity. He contended that whether or not Christ's birth actually took place was no longer at the heart of the story. What mattered was "speechless joy over the unspeakable object." For Schleiermacher "church music could dispense, not with singing, but with definite words." Christmas was about a "living feeling," not a life-giving faith in Christ, leading Karl Barth to write, "Words stand opposed to all which Schleiermacher understands as the genuine miracle of Christmas. Words are hostile to it, detrimental, always powerless to justify it. The man who undertakes to celebrate in words his own 'elevated

16. Tennent, "Gospel Clarity vs. 'The Fog.'"

17. Wiman, *My Bright Abyss*, 11.

humanity' becomes all too easily confusing and incredible to himself." Schleiermacher wanted the feeling without the faith. "All patterns are too stiff for me and all speech too tedious and cold." Schleiermacher longed to be inspired but not with the truth of the Son who is the radiance of God's glory. He wrote, "How fortunate that when we are disturbed and oppressed by the problem of words we can flee to the realm of music, to Christian music and a musical Christianity! Exactly because of its lack of concepts, music is the true and legitimate bearer of the message of Christmas, the adequate expression of the highest and final dialectical level, a level attainable by singing, by playing on flute and piano."[18]

If creation and redemption are only myths and there is no will of God to submit to and no loving God to depend on, we might as well conclude that everything is meaningless and the only thing worth worrying about is our lonely selves. Christians believe otherwise. The incarnation is the grand miracle of the Christian faith. God himself materialized in flesh and blood. "The Word became flesh and lived for a while among us. We have seen his glory, the glory of the one and only Son, who came from the Father, full of grace and truth" (John 1:14). Hebrews is not about a glorious abstraction, a general symbol for celebrating life, but the living Lord Jesus, Immanuel, God with us, the One to be worshiped as the Way, the Truth, and the Life.

Bach's music was inspired by the "Son who is the radiance of God's glory," not ephemeral feelings arising from his music. This is why Bach wrote in the margin of his copy of Abraham Calov's Bible commentary on 2 Chronicles 5:13: "Where there is devotional music, God with his grace is always present." For Bach spirituality revolved around the personal revelation of God rather than in his feelings or in his creative imagination. Worship was not sentiment nor was transcendence self-generated. Yet moderns who appreciate the music of Bach want to transfer the source of inspiration away from the God who has made himself known to the music itself. Conductor John Eliot Gardiner comments on Bach's marginal note, "This strikes me as a tenet that many of us as musicians automatically hold and aspire to whenever we meet to play music, regardless of whatever 'God' we happen to believe in."[19]

18. Schleiermacher, "Celebration of Christmas," quoted in Barth, *Theology and Church*, 157.

19. Gardiner, *Bach*, 17.

The Exact Representation of His Being

How different are these vague notions of Christ in our image compared to the Son who is "the exact representation of his being." "He is the very image of the essence of God—the impress of his being. . .The Greek word *charaktēr*, occurring only here in the New Testament, expresses this truth more emphatically than *eikōn*, which is used elsewhere to denote Christ as the 'image' of God (2 Cor 4:4; Col 1:15)."[20] The Son is the perfect imprint of the Father's identity. "What God essentially is, is made manifest in Christ. To see Christ is to see what the Father is like."[21] There is no generic, nameless, pre-Christian deity to be known. Only God, Father, Son, and Holy Spirit, can be known personally, and only the Son reveals the very being of God. We exegete the Gospels because they exegete the life of Jesus. We expound the epistles because of the truth that is in Jesus (Eph 4:21). This is the bold truth that is celebrated throughout the Bible. The Apostle John writes, "That which was from the beginning, which we have heard, which we have seen with our eyes, which we have looked at and our hands have touched — this we proclaim concerning the Word of life" (1 John 1:1–2).

If the Son is the exact representation of the Father, and if the Bible is all about how God saves and renews the world through the Son, then whatever genre, theme, figure, image, or deliverance story we find in the Bible is ultimately about Christ.[22] On the road to Emmaus, the risen Lord Jesus Christ began with Moses and all the Prophets to explain to his disciples "what was said in all the Scriptures concerning himself" (Luke 24:27).

We cannot know God the Creator apart from knowing God the Redeemer. In his commentary on the Apostles' Creed, Karl Barth stressed that it was no easier to believe in God as our Maker than to believe in God as our Redeemer.

> The first article of faith in God the Father and His work is not a sort of "forecourt" of the Gentiles, a realm in which Christians and Jews and Gentiles, believers and unbelievers are beside one another and to some extent stand together in the presence of a reality concerning which there might be some measure of agreement, in describing it as the work of God the Creator. . . . We

20. Bruce, *Hebrews*, 48.

21. Ibid.

22. Keller, *Preaching*, 70–90.

are not nearer to believing in God the Creator, than we are to
believing that Jesus Christ was conceived by the Holy Spirit and
born of the Virgin Mary. It is not the case that the truth about
God the Creator is directly accessible to us and that only the
truth of the second article needs revelation . . . ."

It is impossible to separate the knowledge of God the Creator
and of His work from the knowledge of God's dealings with
man. Only when we keep before us what the triune God has
done for us in Jesus Christ can we realize what is involved in
God the Creator and His work. . . . What God does as the Creator can in the Christian sense only be seen and understood as a
reflection, as a shadowing forth of this inner divine relationship
between God the Father and the Son. . . . Knowledge of creation
is knowledge of God and consequently knowledge of faith in
the deepest and ultimate sense. It is not just a vestibule in which
natural theology might find a place.[23]

We confess along with the early church "one Lord Jesus Christ, the
Son of God, begotten of the Father; that is, of the essence of the Father,
God of God, Light of Light, very God of very God, begotten, not made,
being of one substance with the Father" (Nicea). The author of Hebrews
and the Apostle Paul are in concert: "The Son is the image of the invisible
God, the firstborn over all creation. . . . He is before all things, and in him
all things hold together. And he is the head of the body, the church; he is
the beginning and the firstborn from among the dead, so that in everything he might have the supremacy. For God was pleased to have all his
fullness dwell in him, and through him to reconcile to himself all things,
whether things on earth or things in heaven, by making peace through
his blood shed on the cross" (Col 1:15–20).

It doesn't take a special methodology or formula to discover that the
Bible is about Christ cover to cover. We cannot read Genesis 1:1 without
thinking of the triune God, Father, Son and Holy Spirit. The spoken Word
of Genesis is none other than the Word that was made flesh and lived for
awhile among us. Abel's sacrifice reminds us of the Lamb that was slain
before the creation of the world. Noah's salvation depends on the victory
of the resurrection. Abraham on Moriah, knife in hand, is a picture of
the agony of the cross. Christ is the one greater than Jacob and Christ is
Joseph's promise bearer. Israel's forty years in the wilderness and Jesus'

23. Barth, *Dogmatics in Outline*, 50, 52.

temptations in the wilderness converge, as does Moses on Mount Sinai and Jesus on the Mount of Beatitudes. The Passover meal is linked to Jesus' Last Supper in the upper room. Mention of David reminds us that Jesus was hailed as the Son of David. Isaiah's Suffering Servant, Jeremiah's Gethsemane life, and Zechariah's mourned and martyred shepherd all point to Christ. God has spoken "through the prophets at many times and in various ways" to prepare us for his final revelation through the Son who is the exact representation of his being. Preaching Christ from all the Scriptures takes the dynamic of divine revelation seriously.

The Being and Becoming of Jesus

There is no tension in the pastor's description of Christ between the being and becoming of Jesus. His eternal essence is one with his historical experience and redemptive accomplishment. The Preacher weaves the essence of who the Son is—"the radiance of God's glory and the exact representation of his being"—together with what Jesus has achieved on the cross and through the resurrection—"after he provided purification for sins." This word "after" is critical to his becoming, but not to his being. The Son is who he has always been. He is after all, the maker of the universe and through the incarnation, crucifixion, and resurrection the Son achieved *for us* salvation and reconciled all things to the Father. "So he became as much superior to the angels as the name he has inherited is superior to theirs" (1:4). "No other book of the New Testament (except the Fourth Gospel) puts the real deity and true humanity of Jesus Christ so clearly side by side."[24]

The Apostle Paul placed the being and becoming of Jesus side by side in his Christ hymn. "Who, being in very nature God did not consider equality with God something to be used to his own advantage," and by reason of his work, "He made himself nothing by taking the very nature of a servant, being made in human likeness. And being found in appearance as a man, he humbled himself by becoming obedient to death—even death on a cross!" The Son is superior to the highest created beings imaginable. "God exalted him to the highest place and gave him the name that is above every name, that at the name of Jesus every knee shall bow, in heaven and on earth and under the earth, and every tongue acknowledge that Jesus Christ is Lord, to the glory of God the Father" (Phil 2:6–11).

24. M. Barth, "The Old Testament in Hebrews," 58.

There is a very real tension between who we are in Christ and who we are becoming in the Spirit of Christ. As we shall see, the pastor is devoted to that struggle, offering spiritual direction that seeks to overcome the tension between our confession and our commitment, between our walking in the Spirit and our love of the world, between faith in Christ and the faith of Jesus. Sad to say, we are often spiritually lopsided. Our identity in Christ is out of kilter with our practical lives. We are in danger of saying, "Lord, Lord," but not doing the will of the Father (Matt 7:21). We are saved by so great a salvation only to become complacent and indifferent to Christ. Instead of growing in our faith, we seem insistent on remaining at the elementary level of what it means to follow Christ (Heb 6:1). We seem to have to go over the basics again and again. But with the Son there is no tension between who he is and what he does.

According to one speculative theory circulating in Palestine through the Qumran sect, the Messiah was a created being subordinate to the archangel Michael.[25] Understandably this theory appealed to Jewish Christians because it preserved the monotheistic transcendence of God without the doctrine of the Trinity and afforded them the opportunity of proclaiming Jesus as the Messiah in accord with popular Jewish messianic thought. Whether or not this heretical notion was lurking in the back of the pastor's mind is debatable. It is more likely that the pastor is focusing on the finality of the revelation of the Son compared to "the message spoken through angels" (2:2). The issue here is not negative, refuting the heretical notion that Son is subordinate to the superiority of angels, but positive, proving the status of the Son not only by virtue of his ontological identity as the Son, but by his suffering, death, and resurrection.

Some Christians may be confused by the language of Hebrews. If Jesus was God in the first place, how did he become superior to the angels? In what sense does the pastor apply Psalm 2:7 to Jesus: "You are my Son; today I have become your Father" (Heb 1:5)? How can he speak of God's "firstborn" (Heb 1:6) without suggesting that the Messiah was created? We are told that Jesus "was made a little lower than the angels" (Heb 2:9), that he belongs to the same family as we do (Heb 2:11), that he was "made like his brothers in every way" (Heb 2:17), that he shared in our humanity (Heb 2:14) and "suffered when he was tempted" (Heb 2:18). How do these statements reconcile with Jesus' deity?

25. Hughes, *Hebrews*, 53.

The pastor is determined to do justice to both the deity and humanity of Jesus Christ. He presents Jesus as having his own spiritual experience of God. He worships and prays to God. He is dependent upon God and exercises trust in God (Heb 1:9; 2:12–13). These are remarkable statements to make for someone who is defending the deity of Christ and his supremacy over the angels. But they are completely consistent with the apostolic understanding of the incarnate One. The apostles believed that Jesus is truly God and that through the incarnation he shares completely in our humanity. He identified with us in the full range of human experience, especially in the trauma and trial of life, including suffering, temptation, and death. The Son's spirituality involved as well the human experience of God, namely, trust, dependence, and faith. The pastor made no attempt to explain the mystery of the incarnation, but he proclaimed the meaning and benefits of that mystery. God became human for the sake of our salvation and participated fully in the human experience except without sin (Heb 2:9–10, 14–17; 12:2). The pastor used the concrete language of *becoming* to describe the human course of Jesus' life of obedience and spiritual pilgrimage.

Jesus did not have to make a name for himself because of who he was in his very being; nevertheless, through his suffering, obedience, and genuine spirituality, he achieved and retained the meaning of that name. It is not surprising that Christians have had difficulty holding together doctrinally and practically the being and becoming of Jesus. But it is absolutely crucial that we hold to this revealed paradox of supernatural reality if we desire to know Christ and become like Jesus. The pastor presents the being and becoming of Jesus boldly and without compromise. We hold this truth in tension. The Word made flesh was full of grace and truth; dwelling in our neighborhood *and* revealing the glory of the only begotten of the Father (John 1:14). "Born of a woman" *and* "the firstborn over all creation" (Gal 4:4; Col 1:15). The incarnate One is not only "gentle and humble in heart" but "the radiance of God's glory and the exact representation of his being, sustaining all things by his powerful word" (Matt 11:29; Heb 1:3). Jesus fit Isaiah's description, "He had no beauty or majesty to attract us to him, nothing in his appearance that we should desire him," even as he fulfilled the Apostle Paul's confession, "He is before all things, and in him all things hold together" (Isa 53:2; Col 1:17). In his very being God, worthy of all praise, and in his humanity, humble and faithful, obedient to death—even death on a cross! The truth of this paradoxical tension calls for imitation and adoration: "Let this mind be in you which was also in Christ Jesus," and "Who has known the mind of the Lord? . . . For from him and through him and to him are all things. To him be glory forever!" (Phil 2:5; Rom 11:33–36).

The positive tension between the divine and human in Jesus is foundational for how we understand the truth and embrace life. The Chalcedonian Definition was hammered out by the early church in 451. The church circumscribed the nature of the Son of God, the Lord Jesus Christ, "the same perfect in divinity and perfect in humanity." They let the revealed mystery stand, by acknowledging "two natures which undergo no confusion, no change, no division, no separation; at no point was the difference between the natures taken away through the union, but rather the property of both natures is preserved and come together into a single person and a single subsistent being; he is not parted or divided into two persons, but is one and the same only-begotten Son, God, Word, Lord Jesus Christ. . . ."[26]

O Christ, the Great Foundation[27]

O Christ the great foundation on which your people stand
To preach your true salvation in every age and land,
Pour out your Holy Spirit to make us strong and pure,
To keep the faith unbroken as long as worlds endure.

Baptized in one confession, one church in all the earth,
We bear our Lord's impression, the sign of second birth:
One holy people gathered in love beyond our own,
By grace we were invited, by grace we make you known.

This is the moment glorious when he who once was dead
Shall lead his church victorious, their champion and their head.
The Lord of all creation his heav'nly kingdom brings:
The final consummation, the glory of all things.

TIMOTHY T'INGFANG LEW, 1933; TRANS. MILDRED A. WIANT, 1966

---

26. Pelikan and Hotchkiss, eds., *Creeds and Confessions of Faith in the Christian Tradition*, vol. 1, 181.

27. McKim, ed., *The Presbyterian Hymnal*, 443.

4

Seven Declarations
(Hebrews 1:5–2:4)

"The main and central action is everywhere and always what God has done, is doing, and will do for us. Jesus is the revelation of that action. Our main and central task is to live in responsive obedience to God's action revealed in Jesus. Our part in the action is the act of faith."

EUGENE PETERSON[1]

ON THE SURFACE IT looks as if the pastor is proof texting when he cites seven Old Testament verses in rapid succession. In proof texting the speaker makes a point by stringing verses together. The verses are often quoted out of context and misinterpreted or manipulated to shore up a speaker's opinion. But the pastor is not thumbing through his Bible (the Old Testament Septuagint) looking for a line here or a line there to bolster his case. On the contrary, he's preaching from the whole Bible, drawing out these prophetic lines to represent the whole counsel of God.

The pastor's eloquent citation of seven Scriptural declarations in defense of the deity and exaltation of the Son confirms the rhetorical power of these texts to synthesize exegetical reasoning and to express the whole counsel of God succinctly. The pastor's selection process conveys in lucid brevity the power of the Son's exaltation and enthronement. None of

---

1. Peterson, *The Message Remix*, 1414.

these verses is isolated from the whole counsel of God nor pulled out of the context of its revelational meaning. They are grouped together more like a string of priceless pearls or the double helix of the DNA code than like a random collection of verses. They serve "to highlight the necessary interpenetration of exegesis and dogmatics."[2] The preacher is not merely listing points or compiling excerpts. He's orchestrating a crescendo of meaning. Or like a florist, he is gathering a bouquet of biblical blossoms into a beautiful arrangement.[3]

The sequence of seven citations begins and ends with questions, "For to which of the angels did God ever say . . . ?" (1:5) and "To which of the angels did God ever say . . . ?" (1:13). The pastor chooses angels, the highest created beings, to contrast the utterly incomparable relationship between the Father and the Son. The comparison is positive, not negative. George Guthrie reasons, along with many other scholars, that "Hebrews should not be read in light of a deficient angelology; rather the author goes to great lengths to drive home the unrivaled superiority of Jesus for specific rhetorical reasons which indeed have a fuzzy Christology as their impetus."[4] The so-called "fuzzy Christology" is in reference to the interpretative freedom employed by the pastor to make his case for the supremacy of Christ. He used seven Old Testament verses, three pairs of two verses each, with a climatic conclusion in Psalm 110:1. The sequence begins and ends with well-established messianic psalms, but the pastor freely applies all seven verses to the Messiah.

This is not sloppy eisegesis. The pastor is creatively and poetically building a biblical case. The truth of the Son's exalted status is meant to be heard as a singular truth, washing over the listener like a wave. This makes dissecting these verses in the sermon, breaking them down, debating their context, tracing their usage, and constructing their background, problematic for effective preaching. The pastor truly intends for us to feel the sweeping impact of these seven citations. This means that the preachers who come closest to matching the pastor's rhetorical effect will be those who share his christological exegesis of the Old Testament texts. We may be amazed at how little commentary the pastor felt compelled to give on these verses. Any effort to explain and illustrate is pushed aside by

2. Allen and Swain, "In Defense of Proof-Texting," 606.

3. *Florilegium* is the Medieval Latin term for this literary gathering. The word derives from the Latin *flos* or flower and *legere* meaning to gather. It literally means a gathering of flowers.

4. Guthrie, "Hebrews," 936.

the pastor who boldly declares in rapid-fire succession seven references with minimal introduction. Each Old Testament reference bears up under closer scrutiny as an inspired testimony to the supremacy of the Son. In the pastor's chain of quotations each line is linked to form "a direct verbal prophecy concerning the perpetual nature of the Son's reign, having been explicitly fulfilled . . . in the exaltation of Jesus to the right hand of God."[5] The pastor knits the couplets together by using catchwords.

For to which of the angels did God ever say,

> "You are my *Son*; today *I* have become your Father" (Ps 2:7).

Or again,

> *I* will be his Father, and he will be my *Son*" (2 Sam 7:14).

And again, when God brings his firstborn into the world, he says,

> "Let all God's *angels* worship him" (Deut 32:43).

In speaking of the angels he says,

> "He makes his *angels* spirits, and his servants flames of fire" (Ps 104:4).

But about the Son he says,

> "*Your* throne, O God, will last forever and ever;
>
> a scepter of justice will be the scepter of your kingdom.
>
> *You* have loved righteousness and hated wickedness;
>
> therefore God, *your* God, has set *you* above your companions
>
> by anointing *you* with the oil of joy" (Ps 45:6–7).

He also says,

> "In the beginning, Lord, *you* laid the foundation of the earth,
>
> and the heavens are the work of *your* hands.
>
> They will perish, but *you* remain; they will all wear out like a garment.
>
> *You* will roll them up like a robe; like a garment they will be changed.
>
> But *you* remain the same, and *your* years will never end" (Ps 102:25–27).

To which of the angels did God ever say,

5. Ibid., 939.

"Sit at my right hand until I make your enemies a footstool for your feet" (Ps 110:1).

First of all, these seven citations proclaim the supremacy of the Son over all creation because of the nature of his relationship with the Father. Second, they affirm that he is worthy to be worshiped by the angels because he transcends them in every way. Third, they declare the exalted enthronement of the Son because of his eternal, holy, and unchanging nature.[6] And finally, they state that his just rule will make everything right. The pastor knew that his Old Testament exegesis of these seven texts was impossible before the illuminating light of Christ appeared in history.[7] Until Jesus came and accomplished his ministry, no one would have preached this sermon.

Some of us grew up reading red letter editions of the New Testament, but for the author of Hebrews the whole Old Testament might as well have been red lettered. It didn't matter who was writing, it was God who was speaking. The pastor hears the voice of God in the Psalms and in the Law and the Prophets, testifying to the exalted status of the Son. Moreover, the object of declaration is no longer the king nor God the Father, but the incarnate One—the Son, who manifests the manifold wisdom of God and fulfills all human responsibility. He is the perfect Prophet, Priest, and King. The pastor has an eye for seeing Christ in the Scriptures. Good preachers know how to do that intuitively. They "can't help but think about Christ even if the text [they] are looking at doesn't seem to be specifically a messianic prophecy. . . . Yet [they] just can't not see him."[8]

The Nicene Creed

At first glance words like "today" and "firstborn" may imply that there was a time before the Son existed. An early fourth century Alexandrian priest by the name of Arius (ca. 280-ca.336) thought this was the case. He taught that if the Father "begat" the Son, there must have been a time when the Son did not exist. Arius took the facts of Jesus' humanity seriously. He believed that Jesus grew in wisdom and favor with God and man (Luke 2:52), and that he was ignorant of the date of the Second Coming

6. O'Brien, *Hebrews*, 65.

7. Cole, *The God Who Became Human*, 89.

8. Keller, *Preaching*, 87.

(Mark 13:32), that he experienced emotional anguish (John 12:27; Mark 14:34), and that, after the suffering on the cross, he was abandoned by God (Mark 15:34).

Arius interpreted these facts from a philosophical and theological perspective that led him to conclude that the Son was ontologically inferior to the Father (Prov 8:22; John 14:28; Col 1:15). His thinking was the product of Greek rationalism, combined with the teachings of Origen (ca. 185–ca.254) on the subordination of the Son. Arius ignored Origen's insistence on the "eternal generation" of the Son, and instead argued that there was a time when the Son did not exist. He wanted to get behind the mystery, explain it, and bring it into line with his concept of God. Arius asserted that God was a remote and inaccessible being, immutable, indivisible, and unique. He "felt no substance of God could in any way be communicated or shared with any other being."[9]

Ironically Arius sacrificed the truth of the incarnation on the ground that he was upholding the logical postulates of the Supreme Being. Therefore in spite of the apostolic testimony, Arius held that the Son was "not the eternal God himself that comes to us in Christ for our salvation, but an intermediate being, distinct from God, while God himself is left out, uncondescending, unredemptive."[10] Where the Bible refers to Christ as God or as the Son of God Arius believed that the use of these titles honored Christ's role rather than defined his being. The titles are merely honorific, "Even if he is called God," wrote Arius, "He is not God truly, but by participation in grace. . . . He too is called God in name only."[11]

Arius's heretical views are relevant today because people still struggle with the relationship between the deity and humanity of Jesus. There are striking similarities between the fourth-century Arianism and the Jehovah's Witnesses cult. Anthony Hoekema believes that the Jehovah's Witnesses' view of the person of Christ is essentially a revival of Arianism. Both movements interpret the begetting and becoming of Christ in literalistic terms.[12] The Son is not equal to the Father and is created by the Father prior to creation. Like Arius, their ancient predecessor, Jehovah's Witnesses do not believe that the Son and the Father are of the same essence. Consequently, they offer a translation of certain biblical passages

9. Walter, "Arianism," 74.

10. Baillie, *God Was In Christ*, 70.

11. Kelly, *Early Christian Doctrine*, 239.

12. Hoekema, *The Four Major Cults*, 327–30.

to remain consistent with their theology. Perhaps the most famous textual revision is John 1:1: "In (the) beginning the Word was, and the Word was with God, and the Word was a god" (New World Translation).

There were times in the fourth century when it looked as though Arianism might triumph in the church, but in the end the Nicene Council prevailed. The creed was formulated at the first ecumenical council in the history of the church. More than 300 bishops, mainly from the eastern provinces of the Roman Empire, where the controversy with Arianism was the greatest, met in AD 325. As the following sections of the creed demonstrate, the bishops strongly affirmed the deity of Christ and directly refuted the Arian position: "We believe . . . in one Lord Jesus Christ, the Son of God, begotten from the Father, only-begotten, that is, from the substance of the Father, . . . begotten not made, of one substance with the Father. . . . But as for those who say, There was when He was not, and Before being born He was not, and that He came into existence out of nothing, or who assert that the Son of God is from a different . . . substance, or is created, or is subject to alteration or change — these the Catholic [i.e., universal] Church anthematizes."[13]

Since its formation, the Nicene Creed has been accepted as an important affirmation of the deity of Christ. Besides refuting the specific tenets of Arianism, it rejected an approach which sought to explain away the mystery of the incarnate One and subject the truth of Christ to philosophical speculation about God. The creed affirms the deity of Christ but does not explain the language used in the Bible for Jesus' humanity. Although the bishops did not see the humanity of Jesus as the critical issue, it was precisely the Bible's references to Jesus' humanity that Arius used to defend his notion of a created Christ. The bishops would have benefitted from following the example of the pastor in Hebrews who presented both the being and becoming of Jesus boldly and without compromise. Apart from the dual thrust, our defense of the deity of Christ obscures our sensitivity to Jesus' human experience of God.

The pastor's reference to "today" corresponds significantly with the messianic trajectory presented in the Gospels. The eternity of Christ's sonship is never in question, but the path of obedience, culminating and climaxing in the cross and the resurrection, is in full view. A deficient understanding of orthodoxy, one that is afraid to think through the meaning of the Gospels, would rather not be bothered by the intricate

13. Kelly, *Early Christian Doctrines*, 232.

and textured weave of Christ's humanity. A childish orthodoxy wants a simple religious proposition repeatable like a mantra rather than the challenge and the inspiration of the being and becoming of Jesus. The popular preference is for faith in Jesus without the faith *of* Jesus. But New Testament Christianity insists on both. Faith and faithfulness are bound together under the Lordship of Christ.

Jesus' response to John's question, "Are you the one who is to come, or should we expect someone else?" was a clear reference to messianic prophecy, but it lacked the explicit affirmation that John undoubtedly sought. Why was Jesus reluctant to say boldly, "I am the Messiah!"? Jesus' elusive response fits a pattern. He avoided direct answers to questions about his authority. He was reluctant to publicize his work. When the Jewish religious leaders confronted him, demanding to know by what authority he taught and acted, he declined to answer (Luke 20:1–8). He repeatedly demanded secrecy from those he healed (Mark 1:44; 5:43; 7:36; 8:26), and he insisted on silence when the demon-possessed cried out that he was the Son of God (Mark 1:34; Luke 4:41). Even the disciples were warned not to tell anyone that he was the Christ (Matt 16:20) or to reveal their experience of Jesus' transfiguration (Matt 17:9).

William Wrede claimed that this so-called secrecy motif in the Gospel of Mark was an attempt to read back into the life of Jesus allusions to his messianic identity that had no historical authenticity. Wrede wrongly concluded that Jesus did not think of himself as the Messiah. He interpreted Jesus' reticence to claim the messianic title as a literary invention used by the early church to emphasize the messianic character of his earthly life.

Jesus' efforts to stifle public exposure and acclaim before his passion have traditionally been interpreted as a conscious attempt to correct the prevailing cultural expectation of the Messiah. Jesus rejected the prevailing Jewish concept of political messiahship. His reticence to claim a title associated with nationalism, political liberation, and freedom from Roman imperial rule is understandable. Just how difficult it was to redefine the meaning of the Messiah is clearly evident in Peter's inability to grasp the true meaning of Jesus' messiahship (Matt 16:21–22).

Contrary to Wrede, the pastor's emphasis on "today" from Psalm 2:7 illustrates the critical timing of Jesus' exaltation and enthronement. Only "after his suffering had proved the completeness of his obedience" was he raised to the Father's right hand.[14] True messianic consciousness is disclosed by Jesus precisely in his endeavor to dissociate himself from popular appeal and power politics. Both the masses and the opposition responded to Jesus in nationalistic fervor, seeing him either as a new hero for a popular uprising or as a fresh threat to the political status quo. On all fronts Jesus sought to redefine his messiahship. For Jesus to have allowed his role to be defined by contemporary messianic expectations, either then or now, would have been tantamount to yielding to the initial temptations in the wilderness. Jesus subjected himself and his followers to a painful course of messianic redefinition that was rooted in the truth of the Old Testament.

Jesus accepted Peter's confession, commending it for its heavenly source, even though he rejected Peter's interpretation of the title (Matt 16:16–17, 21–23). What was true of the title was also true of Jesus' miraculous power. He commanded silence after performing miracles, not because they were not genuine, but because his purpose was to demonstrate the power and compassion of God. Instead of making the miracle a display of power, he sought to make people aware of his mission on a deeper, more demanding, level. Not until the end of his earthly ministry did Jesus clearly and publicly admit he was the Messiah. When the high priest asked, "Are you the Christ, the Son of the Blessed One?" Jesus responded directly, "I am ... And you will see the Son of Man sitting at the right hand of the Mighty One and coming in the clouds of heaven" (Mark 14:61–62).

"It is striking," writes Helmut Thielicke, "that Jesus uses these predicates of majesty when he is being delivered up to death, exposed to humiliation, and plunged into the passion, so that the confession of his messiahship can no longer give a wrong impression of loftiness nor lead to a theology of glory, but engulfs us in the depths of his destiny."[15] Although this perspective is consistent with the pastor's emphasis on "today" another reason ought to be considered. Jesus freely uses the title of Christ only after his resurrection, when he can point to the finished work of the cross and the completion of the Father's will (Luke 24:26, 46). Before he claimed the title for himself and before the Father commended him and enthroned him (Ps 2:7; 110:1), he had to accomplish all that the Father called him to do. Only then, on that day, "today," did the seven cita-

14. Bruce, *Hebrews*, 55.
15. Thielicke, *The Evangelical Faith*, 2:352.

tions find their true fulfillment. Through his actual historical humiliation and exaltation Jesus was shown to be what he knew he was in his very being, the eternal Son of God. He was "acknowledged Messiah in fact not just after his passion and resurrection but *because* of his passion and resurrection as the incarnate One— and, it must be insisted, in continuity with his own self-consciousness during the ministry."[16] (See Acts 2:36; Rom 1:4; Heb 5:8–10.) The rich texture of the pastor's sermon expounds on the developing meaning of Christ's redemptive accomplishment. Both the ancient and modern hearer face a real challenge—to grasp these seven Old Testament texts within the coherent whole of biblical theology.

Angel Helpers

"The reason angels fly," G. K. Chesterton quipped, "is because they take themselves so lightly." I suppose it is a good thing that angels take themselves lightly because we rarely give them much attention. In many churches the subject of angels is rarely raised. Reference is made to angelic choirs on Christmas Eve and angels are featured at the garden tomb on Easter morning, but that is about the extent of it. Angels are not affirmed in our confessions or debated in our theology. But the Bible from beginning to end, consistently refers to angels, not as flighty cherub-like creatures, but as behind-the-scenes messengers on a mission, "sent to serve those who inherit salvation" (Heb 1:14). They worship God, reveal his will, and do his bidding. The basic assumption that angels play a strategic role in the drama of salvation history is undebatable.

Modern versions of spirituality are fine with believing in "an eternal, spaceless, timeless, spiritual Something" but not with the Named God who creates, reveals, and redeems. Believing in "the blinding abyss of undifferentiated spirituality" is one thing, but to believe in angels is quite another. "That is why many believe in God who cannot believe in angels and an angelic world. That is why Pantheism is more popular than Christianity, and why many desire a Christianity stripped of its miracles."[17]

Late modernity can hardly fathom a stealth subject that evades empirical proof. If a subject cannot be weighed, measured, and photographed it is the stuff of myth and legend. That leaves the subject of angels pretty much out of bounds for any thinking modern. But the credibility

16. Longenecker, *The Christology of Early Jewish Christianity*, 74.

17. Lewis, *Miracles*, 159–60.

of the Christian faith does not rest in angels but in Christ. No one has ever been asked to believe in angels; the real focus is always Christ, from whom all other true beliefs and meaningful convictions follow. As our text in Hebrews emphasizes, attention is directed to what God says to his one and only Son, not to what he says to angels.

Pulitzer Prize-winning author and scientist Edward O. Wilson is as secular as they come. He writes, "Human existence may be simpler than we thought. There is no predestination, no unfathomed mystery of life. Demons and gods do not vie for our allegiance. Instead, we are self-made, independent, alone, and fragile, a biological species adapted to live in a biological world."[18] Yet surprisingly Wilson stretches credulity in a most interesting fashion when he encourages belief in extraterrestrial beings. He writes, "The meaning of human existence is best understood in perspective, by comparing our species with other conceivable life-forms and, by deduction, even those that might exist outside the Solar System."[19]

Wilson reasons that given the size and age of the universe there is a distinct possibility of extraterrestrial beings. These "imagined but plausible aliens" are millions of years more advanced technologically and scientifically than we are. Wilson writes, "By chance alone, and given the multibillion year age of the galaxy, the aliens reached our present-day, still-infantile level millions of years ago."[20] Given their phenomenal head-start, aliens will not care so much about our technology, but these "hypothetical aliens" will be interested in our unique cultural evolution—the humanities. Although there is no empirical evidence for extra-terrestrials, Wilson believes it is "possible to produce a logical albeit very crude hypothetical portrait of human-grade aliens on Earth-like planets."[21]

Wilson believes that God is an "idol of the mind" and faith is a product of "the biological evolution of human instinct," but he also believes in the plausible existence of aliens. He offers a detailed description.[22] He reassure us that "our fragile little planet has nothing to fear from extraterrestrials," because they are much smarter than us.[23] Unlike humans, "they would have come to the realization . . . that in order to avoid extinc-

18. Wilson, *The Meaning of Human Existence*, 26.

19. Ibid., 77.

20. Ibid., 54.

21. Ibid., 113.

22. Ibid., 157

23. Ibid., 121.

tion or reversion to unbearably harsh conditions on their home planet they had to achieve sustainability and stable political systems long before journeying beyond their star system."[24] If one of the world's most distinguished evolutionary biologist can write convincingly about aliens, perhaps Christians should believe confidently in what the Bible says about angels.

In comparing the Son to angels, the pastor introduces a strategy that runs through his entire sermon. As great as these supernatural beings are, angels cannot compare to the Son. The argument from lesser to greater holds true throughout the sermon for Abraham, Moses, Joshua, Aaron, the priesthood, and the sacrificial system. The pastor leverages his message on the comparison. "Since the message spoken through angels was binding, and every violation and disobedience received its just punishment" (Heb 2:2), how much more crucial is it for the followers of Christ to remain faithful?

Adrift

The last word of this opening exhortation is a rhetorical question, "Are not all angels ministering spirits sent to serve those who will inherit salvation?" The word *salvation* links these two sections together. In a sentence the pastor deftly shifts from exposition to exhortation. Seven assertions define the character of the Son, followed by seven biblical citations declaring the exalted status of the Son. Fourteen Christ-centered affirmations leading to one compelling admonition for the church. "We must pay the most careful attention, therefore, to what we have heard, so that we do not drift away." The pastor's use of "we" (first person plural) focuses attention on the household of faith rather than the individual believer and admonishes himself along with everyone else. The word *must* conveys the compelling logic of the pastor's admonition. If the Old Testament spoken through angels was binding for the people of God, how much more is the message of salvation delivered by the Son worthy of obedience. The need to "pay more careful attention" implies a serious deficiency requiring immediate attention and change.

The warning is sobering, the danger real, and the application nearly universal. It is difficult to imagine a body of believers that does not need this serious admonition, if not as an indictment, at least as a warning.

24. Ibid.

The pastor will expand and deepen the meaning of apostasy as the sermon builds, but the striking metaphor of drifting away creates a vivid picture for those acquainted with the dangers of the sea. For a number of years our son was an ocean lifeguard in Dominical, Costa Rica. He rescued whole families caught in dangerous rip currents. Rip currents are particularly deceptive because the danger lurks below the surface even on a beautiful sunny day. Unsuspecting swimmers are caught in a fast-moving rip current and before they know it they are drifting out to sea. Inexperienced swimmers grow exhausted fighting the rips and drown if they are not rescued.

The pastor's metaphor underscores the subtle and often undetected nature of the danger of apostasy. His description fits a process that seems especially suited to the American church, where we experience "a gradual, unthinking movement away from the faith."[25] The admonition makes "it plain that our author was afraid that his readers, succumbing to more or less subtle pressures, might become liable to those sanctions—if not by an overt renunciation of the gospel, then possibly be detaching themselves increasingly from its public profession until it ceased to have any influence upon their lives."[26]

The pastor has much more to say about the nature of this deceptively subtle but potentially deadly apostasy as the sermon progresses, but this warning is especially appropriate for believers in the West. The danger of ethical equivocation and theological compromise is real for us. As our convictions diminish, and our spiritual disciplines weaken, and as the integration of theology and ethics unravels, professing Christians will drift away. They will cling all the more to their idea of a consumer Jesus whose purpose is to enhance their self-esteem and happiness. Hebrews is not a scholarly conundrum or a homiletical puzzle narrowly focused on first-century Jewish Christians. Hebrews is a powerful sermon for the church universal and the church global. Hebrews preaches to the modern church, described by our poet-prophets in various ways as Christ-haunted (Flannery O'Connor), or as Christianity without Christ (Kierkegaard), or as watered-down Christianity (C. S. Lewis). Before returning to his positive thrust on Christ and salvation, the pastor asks the critical question that remains at the forefront of the entire sermon: "How shall we escape if we ignore so great a salvation?"

25. O'Brien, *Hebrews*, 84.
26. Bruce, *Hebrews*, 68.

The first reason given for drifting away from Christ is the passive act of ignoring the gospel of salvation. Ironically, the problem of faithlessness is not attributed to either outside opposition or flagrant disobedience. The apparent issue is one of indifference and apathy. Outward religious efforts and observances may be as public as ever, but behind the scenes the believer's passion for the faith has grown passive and complacent. Bible study is a low priority. Personal devotions falls by the wayside. Worship engagement is infrequent. The Bible school hour on Sunday morning is more about sharing personal opinions that it is about growing in the grace and knowledge of the Lord Jesus Christ. Instead of paying attention to the gospel, the gospel is taken for granted. What Christians believe with their head does not necessarily fill their hearts or transform their lives. What they believe does not change how they live. One of the ways we ignore the gospel is by becoming spectators rather than participants in the faith. We emphasize a special call to pastors and forget that the call of God is upon all believers. The biblical meaning of ministry is narrowly focused upon a few, usually men, rather than upon the body of Christ and the church-wide distribution of the gifts of the Spirit. The burden of ministry, which was meant to be shared throughout the household of faith, becomes the special responsibility of the pastor and the church staff. Soul care becomes the responsibility of those approved by an ordination process. We foster a dichotomy between spiritual and secular work and reduce most believers to spectators. The pastor is called to serve "as every person's evangelist, catechist, teacher, overseer, counselor, disciplinarian, liturgist, and preacher." He must also minister to the sick, visit from house to house, and preside at weddings and funerals. For the most part, lay people "are essentially spectators," or at best, third-string players waiting for the chance opportunity to serve when the ordained minister is unable to perform his duties.[27]

Jesus said, "Whoever wants to be my disciple must deny themselves and take up their cross daily and follow me" (Luke 9:23). This simple one-line description of the Christian life underscores the life-changing impact of the gospel of grace in each and every believer. Discipleship is the costly, daily commitment of the ordinary believer. We resist compartmentalizing our faith into separate categories, as if food, work, money, sex, and sport belong to our personal choice. Whereas prayer, worship, Bible reading, and evangelism belong to God. Jesus taught that

27. Hunter, *Radical Outreach*, 105–7.

everything belongs to God and that the spiritual disciplines apply to all of
life. Everything ought to be done in obedience to the will of God. As the
Apostle Paul said, "Whatever you do, whether in word or deed, do it all
in the name of the Lord Jesus, giving thanks to God the Father through
him" (Col 3:17). The pastor's challenge is that we pay the most careful
attention to the gospel so that we do not drift away. The encouragement
for doing so is entirely positive. No matter what the competing interests
could possibly be, they pale in significance when compared to the greatness of our salvation in Christ.

So Great a Salvation

In a word, salvation comprehends all that we have been given in Christ.
We are saved from "sin and death; guilt and estrangement; ignorance
of truth; bondage to habit and vice; fear of demons, of death, of life,
of God, of hell; despair of self; alienation from others; pressures of the
world; a meaningless life."[28] We are saved for a purpose, to love God,
others, and ourselves. Everything we do comes under the Lordship of
Jesus Christ. We are saved for freedom, mission, and community. Salvation changes our relationship with God giving us acceptance with God,
forgiveness, reconciliation, sonship, reception of the Spirit, and everlasting life. Salvation changes us emotionally, giving us confidence, peace,
courage, hopefulness, and joy. Salvation changes us spiritually, giving us
prayer, guidance, discipline, dedication, and service. Salvation changes
us personally, giving us new thoughts, convictions, horizons, motives,
satisfactions, self-fulfillment. Salvation changes us socially, giving us a
new community in Christ, a compassion for others and an "overriding
impulse to love as Jesus has loved."[29]

The pastor commends "this salvation" by identifying the distinctive
ways God has commended his strategic redemptive action. First and foremost the gospel of salvation was "announced by the Lord." Then, it was
"confirmed" by the apostles and others. In addition to these eyewitnesses
who experienced Jesus' ministry directly, God testified to this great salvation "by signs, wonders and various miracles." Finally, the continuing
legacy of the "gifts of the Holy Spirit distributed according to his will,"
commend "this salvation" through the priesthood of all believers."

28. White, "Salvation," 968.
29. Ibid.

The pastor's biblical exposition affirms the finality of the revelation of the Son, declares the exaltation of the Son, and commends the salvation of the Son. All for the purpose of delivering a bold exhortation. His aim is to convince us to pay more careful attention to the gospel "so that we do not drift away."

Love, Divine, All Loves Excelling[30]

Love divine, all loves excelling,
Joy of heaven, to earth come down;
fix in us thy humble dwelling, all thy faithful mercies crown.
Jesus, thou art all compassion, pure, unbounded love thou art;
visit us with thy salvation, enter every trembling heart.

CHARLES WESLEY, 1747

Here is Love[31]

Here is love, vast as the ocean,
Loving kindness as the flood,
When the Prince of Life, our Ransom,
Shed for us His precious blood.
Who His love will not remember?
Who can cease to sing His praise?
He can never be forgotten,
Throughout heav'n's eternal days.

In Thy truth Thou dost direct me
By Thy Spirit through Thy Word;
And Thy grace me need is meeting
As I trust in Thee, my Lord.
Of Thy fullness Thou art pouring
Thy great love and pow'r on me,
Without measure, full and boundless,
Drawing out my heart to Thee.

WILLIAM REES

30. McKim, ed., *The Presbyterian Hymnal*, 376.

31. William Rees (1802–1883), translator, William Edwards, http://hymnary.org/media/fetch/111969.

5

The Pioneer of our Salvation
(Hebrews 2:5–3:6)

"The Son of glory came down, and was slain,
Us whom he had made, and Satan stol'n, to unbind.
'Twas much, that man was made like God before,
But that God should be made like man, much more."

JOHN DONNE, HOLY SONNET 11[1]

THE EXALTED SON, WHO IS "the radiance of God's glory and exact representation of his being," became the incarnate Son to "make atonement for the sins of the people." The pastor moves from exaltation to incarnation to show how Jesus brought many sons and daughters to glory, how he tasted death for everyone, and how he shared in their humanity. The incarnate One transcended his transcendence by obeying the Father's will, by becoming one with us in our humanity, and by suffering death, "so that by his death he might break the power of him who holds the power of death" (Heb 2:14).

Jesus is one with us precisely in the way we need him to be. Solidarity and suffering are the pastor's themes as he develops the big picture of salvation. The pastor would never say something like, "Life goes better with Jesus, because Jesus gives us a better life," but he will say that "the one who makes people holy and those who are made holy are of the same

---

1. Donne, *Selected Poetry*, 205.

family" (Heb 2:11). The pioneer of our salvation, who was made "perfect through what he suffered," is responsible for creating a whole new identity, an identity that depends exclusively on our shared solidarity with Jesus. Yet we are steeped in a competitive individualism that leaves us empty. We are little chiefs with multiple tribal identities: family, school, work, sports, hobbies, church, friends, and entertainment. For many Christians church is one small compartment in this competitive environment. Our multiple tribal identities, each with its own set of cultural customs, rituals, offerings, and obligations, compete for our loyalty. Colleagues at work, next-door neighbors, workout friends, and even family members may not even know we belong to the new tribe.

Once again the pastor compares angels and the Son. "It is not to angels that he has subjected the world to come, about which we are speaking" (Heb 2:5). On both counts, the Son's supremacy over creation and Son's solidarity with humanity, there is no comparison to angels. The cosmic scope of the pastor's theological vision draws a logical comparison between angels and the Son of Man. The pastor builds on the Son's enthronement (Heb 1:13; Psalm 110:1) by retracing the key steps that led him to the right hand of the Father (Heb 2:6–8; Psalm 8:4–8). In the first century, "the most effective way of substantiating the supremacy of the Son" was by comparing him to angels.[2] Since angels were the highest created beings, and there was considerable speculation about their role in the world's administration, it made sense to draw the comparison between angels and the Son.

Pop culture's high-profile celebrity "gods" strike a poor comparison, because no one ever imagines them as being more than ordinary human beings. However, the arts continue to proclaim the human expectation for something more than a material world. Modern cinema is a reminder that there is more to the world than meets the eye. Angels are credible to those who believe "that the universe was formed at God's command" (Heb 11:3). Those who have been redeemed by the blood of the Lamb find it reasonable to believe in the biblical reality of creation and the description of angels. The wild fantasies of a secular world may be a faint hint of the cosmos created by the triune God.

2. Cockerill, *Hebrews*, 100.

Psalm 8 and Human Flourishing

The pastor develops Jesus' solidarity with us in our humanity by drawing on the Psalms, the Prophets, and the Law. In rapid succession he quotes from Psalm 8, Psalm 110, Psalm 22, and Isaiah 8. Then he draws on exodus imagery from Isaiah 41:8–10 and applies the example of Moses from Numbers 12:7. The sweep of biblical insight is impressive. We can learn from the pastor's agile delivery. His energetic movement from text to text intensifies the impact of the truth. The pastor's revelation of Christ goes from heaven's throne to earth's cradle. Having begun with the exaltation of the Son (1:4) he moves to the incarnate Son of Man (2:9). We are led from the Son's exalted status to the Son's solidarity with us. And to do so, he preaches Psalm 8 like it has never been preached before. From his theological vision of Christ on the throne, the pastor explains the meaning of the manger, the cross, and the empty tomb: "But there is a place where someone has testified: 'What is mankind that you are mindful of him or the son of man that you care for him? You made him a little lower that the angels; you crowned him with glory and honor and put everything under his feet'" (Heb 2:6–8).

He gives Psalm 8 a layered theological meaning. The Psalm begins with the greatness of God, "Lord, our Lord, how majestic is your name in all the earth!"and contrasts God's greatness with our smallness. Against the backdrop of the vast cosmos, the psalmist asks, "What is mankind that you are mindful of them, human beings that you care for them?" But the psalmist moves quickly from the littleness of man to the greatness of man. "You have made them a little lower than the angels and crowned them with glory and honor." Our worth is bestowed by God, not created by us. Significance is derived from being made in God's image. We cannot make something of ourselves. Self-worth is not a human achievement. We are made in God's image and endowed with inestimable value. The holy value of the person is built in. It is not optional. Psalm 8 looks back to Genesis: "Then God said, 'Let us make man in our image, in our likeness.'" Not only were we created in God's image but we were mandated to "rule over the fish of the sea and the birds of the air, over the livestock, over all the earth, and over all the creatures that move along the ground" (Gen 1:26). God blessed the first human family and said to them, "Be fruitful and increase in number; fill the earth and subdue it. Rule over the fish of the sea and the birds of the air and over every living creature that moves on the ground" (Gen 1:28). The Bible offers a beautifully balanced estimate of the person. Compare man, male and female, to the vastness of creation and we are minuscule, but compare the person to God and we grow in significance.

Psalm 8 is controversial. Not everyone agrees with the psalmist's anthropology. Distinguished scientist Loren Eiseley describes man as the zenith of the evolutionary process. In the "The Cosmic Orphan" he writes: "The thing that is you bears the still-aching wounds of evolution in body and in brain. Your hands are made-over fins, your lungs come from a swamp, your femur has been twisted upright. Your foot is a reworked climbing pad. You are a rag doll resown from the skins of extinct animals. Long ago, 2 million years perhaps, you were smaller; your brain was not so large. We are not confident that you could speak. Seventy million years before that you were an even smaller climbing creature . . . . You were the size of a rat. You ate insects. Now you fly to the moon."[3] Harvard scientist Stephen Jay Gould (1941-2002) claimed that humanity's significance had to be self-generated. Mankind had to manufacture its own meaning. "We are here because one odd group of fishes had a peculiar fin anatomy that could transform into legs for terrestrial creatures; because the earth never froze entirely during an ice age; because a small and tenuous species, arising in Africa a quarter of a million years ago, has managed, so far, to survive by hook or by crook. We may yearn for a 'higher' answer, but none exists. This explanation, though superficially troubling, if not terrifying, is ultimately liberating and exhilarating. We cannot read the meaning of life passively in the facts of nature. We must construct these answers ourselves—from our own wisdom and ethical sense. There is no other way."[4]

But the pastor is not here to debate the anthropological interpretation of the Psalm. He reads Psalm 8 in the light of the redemptive trajectory of salvation history. The anthropological meaning of the psalm still stands, but in Hebrews the even greater truth of the Son of Man shines through.[5] The pastor freely applies the sweeping anthropological mean-

3. Eiseley, "The Cosmic Orphan," 139.

4. Stephen Jay Gould quoted in Kinnier, *The Meaning of Life*, 108.

5. Psalm 8 relates to the whole of mankind, but it finds its true focus pre-eminently in him who is uniquely the Son of Man and in whom alone the sinfulness of mankind is healed. The phrase "son of man" is used several different ways in the Bible. First of all it is used for all of humankind (Num 23:19; Job 25:6; Ps 80:17; Ps 144:3). Second, it was the title used by Ezekiel, God's prophet and a watchman for Israel, whose ministry parallels the prophetic ministry of the Messiah (used 92 times). Third, Daniel uses it in his prophecy to describe the Messiah, the Anointed One, the one who will rule and

ing of Psalm 8 to the singular person of Jesus. God chose to invest humanity with the dignity and personality of his own image and entrust the human person with the unique capacities and responsibilities of stewards over creation. Jesus shows us how God intended human life to be lived. Through his capacity to love, communicate, think, and worship, he demonstrated not only what it means to be spiritual but what it means to be human. True spirituality belongs to those who love life (Ps 34:11–14) and seek to live it in all its fullness (John 10:10). We were made to know God, but when we reject him we end up rejecting our own humanity.

The early church quoted Psalm 8 to reflect this new and fuller interpretation. What the psalmist applied to humanity in general was now applied to Jesus specifically. Paul wrote, "For he 'has put everything under his feet.' Now when it says that 'everything' has been put under him, it is clear that this does not include God himself, who put everything under Christ" (1 Cor 15:27). "And God placed all things under his feet and appointed him to be head over everything for the church . . ." (Eph 1:22). Peter Craigie writes, "In one sense, this is quite a new meaning, not evidently implicit in the psalm in its original meaning and context. And yet in another sense, it is a natural development of the thought of the psalm, for the dominion of which the psalmist spoke may have had theological reality, yet it did not always appear to have historical reality in the developing history of the human race. The historical reality, according to Paul and the author of the Epistle of Hebrews, is—and will be—fulfilled in the risen Christ."[6] The representative Son of Man became human to meet our need for redemption. "Since the children have flesh

---

reign. "In my vision at night I looked, and there before me was one like a son of man, coming with the clouds of heaven. He approached the Ancient of Days and was led into his presence" (Dan 7:13). Fourth and most importantly, it was the title of choice used by Jesus. It was his favorite self-designation: "Foxes have holes and birds of the air have nests, but the Son of Man has no place to lay his head" (Matt 8:20). ". . . So that you may know that the Son of Man has authority on earth to forgive sins. . . . 'Get up, take your mat and go home'" (Matt 9:6). "The Son of Man is Lord of the Sabbath" (Matt 12:8). "For as Jonah was three days and three nights in the belly of a huge fish, so the Son of Man will be three days and three nights in the heart of the earth" (Matt 12:40). "When Jesus came to the region of Caesarea Philippi, he asked his disciples, 'Who do people say the Son of Man is?'" (Matt 16:13). "The Son of Man did not come to be served, but to serve, and to give his life as a ransom for many" (Matt 20:28). F. F. Bruce: ". . . Ever since Jesus spoke of himself as the Son of Man, this expression has had for Christians a connotation beyond its etymological force, and it had this connotation for the writer of Hebrews" (Bruce, *Hebrews*, 73).

6. Craigie, *Psalms*, 110.

and blood, he too shared in their humanity so that by his death he might break the power of him who holds the power of death" (2:14). The pastor sees the fulfillment of Psalm 8 in Jesus. When he says, "But we do see Jesus," he means that Jesus is the Sovereign Redeemer who brings "many sons and daughters to glory" (Heb 2:10). Jesus entered into our humanity in order to do combat against the devil. The incarnate One is "humanity's champion who does battle on our behalf."[7]

The poetic description of Jesus' solidarity with humanity is powerful:

> "But we do see Jesus,
> who was made lower than the angels for a little while,
> now crowned with glory and honor because he suffered death,
> so that by the grace of God he might taste death for everyone."

The pastor wants the congregation to know that Jesus' suffering death follows from his supremacy over all creation and his solidarity with all humanity. The need for redemption because of our fallen human condition lies behind everything in the sermon. The pastor keeps this reality before us: "After he had provided purification for sins, he sat down at the right hand of the Majesty in heaven"(Heb 1:3).

The pastor intended a synergy between Jesus' solidarity with us and his suffering for us. He is the representative Son of Man and the Pioneer of our salvation. The themes of supremacy, solidarity, and suffering are woven together: "In bringing many sons and daughters to glory, it was fitting that God, for whom and through whom everything exists, should make the pioneer of their salvation perfect through what he suffered. Both the one who makes people holy and those who are made holy are of the same family" (Heb 2:10-11).

Jesus' atoning sacrifice on our behalf makes us into one family.[8] His redemptive suffering destroys any sense of moral merit or ethnic privilege. The Pioneer of our salvation has created one new family. He was made perfect through what he suffered so that we might be made holy. "He is the Savior who blazed a trail of salvation along which alone God's

---

7. Cole, *The God Who Became Human*, 132-33.

8. The rich and varied metaphors used to describe the creation of this family complement and reinforce one another. Whether by birth (John 1:11-12), adoption (Rom 8:14-17), or election (Eph 1:4), we are the sons and daughters of God through Christ, the Lamb that was slain before the creation of the world. Cockerill may make an unwarranted distinction when he warns against John and Paul's perspectives on the children of God prejudicing our understanding of Hebrews (Cockerill, *Hebrews*, 137).

"many sons and daughters" could be brought to glory."[9] There is no basis for any person, group, race, tribe, nation, or nations to feel superior. Our depravity is overcome, not because of what we have done, but because of "the one who makes people holy" (Heb 2:11).

Psalm 22 and Isaiah 8

The Apostle Paul is able to say, "For I am not ashamed of the gospel, because it is the power of God that brings salvation to everyone who believes . . ." (Rom 1:16), because Jesus "is not ashamed to call them brothers and sisters (Heb 2:11)." The pastor quotes Psalm 22 as the very words of Jesus to emphasize this deep relational truth. The messianic psalm begins with lament, "My God, my God, why have your forsaken me?" and continues with a vivid description of the cross. But of the psalm's two themes, lament and praise, suffering and solidarity, the pastor chooses to emphasize the latter. Jesus says, "I will declare your name to my brothers and sisters; in the assembly I will sing your praises."

The quick transition from Psalm 22 to Isaiah 8 is like an artist splashing colors, a dash here and a dash there. Our poet-pastor quotes two brief lines from Isaiah 8 without commentary and explanation. But these two lines speak volumes. In an instant we are transported back to another well-known messianic text.[10] Jesus is the full embodiment of trust in God, the trust that was foreshadowed in the prophet Isaiah and rejected by king Ahaz.

The pastor quotes Jesus saying, "I will put my trust in him" (Heb 2:13; Isa 8:17). The roots of the testimony go back to the seventh and eighth chapters of Isaiah. Isaiah declares the coming of the Davidic-Messiah. "The virgin will conceive and give birth to a son, and will call him Immanuel" (Isa 7:14). This is in keeping with the promise to David that his throne would be established forever (2 Sam 7:11–16) and fulfills the high expectations of the Anointed One, the Son of God, celebrated in Psalm 2 and anticipated in Psalm 45. The title *Immanuel* is unique to Isaiah, but it highlights earlier prophecy of the coming Messiah.

9. Bruce, *Hebrews*, 80.

10. Ibid., 82—Bruce writes, "This is a good example of C. H. Dodd's thesis that the principal Old Testament quotations in the New Testament are not isolated proof-texts, but carry their contexts with them by implication."

King Ahaz and the prophet Isaiah represent two radically different commitments to the Word of God.[11] Although they worshiped in the same temple they had different faiths. Ahaz was self-reliant, fearful, and opportunistic. Isaiah placed his trust in Yahweh. There was no middle ground between them. Ahaz refused to hear and understand the Word of God. He epitomized the hard-hearted response to Isaiah's Spirit-filled proclamation of the Word of God (Isa 6:9-10). He embodied the rejection that God had warned Isaiah to expect. Isaiah and Ahaz were polar opposites, representing the fear of God and the fear of man. For his part, Isaiah depended on the Word of the Lord. And even though the circumstances countered his faith, Isaiah was confident. "Bind up the testimony and seal up the law among my disciples. I will wait for the Lord, who is hiding his face from the house of Jacob. I will put my trust in him" (Isa 8:16-17). Isaiah and his family embodied the message of God. Twenty years after his call and commissioning (Isa 6:8), Isaiah declared, "Here am I, and the children the Lord has given me. We are signs and symbols in Israel from the Lord Almighty, who dwells on Mount Zion" (Isa 8:18). The prophet and his family were God's ordained visual aid pointing forward to Jesus Christ. They embodied the cruciform lifestyle that Immanuel was destined to fulfill. This is why the pastor drew on Isaiah's prophecy to underscore Jesus' solidarity with us in our redemptive need.

A Merciful and Faithful High Priest

Every time the pastor stresses the Son's solidarity with us he emphasizes the Son's suffering for us. Jesus is crowned with honor and glory because

11. Under Ahaz, the house of David was led by a king who wanted nothing to do with Yahweh, a conviction he seemed bent on proving. He "cast idols for worshiping the Baals" and "offered sacrifices and burned incense at the high places" (2 Chr 28:2,4). He "even sacrificed his son in the fire, following the detestable ways of the nations the Lord had driven out before the Israelites" (2 Kgs 16:3). Eventually, he stripped the temple of God of its furnishings, and sent the silver and gold to the king of Assyria. He said to the king of Assyria what he could not bring himself to say to Yahweh, "I am your servant and vassal. Come up and save me out of the hand of the king of Aram and of the king of Israel, who are attacking me" (2 Kgs 16:7-8). Chronicles reports that Ahaz "shut the doors of the Lord's temple" (2 Chr 28:24), but the account in Kings indicates that he remodeled the temple to please the Assyrians. Apparently Ahaz was especially proud of the new altar that he had built according to a design he saw in Damascus (2 Kngs 16:10-18). Through his acts of desecration, Ahaz effectively closed the temple down, but Uriah the priest still presided over this open-minded blending of diverse religious traditions. For his part, Ahaz was undoubtedly proud of his religious accomplishments. He "set up altars at every street corner in Jerusalem" (2 Chr 28:24).

"he suffered death, so that by the grace of God he might taste death for everyone" (Heb 2:9). We are made into a holy family by the pioneer of our salvation who was made "perfect through what he suffered" (Heb 2:10). Our bondage to sin and fear is broken because the Son, who shared in our humanity, died that we might live (Heb 2:14). We are the children of Abraham because Jesus became "fully human in every way, in order that he might become a merciful and faithful high priest in service of God, and that he might make atonement for the sins of the people" (Heb 2:17). The exalted Son's *solidarity with us* and *suffering for us* cannot be separated. His being and becoming are one. His deity can no more be divorced from his humanity than his humanity can be separated from his deity. The meaning of the incarnation and the purpose of redemption are understood together or not at all. We cannot fathom Christmas without embracing Good Friday and Easter.

Today's cultural ethos takes us back to Ahaz the ancient king of Judah. For all our talk of independence and self-fulfillment we are a needy people, filled with anxiety and fear. If we have money, we pay to have our home decorated, our lawn landscaped, our children tutored, our hair colored, our clothes tailored, our finances audited, our food prepared, and our property protected. If we don't have money, we envy those who do and dream about the freedom they enjoy. What we want out of life fuels our consumer culture. We want to be entertained, networked, managed, conditioned, and medicated. We need constant reassurance from our friends and family that we are loved and that our lives mean something. We crave excitement, escape, adventure, fun, and tender loving care. We are dependent on a host of experts, advisors, providers, suppliers, doctors, technicians, counselors, agents, lawyers, consultants, adjustors, therapists, designers, and life coaches. We know we need help in virtually every area of life but one. We don't need our sins forgiven. We don't need a merciful and faithful high priest in service to God, who makes atonement for our sins. Yet what we want and what we need can be two different things. And sooner or later we face a crisis of need, a clash between what we think we need and our true needs—our deepest needs. "We all, like sheep, have gone astray, each has turned to our own way; and the Lord has laid on him the iniquity of us all" (Isa 53:6).

The exalted Son's solidarity with us is for the purpose of overcoming the power of death and freeing us from the bondage of sin and death. But before we can truly appreciate what God in Christ has done for us we need to understand the deep-seated need of the human condition.

Humanity reduced to bunch of consumers in need of products and services fundamentally contradicts who we really are as image-bearers of God in need of salvation. Our great need is for atonement, not affirmation. We are much more than the sum total of our consumer wants and needs. Our soulful longings are not false, but real, and we need a merciful and faithful high priest. The pastor will have much more to say about our great high priest and his atoning sacrifice, but he introduces the gift of divine redemption in the light of the purpose of the incarnation. The atoning sacrifice of Christ follows from the Son's exalted status and suffering solidarity.

The Household of Faith

"Therefore, holy brothers and sisters, who share in the heavenly calling, fix your thoughts on Jesus, whom we acknowledge as our apostle and high priest" (Heb 3:1).

The pastor's tight textual weave of exposition and exhortation pivots on carefully selected key words, such as *high priest, holy,* and *brothers and sisters,* that propel the sermon forward. The pastor's agility in moving from one section to another "conveys underlying passion" and increases the drama of the delivery.[12] The pastor preaches to the community first and then to the individual, as can be seen by his emphasis on the descendants of Abraham, "holy brothers and sisters," and Christ's "atonement for the sins of the people." He develops the metaphor of God's house to underscore this corporate identity. "We are his house, if indeed we hold firmly to our confidence and the hope in which we glory" (Heb 3:6). Today we tend to focus on the individual and cater to personal felt needs with the result that the effectiveness of the sermon rides on whether or not the listener is moved emotionally. Sometimes it is the power of the preacher's stories and humorous anecdotes that impress the mind of the listener rather than the truth of the biblical text. But the pastor insists on keeping the focus on the main thing, the shared impact of gospel truth. Theologian David Wells wisely observed, "The self is a canvas too narrow, too cramped, to contain the largeness of Christian truth."[13]

---

12. Millar and Campbell, *Saving Eutychus,* 108.

13. Wells, *No Place For Truth,* 183.

The pastor celebrates the identity and dignity of the people of God by calling them "holy brothers and sisters," and by affirming that they all "share in the heavenly calling." There is no call more special than this heavenly calling. The call to discipleship and vocational holiness is the call of each and every believer. The challenge before all of us who follow Christ is to live a life worthy of the calling we have received "so that the body of Christ may be built up until we all reach unity in the faith and in the knowledge of the Son of God and become mature, attaining to the whole measure of the fullness of Christ" (Eph 4:1–13). All Christ's followers share this call. We have no biblical support for narrowing the call to a select few. All the saints are called to salvation, service, sacrifice, and simplicity. The key to fulfilling the purpose for which we were created (Gen 1:27–28; Ps 8:6–8) and the open secret to human flourishing (John 10:10) is found in the enthusiastic embrace of this calling.

The pastor follows up his first exhortation to "pay the most careful attention" to the gospel, so that we do not drift away (Heb 2:1–4), with a second exhortation: "Fix your thoughts on Jesus, whom we acknowledge as our apostle and high priest" (Heb 3:1). The purpose of the incarnation is affirmed in three ways: the Son's supremacy over us, his solidarity with us, and his sacrifice for us. The pastor uses two titles, "apostle" and "high priest," to define the identity of Jesus.[14] He is not only God's envoy, apostle, and pioneer, but he is also our merciful and faithful high priest who makes atonement for our sins. Jesus not only saves us by faith he shows us how to be faithful. In him we see what salvation looks like. This is the perfection of the incarnation. "He was faithful to the one who appointed him, just as Moses was faithful in all God's house." Faith *in* Jesus means practicing the faith *of* Jesus. He's not only the truth; he's the way. He's not only the creed; he's the commitment. He's not only the doctrine; he's the praxis and the plan. To believe in Jesus is to follow the example of Jesus.

One Greater Than Moses

"Jesus has been found worthy of greater honor than Moses, just as the builder of a house has greater honor than the house itself. For every house is build by someone, but God is the builder of everything. 'Moses was faithful as a servant in all God's house' (Num 12:7), bearing witness to what would be spoken by God

14. O'Brien, *Hebrews*, 129.

in the future. But Christ is faithful as the Son over God's house. And we are his house, if indeed we hold firmly to our confidence and the hope in which we glory" (Heb 3:3).

Moses was sent by God to deliver his people out of bondage. He "was faithful in all God's house," humbly and faithfully seeking to lead the people of God according to the will of God. When Miriam and Aaron opposed Moses, God came to his defense and affirmed his superiority over all the other prophets. "When there is a prophet among you, I, the Lord, reveal myself to them in visions, I speak to them in dreams. *But this is not true of my servant Moses; he is faithful in all my house.* With him I speak face to face, clearly and not in riddles; he sees the form of the Lord. Why then were you not afraid to speak against my servant Moses?" (Num 12:6–8).

But as great as Moses was, Jesus is far greater. Moses was a servant in God's house, but Jesus is the Son. Jesus is not just faithful *in* God's house; he is faithful *over* God's house. Once again the comparison between the lesser and the greater does not diminish the lesser, but shows how much greater God's final and definitive revelation is in the Son. The legacy of Moses's faith and faithfulness gives way to the far better faith and faithfulness of Jesus. Obviously, no "Moses" figure ought to stand in place of the Messiah. Pastors, teachers, parents, mentors, and friends are all servants practicing the faithfulness of Jesus. Their responsibility is to point to Jesus, not to themselves. We fix our eyes on Jesus, the object of our faith and the model for our faithfulness. We want to have both faith *in* Jesus and the faith *of* Jesus.

One final word of exhortation remains, a positive challenge that will only grow in depth and passion as the pastor continues: "We are his house, if indeed we hold firmly to our confidence and the hope in which we glory" (Heb 3:6). The challenge is not to the individual believer alone but to the people of God. Our shared identity in Christ depends on continuing faithfully in the faith we confess. The real test of genuine faith is found in faithfulness to the end. The pastor's challenge is twofold. We must hold firmly to our confidence (*parrhēsia*) in the gospel and we must hold firmly to "the hope in which we glory." The English word *confidence* may suggest inner self-assurance or peace of mind, but the Greek word *parrhēsia* goes beyond internal assurance and describes a confidence "that issues in a bold freedom of speech."[15] Instead of a private religious

15. O'Brien, *Hebrews*, 137.

confidence that satisfies the cowardly self, the pastor calls for a bold personal faith that has salt and light impact in the public arena. This is the confidence that requires courage and humility. To fix our thoughts on Jesus is to possess an authentic boldness that cannot be hidden or faked. The Holy Spirit gives believers the confidence to live for Christ "before an unbelieving world."[16]

The second part of this challenge is to hold fast to "the hope in which we glory." Once again, the faithful disciple can hardly suppress what he or she truly boasts or glories in. If our real hope is in Christ our priorities and ambitions are bound to change and the world will notice.[17] To glory in this hope is to live "with a robust faith in God's future reward rather than in pursuit of the temporal, visible rewards offered by the present world."[18] Wisdom requires that faithful disciples discern between the blessings of God that call forth praise and gratitude and the rewards of the world that fuel a worldly quest for success. Earthly rewards and blessings are received by those engaged in God's kingdom work and should be welcomed as a foretaste of the believer's heavenly reward. But we are all susceptible to the danger of being driven by "the lust of the flesh, the lust of the eyes, and the pride of life," the things that come "not from the Father but from the world" (1 John 2:15–17).

The little word *if* is a critical word in this exhortation. "We are his house, if indeed we hold firmly to our confidence and the hope in which we glory" (Heb 3:6). Then, the pastor repeats his emphasis, "We have come to share in Christ, if we hold our original conviction firmly to the

---

16. Cockerill, *Hebrews*, 173.

17. The Hebrews' Sermon resonates with the message of First Peter. Peter encouraged the "elect exiles" to embrace with joy the new reality chosen for them by the triune God. They are given new birth into a "living hope," into "an inheritance that can never perish, spoil or fade." They live into a new reality that far outweighs the social reality of being resident aliens. They eagerly await "the coming salvation that is ready to be revealed in the last time." Instead of suffering resentment because of their gospel-induced alienation, First Peter's chosen outsiders are "filled with an inexpressible and glorious joy." Believers are challenged to engage mentally and emotionally in the hard work of setting their hope on the grace of Christ. This is the hope that drives out fear because we have been given new birth into a living hope. Our identity in God the Father, Son, and Holy Spirit cannot be stolen. Our eternal salvation, experienced now and in the future, cannot be taken from us. Our destiny cannot be diverted. This is the hope that "does not close doors to relationship with other people out of either fear or hate. It turns, rather, in openness to others just as it turns to God" (Goppelt, *1 Peter*, 243).

18. Cockerill, *Hebrews*, 173.

very end" (Heb 3:14). F. F. Bruce writes, "Nowhere in the New Testament more than here do we find such repeated insistence on the fact that continuance in the Christian life is the test of reality. The doctrine of the final perseverance of the saints has as its corollary the salutary teaching that saints are the people who persevere to the end."[19] Bruce sees in Jesus' parable of the Sower a fitting illustration for the pastor's exhortation against the transitory nature of spurious faith. The seed that fell on rocky ground "sprang up quickly, because it did not have much soil. But when the sun came up, the plants were scorched, and they withered because they had no root" (Mark 4:5–6). Bruce concludes, "This is precisely what our author fears may happen with his readers; hence his constant emphasis on the necessity of their maintaining fearless confession and joyful hope."[20]

At the Name of Jesus[21]

At the name of Jesus every knee shall bow,
　Every tongue confess him King of glory now;
'Tis the Father's pleasure we should call him Lord,
　Who from the beginning was the mighty Word.

Humbled for a season to receive a name
　From the lips of sinners unto whom he came,
Faithfully he bore it spotless to the last,
　Brought it back victorious, when from death he passed.

Bore it up triumphant, with its human light,
　Through all ranks of creatures, in the central height,
To the throne of Godhead, to the Father's breast,
　Filled it with the glory of that perfect rest.

Christians, this Lord Jesus shall return again,
　With his Father's glory o'er the earth to reign;
For all wreaths of empire meet upon his brow,
　And our hearts confess him King of glory now.

MARIA NOEL CAROLINE, 1870

19. Bruce, *Hebrews*, 94.
20. Ibid.
21. McKim, ed., *The Presbyterian Hymnal*, 148.

How Deep The Father's Love For Us[22]

How deep the Father's love for us
How vast beyond all measure
That He should give His only Son
To make a wretch His treasure
How great the pain of searing loss
The Father turns His face away
As wounds which mar the Chosen One
Bring many sons to glory

STUART TOWNSEND

22. Stuart Townend, Copyright © 1995 Thankyou Music (Adm. by CapitolCMG-Publishing.com excl. UK & Europe, adm. by Integrity Music, part of the David C Cook family, songs@integritymusic.com).

6

Wilderness Generation
(Hebrews 3:7–4:13)

"I am honestly afraid that American evangelicalism is guilty of idolatry. It is bowing down, if I may borrow a biting phrase from philosopher William James, before the bitch goddess of success."

VERNON GROUNDS[1]

THE PASTOR'S EXPOSITION OF Psalm 95 supports his warning against hardhearted unbelief and inspires his vision for firm-to-the-end faithfulness. He presses home the urgency of his warning and the immediacy of his challenge by repeating *today* five times. The pastor's confidence is not in his personal powers of persuasion but in the Word of God that he describes as living and thus active, sharper than any double-edged surgical knife. The "laser-like penetrating quality" of God's Word can "divide the indivisible."[2] The preached Word penetrates the impenetrable and exposes the hidden recesses of the human heart. "Everything is uncovered and laid bare before the eyes of him to whom we must give account" (Heb 4:13). The Word of God "probes the inmost recesses of our spiritual being and brings the subconscious motives to light."[3]

1. Grounds, "Faith for Failure," 4.
2. Cockerill, *Hebrews*, 216.
3. Bruce, *Hebrews*, 113.

This description of the Word of God is remarkably parallel to the Apostle John's vision of the Son of Man in Revelation, whose penetrating gaze purifies and whose voice roars like white water thunder. This is the voice that no power on heaven or earth can silence. "Nations are in uproar, kingdoms fall; he lifts his voice, the earth melts"(Ps 46:6). "The voice of the Lord is over the waters; the God of glory thunders, the Lord thunders over the mighty waters. The voice of the Lord is powerful; the voice of the Lord is majestic. The voice of the Lord breaks the cedars" (Ps 29:3–4). The pastor describes the Word of God as a double-edged sword, recalling the words of Isaiah, "He will strike the earth with the rod of his mouth; with the breath of his lips he will slay the wicked" (Isa 11:2,4). The wisdom of God cuts through all the rhetoric and propaganda like a sword. It is like a double-edged surgical knife penetrating our defenses and exposing our strategies of self-deception. It slices open our self-justifying excuses, exposing our sinful actions. The pastor knows that "the art of preaching is to somehow or other get around our third-person defenses and compel a second-person recognition ["You are the man!" 2 Sam 12:7], which enables a first-person response."[4] It even cuts through all of our efforts to systematize and package the Word. We cannot box it up for easy consumption, and domesticate it for our convenience.

The pastor begins with the Holy Spirit and ends with the Word of God. The pastor's expressed confidence is in the Word and Spirit of God. His urgent warning and bold challenge are based exclusively on the authority of God's Word, which is his only hope for penetrating the hidden hardness of the believer's heart. His biblically based sermon draws on God's precedent-setting judgment against the Israelites in the wilderness. Psalm 95 takes us back to Israel's failure in the wilderness, when the beneficiaries of the Exodus quarreled with Moses over water at Rephidim (Exod 17:7) and rebelled against the Lord at Kadesh (Num 14). Their refusal to go into the promised land summed up their chronic contempt for God. "Kadesh became the symbol of Israel's disobedience, the place where God's past redemption was forgotten and where divine promise no longer impelled the people to obedience."[5] Psalm 95 goes beyond isolated instances of sin and exposes a persistent pattern of stubborn rebellion and hardhearted resistance to the will of God. Their constant waywardness is

4. Peterson, *Leap Over A Wall*, 185.

5. Lane, *Hebrews*, 1:85.

captured in the Lord's verdict: "Their hearts are always going astray, and they have not known my ways" (Heb 3:10).

As noted earlier, the pastor is concerned that the recipients of his sermon are in danger of drifting away (Heb 2:1) and falling into a pattern of unbelief. In this second exhortation, he intensifies his admonition: "See to it, brothers and sisters, that none of you has a sinful, unbelieving heart that turns away from the living God" (Heb 3:12). This warning coupled with his emphasis on the penetrating power of the Word of God suggests that the congregation may not be aware of the danger it is in. In hindsight the rebellion of the Exodus generation "is not simply lack of trust or passive disbelief, but a positive refusal to believe, an active disobedience to God."[6] But in the moment, when the fear of running out of the water was real and when they heard the majority report describe giants in the land (Num 14:31–33), the Israelites undoubtedly felt that their concerns were reasonable if not justified. What Moses saw as rebellion, they saw as common sense, and what Caleb and Joshua saw as a God-given opportunity, they saw as foolhardy. They were truly guilty "of rampant unbelief and faithlessness," but because of the hardness of their hearts they did not see it that way.[7] Such is the deceptiveness of sin that it is difficult to discern our passive resistance to the will of God.

The pastor sees a close parallel between the wilderness generation and the recipients of his sermon. He links Exodus typology to the wilderness Israelites and the church. F. F. Bruce explains, "The death of Christ is itself called an 'exodus' (Luke 9:31); he is the true passover, sacrificed for his people, 'a lamb without blemish and spot' (1 Pet 1:19). They, like Israel in early days, are 'the church in the wilderness' (Acts 7:38); their baptism into Christ is the antitype of Israel's passage through the Red Sea (1 Cor 10:1f); their sacramental feeding on him by faith is the antitype of Israel's nourishment with manna and the water from the rock (1 Cor 10:3f). Christ, the living Rock, is their guide through the wilderness (1 Cor 10:4b); the heavenly rest which lies before them is the counterpart to the earthly Canaan which is the goal of the Israelites."[8]

6. O'Brien, *Hebrews*, 146.

7. Ibid., 154.

8. Bruce, *Hebrews*, 96–97; see Jude 5.

Today's Congregation

We tend to *overhear* this sermon as a message intended for someone else, but if we are honest the pastor is speaking to us. Believers who are in danger of becoming "hardened by sin's deceitfulness" do not see the threat. They blend into the prevailing culture and imbibe the religious practices of the day. They acclimate to the mores and manners, ethics and ethos, of the surrounding culture. They tone down the message of the gospel. Sermons aim to uplift the human spirit and bolster self-esteem. Christians want to make Christianity look attractive and appealing to the world. The line between church and world is blurred in an effort to justify our existence to the world. We publicize our humanitarian efforts and downplay the truth of the gospel. We equivocate on sexual ethics and build our institutions with the marketing principles of the world. Like the believers in Rome, if we have any hope of redeeming our witness, we will have "to disentangle the life and identity of the church from the life and identity of American society." Sociologist James Hunter continues, "For conservatives and progressives alike, Christianity far too comfortably legitimates the dominant political ideologies and far too uncritically justifies the prevailing macroeconomic structures and practices of our time . . . . The moral life and everyday social practices of the church are also far too entwined with the prevailing normative assumptions of American culture . . . . Christianity has uncritically assimilated to the dominant ways of life in a manner dubious at the least. Even more, these assimilations arguably compromise the fundamental integrity of its witness to the world."[9]

In the mainline church the "weird stuff" like the virgin birth, the incarnation, the bodily resurrection of Jesus, and belief in a real heaven and hell, are often relegated to private belief and personal opinion. The weekly recital of the creedal confession caters more to nostalgia than to the bold confession of countercultural truth. Both mainline Protestants and popular evangelicals are struggling with evangelism in a post-Christian culture. It has become difficult to offer the gospel of Jesus Christ in a distinctive voice. Our evangelism sounds either like spiritualized political correctness or Christianized self-help.

We are more like the Israelites in the wilderness than we care to admit. We are guilty of turning "away from the living God" in self-justifying ways that impress us as preeminently reasonable. Like the majority report of the twelve spies we are ready to capitulate to the perceived strength of

9. Hunter, *To Change the World*, 184–85.

the prevailing culture. The culture before us is stronger than we are and we lack the faith and resolve to boldly proclaim and live the gospel. We have chimed in with the "bad report" and concluded, "We seemed like grasshoppers in our own eyes, and we looked the same to them" (Num 13:33).

This is why we need the double-edged surgical knife of God's Word to cut through the equivocations, distortions, and excuses. We need everything uncovered and "laid bare before the eyes of him to whom we must give account" (Heb 4:13). Or else, we will end up like the wilderness generation wandering about aimlessly until we die.

Six Strategies of Self-Deception

The pastor's concern and goal is to expose the "beguiling lines of rationalization" that seduce and weaken our resolve to obey Christ and witness boldly.[10] "The deceptive power of sin is not an excuse for disobedience but an urgent call for vigilant resistance."[11] We must not allow ourselves to be hardened.[12] "But encourage one another daily, as long as it is called 'Today,' so that none of you may be hardened by sin's deceitfulness" (Heb 3:13). The process of petrification of wood is a helpful analogy to what happens to sin-hardened hearts. In the slow conversion of wood to stone, "the organic material of the wood is replaced by inorganic minerals . . . leaving a stone mold in place of the original form."[13] "In the same way," writes Robert Saucy, "we can almost unconsciously harden our hearts by drifting through life without attention to the choices we are making every day. . . . We can let the vitality of our spiritual life begin to decay and allow the nonliving materials of our environment to seep into our heart and very slowly replace the tissues of the soft, pliable new heart with the hard, lifeless—death-dealing—material of the world around us."[14]

Discerning the complex disguises of self-deception is every disciple's personal challenge. It is only by the grace of God that we will have the wisdom and discipline to detect sin's persistent insidiousness. Diagnosis requires prayer, diligence, and insightful spiritual directors. Classic

10. Bruce, *Hebrews*, 101.

11. Cockerill, *Hebrews*, 187.

12. Ibid.

13. Saucy, *Minding the Heart*, 59.

14. Ibid.

works on the Christian life describe these petrifying tendencies that inevitably lead to hardness of heart. Authors like Richard Baxter, Søren Kierkegaard, William Wilberforce, and C. S. Lewis identify six patterns of self-deception. These are the subtle strategies that lead to an "unbelieving heart that turns away from the living God" (Heb 3:12). The pastor challenges us to "encourage one another daily, as long as it is called 'Today,' so that none of you may be hardened by sin's deceitfulness" (Heb 3:13).

1. *Self-Serving Bias:* Danish Christian philosopher Søren Kierkegaard suggested that becoming aware of our sin is like trying to see our own eyeballs. We have a natural inclination to pacify and placate our conscience. We tend to grade ourselves on a curve, like the Pharisee in Jesus' parable, who looked down on the tax collector and thanked the Lord that he was not like "this tax collector" (Luke 18:9–14). We excuse ourselves by judging others. British abolitionist William Wilberforce warned that we have a "natural proneness to think too favorably of ourselves." Selfishness disposes us to "overrate our good qualities, and to overlook or excuse our defects." We are misled in our self-evaluation by "the favorable opinions of others" and by substituting good intentions for meaningful moral and spiritual change.[15]

2. *Moral Indifference:* Wilberforce contended that moral ambiguity produced a false comfort and led to self-justifying ways. We present Christian faith and practice in vague moral generalities which leave specific sins unchecked. "Instead of tracing and laying open all the secret motions of inward corruption, and instructing their hearers how best to conduct themselves in every distinct phase of the Christian warfare, they generalize about it . . . . They will confess in general terms to be 'miserable sinners.' But it is an expression really of secret self-complacency."[16] The only reason we are not as strong and vital as the early church is not due to our ignorance or inability but because we never intended to change our ways.[17]

3. *Theoretical Niceness:* We think we are better than we are by taking credit for untested righteousness. We commend ourselves for our theoretical goodness, but as C. S. Lewis observed, our goodness is untested. "If, being cowardly, conceited and slothful, you have never yet done a fellow creature great mischief, that is only because your neighbor's welfare

15. Wilberforce, *Real Christianity*, 114–15.

16. Ibid., 125.

17. Lewis, *Problem of Pain*, 66.

has not yet happened to conflict with your safety, self-approval, or ease."[18] Seventeenth-century Puritan pastor Richard Baxter honed in on the gap between theory and practice. People are happy to have the Word of God preached. They may in fact insist on it, but they have no intention of changing and becoming obedient to the Word. Baxter warns the pastor, "They will give you leave to preach against their sins, and to talk as much as you will for godliness in the pulpit, if you will but let them alone afterwards, and be friendly and merry with them in your conversation. For they take the pulpit to be but a stage."[19]

4. *Ethical Amnesia:* We overlook wrongs that we committed in the distant past. "We have a strange illusion," C. S. Lewis said, "that mere time cancels sin." We recount past sins of our youth with laughter, as if the sins themselves make us more interesting people. "But mere time does nothing either to the fact or to the guilt of a sin. The guilt is washed out not by time but by repentance and the blood of Christ."[20] William Wilberforce observed, "We tend to see only those things which we have recently fallen into, and overlook wrongs committed awhile back. If recent, we will have deep remorse for such sins and vices. But after a few months or years, they leave but very faint traces in our recollection."[21]

5. *Cultural Bias:* One of the many disguises of self-deception diagnosed by both Wilberforce and Lewis is our inclination to feel superior to people in other times and cultures because we do not practice their particular sins. We should ask ourselves, Lewis says, "whether God ought to have been content with the cruelty of cruel ages because they excelled in courage and chastity." God neither overlooks their cruelty nor approves "our softness, worldliness, and timidity."[22] Wilberforce warned that we are apt to overlook the persistent sin, the sin that we have grown used to, "the sin that so easily entangles," and pride ourselves on some over-exaggerated virtue. Self-deception is also compounded by claiming victory over a particular sin we have simply lost interest in or grown out of. Wilberforce observed, "The youth of one sex may indulge occasionally in licentious excesses. Those of the other may be given over to vanity and pleasure. Provided they are sweet-tempered, and open, and not disobedi-

---

18. Ibid., 65.
19. Baxter, *The Reformed Pastor*, 85.
20. Lewis, *Problem of Pain*, 61.
21. Wilberforce, *Real Christianity*, 114.
22. Lewis, *Problem of Pain*, 64.

ent to their parents and superiors, the former are deemed good-hearted young men, and the latter innocent young women."[23]

6. Selective Morality: Wilberforce wasn't buying the excuse that youth will be youth and that it is normal for them to sow their wild oats. He contended that such a view overlooks the grave danger of divine displeasure and makes light of sin. Young people appear to outgrow sexual promiscuity and vanity, when they get married and settle down, but the guilt of past sins remains. The old sins of self-indulgence morph into the new sins of selfish ambition and materialistic pursuits. Middle-aged people "congratulate themselves on having removed vices, which they are no longer strongly tempted to commit."[24] In old age, we are tempted to condone and excuse sin, making light of it in young people, expecting it in mid-lifers, and justifying our opinionated, selfish ways. "Thus throughout the whole of life," Wilberforce concludes, "we devise some means or other for stifling the voice of conscience. 'We cry peace, when there is no peace!'"[25]

When my wife Virginia and I lived in a one-bedroom apartment in Toronto, we had a problem with cockroaches. Late at night I would go into the kitchen, flip on the light, and see these creatures scurry across the floor or counter. A light sleeper by nature, I developed a nocturnal habit of hunting down cockroaches at 3 AM. After several weeks of this admittedly odd habit I decided it was time to get serious and find out where all the cockroaches were coming from. What I discovered shocked me. In the crack between the kitchen cabinets and the ceiling were literally hundreds of cockroaches, nesting right above our food. My nightly antic of hunting down a few cockroaches was nothing more than playing with the problem. We had to clear everything out of the kitchen and call in an exterminator. When I am tempted to deal lightly with my sin, I remember how I deceived my self into thinking that knocking off a few cockroaches would solve the problem. Sometimes we play with our sin. We know sin is there and we stomp on it occasionally, but we don't deal with the source.

The pastor calls us to detect the complex strategies of self-deception. We are warned that we have a built-in insensitivity to our true spiritual state. We easily succumb to a moral indifference made worse

23. Wilberforce, *Real Christianity*, 115.

24. Ibid.

25. Ibid.

by overexposure to certain sins and distracted by busy lives. We become desensitized to greed, accustomed to gossip, callous to those in need, complacent with premarital sex, indifferent to a steady diet of media violence. Like the proverbial frog in the kettle, we don't notice the steadily rising temperature. We find "safety in numbers" and in the excuse "everybody does it." Our actions and attitudes might impress believers from Africa and China as scandalous, but we have become accustomed to our private excesses, spiritual complacency, and moral laxity. What strikes them as sinful and abnormal behavior, especially for sincere believers, has become the new normal for us.

The pastor is convinced that faithfulness to the end proves faith from the beginning. "We have come to share in Christ, if indeed we hold our original conviction firmly to the very end" (Heb 3:14). He is also concerned that professing believers can be hardened by sin's deceitfulness. They can possess a sinful, unbelieving heart. Like the mass of Israelites who had experienced the redeeming power of God, but who were denied entrance into the promised land, professing believers must hold to their original conviction if they expect to enter their promised rest. "The parallel between those Israelites and the people of God in the new age is impressive enough for the disaster which befell the former to serve as a warning to the latter."[26]

Our responsibility is to let the Word of God perform its diagnostic work. Its not so much we who interpret the Bible as it is the Bible that interprets us. The pastor has the utmost confidence in the penetrating power of the Word and Spirit of God to lead to discernment. "The word of God is living and active. Sharper than any double-edged sword, it penetrates even to dividing soul and spirit, joints and marrow; it judges the thoughts and attitudes of the heart" (Heb. 4:12). Much is hidden from our eyes, but "nothing in all creation is hidden from God's sight," therefore it is crucial to listen to God's Word with open ears and an open mind (Heb 4:13).

There are many ways the devil seeks to destroy the gospel in people's lives. How difficult it must be for an abused child to believe in the love of God and a spoiled, materialist child may not fare much better. The devil uses many things to harden our hearts: money, sex, and power, to name three. But we should never say that it is impossible for anyone, including ourselves, to hear the gospel, because we know that the Word of God "is

26. Bruce, *Hebrews,* 105.

sharp as a surgeon's scalpel, cutting through everything, whether doubt or defense, laying us open to listen and obey." We agree with the writer of Hebrews, "Nothing and no one is impervious to God's Word" (Heb 4:12–13, *The Message*).

True Rest

The pressing importance of the pastor's exhortation is emphasized by the repetition of the word *today* five times. The eschatological vision of authentic faithfulness is accented by thirteen references to *rest*. These two words, *today* and *rest*, form a dynamic *already, not yet* tension. Daily faithfulness and everlasting rest are inseparably linked. When the next generation of Israelites finally entered God's promised land, they experienced rest from their enemies (Deut 12:10; Josh 23:1), but that rest was only a type of the everlasting rest promised in Christ. The psalmist clearly meant a rest that goes beyond the experience of Joshua. "For if Joshua had given them rest, God would not have spoken later about another day" (Heb 4:8). The pastor sees the ground for this everlasting rest at the beginning of time in creation's seventh day. "There remains, then, a Sabbath rest for the people of God; for anyone who enters God's rest also rests from their works, just as God did from his" (Heb 4:9–10). Taken together these two types, Israel in the land and God resting on the seventh day, point forward to God's everlasting rest (Rev 14:13). But as we go deeper into Hebrews we will see the significance of Christ's high priestly work in achieving this ultimate rest by fulfilling the Day of Atonement ("a day of sabbath rest," Lev 16:31) and we will see that "the imagery of rest is best understood as a complex symbol for the whole soteriological process."[27]

The pastor has much more to say about salvation and how Jesus is "our apostle and high priest" (Heb 3:1), but for now he introduces the goal for which we ought to strive. This is the promised rest that invokes "the longing for a better country—a heavenly one" (Heb 11:16); that awakens a deep godly fear that we not fall short of it (Heb 4:1); and that we "make every effort to enter into this rest" (Heb 4:11). This challenge is for every disciple and requires constant vigilance. Our English translation, "make every effort," hardly does justice to the intensity of the Greek phrase. It means, "Take pains," "Spare no effort," "Give it all you've got." Obviously the pastor intends an all-out effort. A lackadaisical attitude will never

27. Guthrie, "Hebrews," 959.

accomplish what the pastor has in mind. Any hint of passivity or a laid-back attitude is excluded. "This blissful rest in unbroken fellowship with God is the goal to which his people are urged to press forward."[28] How shall we interpret the pastor's exhortation in today's climate of easy grace and moral permissiveness? We are quick to give ourselves grace and to appease our consciences by comparing ourselves to others who we judge to be worse than we are. We tend write off the hard work of righteousness as works righteousness and conclude our services with the mantra, "There is now no condemnation to those who are in Christ," without seriously considering what it means to be in Christ today.

If Thou But Trust in God to Guide Thee[29]

If thou but trust in God to guide thee, with hopeful heart through all thy ways,
 God will give strength whate'er betide thee, to bear thee through the evil days.
Who trusts in God's unchanging love builds on the Rock that none can move.

Only be still, and wait God's leisure in cheerful hope, with heart content
 To take whate'er thy Keeper's pleasure and all-discerning Love hath sent.
No doubt our inmost wants are clear to One who holds us always dear.

Sing, pray, and swerve not from God's ways, but do thine own part faithfully;
 Trust the rich promises of grace, so shall they be fulfilled in thee.
God never yet forsook at need the soul secured by trust indeed.

GEORG NEUMARK, 1657, TRANS. CATHERINE WINKWORTH, 1855

28. Bruce, *Hebrews*, 110.
29. McKim, ed., *The Presbyterian Hymnal*, 282.

7

A Warning Against Apostasy
(Hebrews 4:14–6:20)

"There is an admirable conjunction of diverse excellencies in Jesus Christ: infinite highness and infinite condescension, infinite justice and infinite grace, infinite glory and lowest humility, infinite majesty and transcendent meekness, equality with God and the deepest reverence towards God, infinite worthiness of good and the greatest patience under sufferings of evil, and absolute sovereignty and perfect resignation."

JONATHAN EDWARDS[1]

THE PASTOR DEEPENS HIS exposition and intensifies his exhortation by focusing on Jesus our great high priest. He proclaims the supremacy, solidarity, and sacrifice of Christ. He challenges us to fix our thoughts on Jesus (Heb 3:1). He exhorts us to do for ourselves what no one can do for us, to "hold firmly to the faith we profess" (Heb 3:6; 4:14). The sermon's alternating force of exposition and exhortation jackhammer our petrified hearts. The pastor knows how religion can subvert the faith and suppress the truth. He identifies nominal Christianity as the believer's primary problem. He warns against drifting away from "so great a salvation" (2:1–3) and turning "away from the living God" (3:12). The pastor targets a religious culture that is familiar with Christianity and diminishes

1. Edwards, *The Excellency of Christ.*

86

genuine faith in Christ. His only hope is for the penetrating power of the Word of God "to help us in our time of need" (Heb 4:16).

Our Great High Priest

The focus in the middle section of the sermon (Heb 4:14–10:25) is on Jesus our great high priest. The pastor begins and ends with the positive admonition to draw near to God: "Let us then approach God's throne of grace with confidence . . ." (Heb 4:16), and "Let us draw near to God with a sincere heart and with the full assurance that faith brings . . ." (Heb 10:22). The pastor's central theological argument demonstrates the superiority of Jesus over the Aaronic priesthood (Heb 5:1–10); the fulfillment of God's promises to Abraham through Jesus the superior high priest in the order of Melchizedek (Heb 6:13–7:28); the superiority of Jesus' sacrificial ministry through the new covenant (Heb 8:1–9:10); and the perfection of Jesus' once-and-for-all sacrifice of himself for our sins (Heb 9:11–10:18).

The consistent refrain throughout the pastor's Christ-centered manifesto is a warning against immaturity and apostasy. All believers are challenged to be diligent to the end and not to throw away their confidence. These pastoral exhortations (Heb 5:11–6:12; 10:19–39) are not digressions but the very purpose for the theological expositions. A faithful exposition of Hebrews seeks to keep pace with the pastor and allow the momentum of his message to build. Verse by verse exposition tends to flatten the text and rob Hebrews of its impact.[2] The pastor's straightforward exposition proves the supremacy of Jesus' high priestly ministry, the superiority of the new covenant, and the perfection of his atoning sacrifice. There is plenty of material here for scholars to explore in depth, but the thrust of the pastor's comprehensive argument must be allowed to come through. We must keep in mind that this was a sixty-minute sermon delivered to a worshiping congregation. The spiraling impact of theological exposition and pastoral exhortation ought to be held together in tension. By breaking the text down into small units, the preacher narrows his focus and his sermon loses energy. The thrust of the message

---

2. James Earl Massey writes in *Preaching Hebrews*, 124–25, "The lengthy and involved argument presented in Hebrews does not yield readily to an easy break-down for sermonizing and many blocks of material deal with the same aspect of thought, although ascensively."

may be lost in the details of the text. It is better to follow the tension in the text to the passion of the passage.

The pastor places polar opposite truths, absolute transcendence and deep empathy, in radical juxtaposition. In Christ, we have a high priest who is both the Son of God and the Son of Man. The incarnate One transcends his transcendence and takes on our weakness in every respect except without sin. He became "fully human in every way, in order that he might become a merciful and faithful high priest in service of God, and that he might make atonement for the sins of the people" (Heb 2:17). As the ascended Lord, Jesus "sat down at the right hand of the Majesty in heaven" (Heb 1:3); as the incarnate One, Jesus knows our needs, understands our temptations and empathizes with our weaknesses. "Sympathy with the sinner in his trial does not depend on the experience of sin which only the sinless can know in its full intensity. He who fails yields before the last strain."[3]

Jesus alone is worthy of all "power and wealth and wisdom and strength and honor and glory and praise" (Rev 5:12), because he alone has experienced powerlessness, poverty, weakness, dishonor, and shame without sin. To receive empathy from people who have failed as we have failed may make us feel better, but we need the empathy that leads to redemption. Pity offers slight consolation, but real comfort comes through atonement. Only in Jesus do we have the grace to draw near to God.

Every high priest "is able to deal gently with those who are ignorant and are going astray, since he himself is subject to weakness" (Heb 5:2). His empathy is due to the fact that he is a sinner like everyone else. "This is why he has to offer sacrifices for his own sins, as well as for the sins of the people" (Heb 5:3). The authority of the high priest lies not in his sinful self, but in God. His value lies in his divine appointment: "no one takes this honor on himself, but he receives it when called by God, just as Aaron was" (Heb 5:4).

The pastor takes up both themes, divine appointment and human empathy, and applies them in reverse order to Jesus. "Christ did not take on himself the glory of becoming a high priest" (Heb 5:5). He was called of God, who said to him, "You are my Son; today I have become your Father" (Ps 2:7). "And he says in another place, 'You are a priest forever, in the order of Melchizedek'" (Ps 110:4). By quoting from these two psalms, the pastor reiterates the first and the last verses quoted in his overture

---

3. B. F. Westcott, quoted in Bruce, *Hebrews*, 116.

(Heb 1:5–13). He opened with seven declarations heralding Christ's divine appointment. He continues here with an emphasis on Jesus' humanity and empathy (Heb 5:7–10). Jesus' priestly empathy is rooted in his experience of suffering.

Learned Obedience

The pastor begins by saying, "During the days of Jesus' life on earth" (Heb 5:7). He does this to draw out Jesus' exemplary faithfulness. The One who is "the radiance of God's glory and the exact representation of his being" offered up "prayers and petitions with fervent cries and tears to the one who could save him from death" (Heb 5:7). If "he was heard because of his reverent submission," should we not expect to pray as he prayed? If he who knew no sin learned "obedience from what he suffered" (Heb 5:8), should we not expect the same? The unexpected twist comes when the pastor assumes Jesus' essential deity with the quick phrase, "Son though he was," and then proceeds to emphasize the long, hard struggle of faithfulness. The One who was already perfect *became* perfect by the things that he suffered. The Savior from all eternity became "the source of eternal salvation" (Heb 5:9). The heir of all things was "designated by God to be the high priest in the order of Melchizedek" (Heb 5:10). The pastor has a clear view of the being and becoming of Jesus, but here he emphasizes the becoming of Jesus so that we will identify with him and his long obedience to the end.

The picture of Jesus offering "up prayers and petitions with fervent cries and tears to the one who could save him from death," recalls his Gethsemane experience (Mark 14:33–36). It was in the garden that Jesus grappled with the "the horrifying cup of vicarious suffering."[4] The imminent prospect of severe physical abuse and the extreme torture of crucifixion undoubtedly caused intense emotional pain. But the real trauma of Gethsemane was his contemplation of the Father's abandonment. The full impact of the sin of all humanity bore down on him. His painful struggle was real, his humanity true, and his courage undaunted.

Although Jesus' experience of Gethsemane was unique, the pastor means for us to learn from his example. The human experience of God and God's experience of humanity are not mutually exclusive. Jesus' Gethsemane defines the strength that is made perfect in weakness.

4. France, *Matthew*, 373.

Likewise, all of us who take up our cross and follow Jesus will have our own "Gethsemanes." This is when the will of God takes us where we do not want to go. But it is only by virtue of his Gethsemane that our Gethsemanes make sense. Salvation depends on his death and resurrection.

The pastor will resume his theology of Christ when he returns to the Melchizedek theme (Heb 7:1ff), but first he feels compelled to address pressing pastoral concerns. Exposition and exhortation are woven together so tightly that they are inseparable.

Sluggishness

The pastor's transition from exposition to exhortation conveys real concern for his "dear friends" (Heb 6:9). Pastors can empathize with him when he says, "We have much to say about this, but it is hard to make it clear to you because you no longer try to understand" (Heb 5:11). His assessment of the congregation's ability to grasp his message is straightforward and honest. Apparently he doesn't consider them to be very teachable. He chooses a colorful word (nōthroi), variously interpreted as "sluggish," "dull," or "lazy," to describe the congregation's failure to understand. The word "usually connoted culpable negligence."[5] Instead of being able to teach and disciple others, they were still going over the ABC's of the faith. They were stuck on the elementary elements of the Christian faith. This key word, sluggish, begins and ends this section (Heb 5:11–6:12), forming an inclusio. To paraphrase, "clarity is difficult because you are so sluggish" (Heb 5:11), and "don't grow sluggish, but imitate the faithful" (Heb 6:12).

If the first generation of believers in Rome were in danger of sluggishness, I wonder how much more difficult it is today when spiritual laziness has become for many professing Christians an ingrained religious habit. Few believers seem motivated to delve into the meaning of the gospel for their daily lives. Young people go off to university with a poor grasp of what they believe. Families seem more interested in admiring Jesus from their suburban comfort zone than following Jesus into Sermon on the Mount faithfulness. Believers may know a few tenets of the faith but they have not "trained themselves to distinguish good from evil" (Heb 5:14). Adults show little interest in understanding how God's word applies to their vocational lives. The pastor's chief concern is not their intellectual capacity or mental laziness as much as it their willful

5. O'Brien, Hebrews, 205.

neglect and spiritual resistance.[6] N. T. Wright asks why "so many Christians are not only eager to stay with a diet of milk, but actually get cross at the suggestion that they should be eating something more substantial?" Wright observes,

> In my own country I meet a settled prejudice, even among people who are highly intelligent in other areas, who work in demanding professions, who read serious newspapers and magazines and who would be ashamed not to know what was going on in the world, against making any effort at all to learn what the Christian faith is about. As a result we find, both inside the churches and outside, an extraordinary ignorance of who Jesus really was, what Christians have believed and should believe about God and the world. . . . Some Christians are indeed eager and ready for solid food. But I deeply regret that, in many churches in Western Europe at least, it seems that the most people can be persuaded to take on board is another small helping of warm milk.[7]

Solid food unites knowing and obeying God. Faith and practice form a dynamic synergy. Theology informs ethics and ethics informs theology. "But solid food is for the mature, who by constant use have trained themselves to distinguish good from evil" (Heb 5:14). As Bonhoeffer said, "Only he who believes is obedient, and only he who is obedient believes."[8] The holistic life of obedience and devotion is a major concern of all the New Testament writers. The costly work of the crucified Son inspires the believer's obedience. The apostle Peter used a working-class metaphor to describe the believer's active pursuit: "Therefore, having girded up the loins of your mind set your hope on the grace to be brought to you when Jesus Christ is revealed in his coming" (1 Pet 1:13). The mental image is of a Near Eastern laborer tucking up a long robe in his belt so that he could go about his work unhindered. Peter challenges believers to mentally and emotionally engage in the hard work of setting their hope on the grace of Christ.

Every aspect of mental effort, emotional affection, and vocational responsibility is gathered up and focused on the life and teaching of Christ. The Apostle Paul described it this way: "Let this mind be in you which was also in Christ Jesus" (Phil 2:5) and, "Do not conform to the pattern

6. Ibid., 206.

7. Wright, *Hebrews*, 52.

8. Bonhoeffer, *Cost of Discipleship*, 69.

of this world, but be transformed by the renewing of your mind" (Rom 12:2). The pastor's prescription is clear: "Let yourself move forward"—or in other words, "So come on, let's leave the preschool finger-painting exercises on Christ and get on with the grand work of art. Grow up in Christ" (Heb 6:1, *The Message*). He describes "the elementary teachings about Christ" in three pairs of six items:

(1) repentance from acts that lead to death and faith in God;

(2) instruction about cleansing rites and the laying on of hands;

(3) the resurrection of the dead and the eternal judgment.

F. F. Bruce observes that these "rudiments" are not uniquely Christian but could have their "place in a fairly orthodox Jewish community."[9] Although Christianity gave each item new significance and meaning, they posed "a subtle danger" for Jewish Christians "which could not be experienced by converts from paganism."[10] Pagan converts had to make a clear break from their former paganism. There was little temptation to revert back to paganism unless they were prepared to reject the Christian faith outright. Apparently the letter's original recipients were tempted to revert back to their religious traditions. It was possible for them to gradually give up what was distinctively Christian while retaining their traditional religious roots.

A similar danger exists today for Christians, regardless of their denominational heritage, to substitute their religious tradition for life-transforming discipleship. These elementary teachings can be transposed into different traditions. For example, "Repentance from acts of that lead to death," is the equivalent of coming forward in an evangelistic crusade. "Faith in God" is a cliché for believing in the importance of spirituality. "Cleansing rites" and "laying on of hands" involves compliance with entrance requirements for church membership. And "the resurrection of the dead and the eternal judgment" boils down religious slogans such as "once saved always saved." The elementary teachings can become twisted into a quasi-Christian folk religion. A Christless Christianity involves checking the boxes: baptism, confirmation, membership, church attendance, and tithing. But the nominal Christian experiences little genuine faith in Christ and no life transformation "in accordance with the truth that is in Jesus" (Eph 4:21). The outward show of religion replaces

9. Bruce, *Hebrews*, 139.

10. Ibid., 143.

authentic Christian discipleship. Hebrews warns against a form of Christianity that competes against true faith in Christ "by being inoculated with something which, for the time being, looks so like the real thing that it is generally mistaken for it."[11]

Religious Admirers

Søren Kierkegaard believed that Christians in his day were assimilated into the culture so completely that there was no real difference between a Christian and a non-Christian. Everyone was a Christian, because no one was a Christian. Kierkegaard lamented that "Christianity marches to a different melody, to the tune of 'Merrily we roll along, roll along, roll along'—Christianity is enjoyment of life, tranquilized, as neither the Jew nor the pagan was, by the assurance that the thing about eternity is settled, settled precisely in order that we might find pleasure in enjoying this life, as well as any pagan or Jew."[12]

Kierkegaard might have preferred to topple shrines and break stained glass windows, but he determined that violent gestures would prove nothing because there was nothing wrong with the externals in themselves. The church's doctrine and hymnal were orthodox. The problem wasn't with the outward form of the church; the problem was the heart of the matter. Christianity had been surreptitiously turned into a cheap imitation knock-off. Establishment religion had replaced New Testament Christianity. Today we would call it cultural religion. Kierkegaard was frustrated because his stringent criticism of the church didn't even cause a ripple. Thus, he determined that "Henceforth I will write in such a way as to irritate people into facing the issues."[13]

Flannery O'Connor was another writer who contended with cultural Christianity. "I think it is safe to say that while the South is hardly Christ-centered," she wrote, "it is most certainly Christ-haunted."[14] Her grotesque fictional characters were often professing Christians whose thin veneer of cultural Christianity was exposed, revealing the dark side of unredeemed humanity. Like a prophet, she used her "Christian" freaks to expose the dark side of cultural Christianity.

11. Ibid., 144.

12. Kierkegaard, *Attack Upon 'Christendom*,' 35.

13. Ibid., xxvi.

14. O'Connor, "The Catholic Novelist in the South," 861.

Kierkegaard's "freak" was Bishop Mynster, who, Kierkegaard claimed, managed in his preaching and his living to soft-pedal, slur over, suppress, and omit anything that was decisively Christian.[15] When Bishop Mynster died, he was praised "as one of the genuine witnesses to the truth" in the strongest and most decisive terms possible. Kierkegaard found this claim outrageous. Mynster may have been a great admirer of Jesus, but as far as Kierkegaard was concerned, he didn't know the first thing about preaching repentance or taking up the cross and following Jesus. Kierkegaard could no longer write off the "impudent indecency" of cultural Christianity. For him, it was a case of open apostasy.[16]

Kierkegaard labeled this religious Christianity as Christianity without Christ. He claimed that Christianity without Christ raises anxiety over our problems without genuine repentance and the message of the cross. It promotes individual empowerment without teaching self-denial and the way of the cross. Christless Christianity redefines faith as a private, hidden inwardness instead of a total life commitment to Jesus Christ. Evangelism seeks to entertain people, rather than convict them of their sin and draw them to Christ. Missions aims to convince the world that the church is relevant and helpful. Ethics is based on the spirit of the times and cultural respectability. Christianity without Christ substitutes the rich young ruler for the cross-bearing disciple. For Kierkegaard the difference between those who admired Jesus and those who followed Jesus was meaningless, because there was no real difference. Everyone admired Jesus; no one followed him.

Kierkegaard lamented that we have plenty of pastors, "eminently learned, talented, gifted, humanly well-meaning . . . but not one of them is in the character of the Christianity of the New Testament."[17] We have magnificent buildings and programs, but we're only playing Christianity.[18] Spiritual "swindlers" have taken possession of "the firm 'Jesus Christ' and done a flourishing business under the name of Christianity."[19] Everyone is "playing at Christianity, transforming everything into mere words."[20]

Christless Christianity replaces the crucified and risen Christ with a culturally compatible Jesus who inspires popular admiration. Kierkegaard

15. Kierkegaard, *Attack upon 'Christendom,'* 5.

16. Ibid., 19.

17. Ibid., 29.

18. Ibid., 140.

19. Ibid., 117.

20. Ibid., 108.

acknowledged that it was easy to blur the distinction between admiration and obedience and mistake an admirer for a follower. Jesus may be celebrated as the answer for every question, the slogan for every praise, and the solution for every problem, but admirers don't really know the Jesus presented in the New Testament. Jesus is a symbol for success, but no one cares to listen to him, let alone obey him. Everyone assumes that they already know what they need to know about Jesus. The admirers' eyes are blinded to the meaning of Jesus. Instead of the crucified Lord, who calls us to take up our cross and follow him, their fantasy Jesus presides over their personal vision of success.

Kierkegaard believed that the life of Jesus "from beginning to end, was calculated only to procure followers, and calculated to make *admirers* impossible. . . . His life was *the Truth*, which constitutes precisely the relationship in which admiration is untruth . . . . But when *the truth*, true to itself in being the truth, little by little, more and more definitely, unfolds itself as the truth, the moment comes when no admirer can hold out with it, a moment when it shakes admirers from it as the storm shakes the worm-eaten fruit from the tree."[21]

The pastor is not talking about an advanced level of spirituality or a higher order of commitment, but basic New Testament Christianity. Disciples are called to become like Jesus. If Jesus "offered up prayers and petitions with loud cries and tears to the one who could save him from death, and he was heard because of his reverent submission," then his followers can expect to experience along the path of obedience their own dark night of the soul. Jesus "learned obedience from what he suffered" and we cannot expect anything less (Heb 5:7).

Søren Kierkegaard held that the desire to admire Jesus instead of to follow him was not the invention of bad people; "no, it is the flabby invention of what one may call the better sort of people, but weak people for all that, in their effort to hold themselves aloof."[22] Instead of working out their salvation with fear and trembling (Phil 2:12), admirers choose the features of Christianity that they like best. They are drawn to inspirational services and self-help programs. So-called successful churches cater to these felt needs and attract large numbers of admirers, but there is little talk of the cost of discipleship and what it means to follow the crucified and risen Lord Jesus Christ.

21. Ibid., 232, 239.
22. Ibid., 237.

The Danger of Apostasy

"Impossible!" The pastor is emphatic. He draws out the full impact of the word by placing it first. "It is impossible for those who have once been enlightened, who have tasted the heavenly gift, who have shared in the Holy Spirit, who have tasted the goodness of the Word of God and the powers of the coming age and who have fallen away, to be brought back to repentance" (Heb 6:4–5). Given his rich description of the benefits of true faith in Christ, we expect the pastor to say that it is impossible for anyone to fall away, but instead he shockingly says the opposite.

The pastor's lavish description of Christian experience is in marked contrast to his rather prosaic recital of elementary teachings. He compares the equivalent of a religious checklist (conversion, baptism, confirmation, membership, evangelism) to the deeply personal experience of faith in Christ. He insists on moving us beyond the elementary ABCs of the faith, and concludes, "God permitting, we will do so" (Heb 6:3). But then he seems to open up the real possibility of sincere believers falling away, believers who have been enlightened, who have experienced the power of conversion, who have tasted the heavenly gift, and who understand God's gracious gift of salvation. They have even experienced the power of the Holy Spirit, the goodness of the Word of God, and the powers of the coming age.

The pastor is emphatic. If these people who have experienced so much in Christ fall away they cannot be brought back to repentance. This is not a straw-man argument. "The warning of this passage was a real warning against a real danger which is still present so long as 'an evil heart of unbelief' can result in 'deserting the living God' (Heb 3:12)."[23] "Let him pose his sharp and uncomfortable question directly to us. Are we—or some within our Christian fellowship—in danger of turning our backs on the faith, and joining in the general tendency to sneer at the gospel and the church?"[24]

Let's be clear. The pastor's point is not that God refuses to forgive repentant believers. The only unpardonable sin is the persistent refusal to repent and turn to God. Jesus said, "Truly I tell you, people can be forgiven all their sins and every slander they utter, but whoever blasphemes against the Holy Spirit will never be forgiven; they are guilty of eternal sin" (Mark 3:28–29). The "unpardonable sin" or "the sin that leads to

23. Bruce, *Hebrews*, 148.
24. Wright, *Hebrews*, 60.

death" (1 Jn 5:16) describes the person who is unresponsive and resistant to the Spirit's witness.[25] The pastor's admonition is for unbelieving believers who have experienced the intimacy of the faith and the power of the Spirit, but in their hard-hearted rebellion and resistance refuse to repent and follow Christ.

For the pastor the perseverance of the saints stands in marked contrast to the persistent sinfulness of former professing believers who wilfully and intentionally reject their once vivid experience of Christ. The pastor expresses this hellish state of unbelief in the most graphic way possible: "To their loss they are crucifying the Son of God all over again and subjecting him to public disgrace" (Heb 6:6). Apostates subject Jesus to public disgrace all over again. It is as if they are re-enacting the crucifixion.[26] What is significant to note is that those who re-crucify Christ are not militant atheists or radical jihadists but professing believers who have turned away from the living God. The pastor appears to have in mind unbelievers who have turned away from Christ without forsaking their religion! Scary

The pastor concludes this section with an easily understood object lesson. Against the vivid picture of the re-crucified Son of God, the pastor calmly sketches a landscape (Heb 6:7-8). He compares fertile farmland that receives God's blessings with a barren wasteland "in danger of being cursed." The illustration recalls various Old Testament texts that use the land as a sign of God's blessing or God's curse, such as Isaiah's Song of the Vineyard (Isa 5:1-7).[27] Believers who respond to God's grace and persevere in their faith in Christ are blessed. They produce the fruit of righteousness. But those who reject God's grace and turn away from the living God are cursed. They have nothing to show for their religion but "thorns and thistles." Their worthless effort is good for nothing but to be burned, "for our God is a consuming fire" (Heb 12:29).[28]

---

25. Edwards, *Mark*, 123. Edwards writes, "The sin against the Holy Spirit is thus not an indefinable offense against God, but a specific misjudgment that Jesus is motivated by evil rather than by good, that he is empowered by the devil rather than by God. . . . By addressing the warning to the scribes, Mark signifies the unique pitfall that this sin can pose for religious people."

26. O'Brien, *Hebrews*, 227.

27. Guthrie, "Hebrews," 962-63.

28. Bruce, *Hebrews*, 150.

Encouraging Dear Friends

An abrupt change of tone is signaled by a shift from the third person (*those who*) to the second person (*you and yours*) and by addressing the hearers as "dear friends," or "beloved."[29] His tone of endearment resonates with the humility of one who truly wants to communicate clearly. The pastor speaks the truth in love, saying what he means to say, as if he was talking to a loved one.[30] He delivers his strong message against apostasy with love and concern. The pastor is like a caring doctor informing a vulnerable patient that he or she has cancer.

When I was eighteen an oncologist looked me in the eye and said with his hand on my knee, "I'm sorry. I have some bad news. You have Non-Hodgkin's lymphoma." My doctor promised to do everything he could to help me deal with it. My cancer became his challenge and I was impressed with his devotion to my healing. He entered into my struggle as if it was his war to fight. It is that kind of empathy and heartfelt concern that can be seen in the pastor's concern for his hearers.

 When we teach and preach Hebrews we want to follow the tenor and tone of the pastor's prophetic critique against Christless Christianity. We want to strive for the impact of the original sermon and capture the juxtaposition of intense concern and powerful hope. We want the boldness of the pastor's challenge to come through convincingly and to encourage "diligence to the very end" (Heb 6:11). As the pastor says, "Even though we speak like this, dear friends, we are convinced of better things in your case—things that have to do with salvation" (Heb 6:9). Hope lies in God's justice. Confidence comes through their proven track record of Christian service.[31] "God is not unjust; he will not forget your work and the love you have shown him as you have helped his people and continue to help them" (6:10). God takes our good works personally! As Jesus said, "Whatever you did for one of the least of these brothers and sisters of mine, you did for me" (Matt 25:40). The pastor's encouragement here is consistent with the Apostle Paul's theology: "For it is by grace you have been saved, through faith—and this is not from yourselves, it is the gift of God—not by works, so that no one can boast. For we are God's workmanship, created in Christ Jesus to do good works, which God prepared in advance for us to do" (Eph 2:8–10). The Reformers insisted that we are

29. O'Brien, *Hebrews*, 230.

30. Chapell, *Christ-Centered Preaching*, 99.

31. O'Brien, *Hebrews*, 231.

saved by faith alone, but saving faith is never alone. True faith in Christ is always accompanied by the works of Christ. We not only have faith *in* Jesus but we demonstrate the faith *of* Jesus. Beatitude-based living begins with grace and continues with the works of grace.

In Jesus' parable of the sheep and the goats, the righteous are commended for feeding the hungry, giving water to the thirsty, showing hospitality to the stranger, clothing the needy, caring for the sick, and befriending the imprisoned (Matt 25:31–46). Moreover, it is in their nature to do this. They don't give it a second thought, or maybe we should say that when they see someone in need they cannot stop thinking about the needy until they meet their need. They follow Jesus and this is what disciples who are saved by grace through faith do with their lives. The gospel of Jesus Christ plays itself out in 10,000 ways in the daily routine of ordinary selfless concern for the other. Life is marked by the principle of the cross: my life for yours, not your life for mine. There is something beautiful about the ignorance of those who ask: "Lord, when did we see you hungry and feed you, or thirsty and give you something to drink? When did we see you a stranger and invite you in, or needing clothes and clothe you? When did we see you sick or in prison and go and visit you?" This is an ignorance that runs contrary to the presumption of works righteousness. It fits with "so-that-no-one-can-boast" salvation by grace through faith. Because of Jesus Christ the righteous care for the needy and they do so without showy piety or inflated spirituality.

James said it well: "Religion that God our Father accepts as pure and faultless is this: to look after orphans and widows in their distress and to keep oneself from being polluted by the world" (Jas 1:27). Instead of being lazy or sluggish, the pastor says in effect, "Get a life. Mix it up. Put yourself in the company of the needy. Keep your eyes peeled for poor widows. Don't divert your eyes from the lame. Pay attention to them. Let's not make ministry into a mystery. Get in the game. Just do it!" He makes this appeal for *faithfulness to the end* personal. "We want each of you to show this same diligence to the very end," even as he leverages their personal hopes and aspirations as a motive for effort, "so that what you hope for may be fully realized" (Heb 6:11). His parental-like spiritual direction shows more compassion than frustration. He makes his appeal with their best interests at heart. "We do not want you to become lazy," is the coach's call for "energy, enthusiasm, faithful effort and patient hard work."[32] The

32. Wright, *Hebrews*, 63.

pastor has much more to say about imitating "those who through faith and patience inherit what has been promised" (Heb 6:12; see 11:1–40).

God's Promise Pictured

How God's covenant promise should be given and received is on full display in the life of Abraham. The ancient patriarch illustrates justification by faith in Paul's letter to the Romans and faithfulness to the end in Hebrews. After Abraham's faith was tested on Mount Moriah, the Lord said, "Now I know that you fear God, because you have not withheld from me your son, your only son" (Gen 22:12). Abraham was asked to take God at his word, just as we are. There is no one greater than God to vouch for God. The "unchanging nature of his purpose" is rooted in God's unchanging character. God not only gave the promise, God confirmed it with an oath. And on both counts, the promise declared and the oath confirmed, "it is impossible for God to lie" (6:18). We have God's Word on it, and God cannot lie. Consequently, "we who have fled to take hold of the hope set before us may be greatly encouraged" (Heb 6:18).

Although the main issue here is the integrity and certainty of God's promise, Abraham's faithful patience is presented as an example for us worthy of emulation.[33] Instead of either drifting away (Heb 2:1) or becoming lazy (Heb 5:11; 6:12), the pastor envisions believers who are "greatly encouraged" (Heb 6:18). They embrace the hope that is set before them with passionate eagerness. Instead of wandering around in the wilderness, they have found their strength in the Lord and their hearts are set on pilgrimage (Ps 84:5). They share the Apostle Paul's conviction, "I press on to take hold of that for which Christ Jesus took hold of me" (Phil 3:12).

The pastor portrays hope as "an anchor of the soul, firm and secure." His image reminds us that our lives have been securely anchored to an unmovable object. "We are refugees from the sinking ship of this present world-order so soon to disappear," writes F. F. Bruce. "Our hope is fixed on the eternal order, where the promises of God are made good to his people in perpetuity. Our hope, based upon his promises, is our spiritual anchor."[34]

This is the hope that enters what the preacher calls the inner sanctuary. With this reference to the holy of holies his hearers immediately

33. Cockerill, *Hebrews*, 286.
34. Bruce, *Hebrews*, 154.

picture the wilderness tabernacle and the inner sanctum containing the ark of the covenant. A curtain separated the Holy Place from the Most Holy Place. Once a year on the Day of Atonement the great high priest entered the Most Holy Place and offered the prescribed sacrifice for all the members of the community (Lev 16:29–34). Hope enters the inner sanctuary in the person of Jesus our forerunner. He is the pioneer and perfecter of faith. He goes before us on our behalf. He sets precedent and makes the redemptive provision for us. He is our propitiatory precursor, our guarantee of admission into the dwelling of God.[35] He has "entered on our behalf." He has gone to prepare a place for us (John 14:2). The final image of hope is a picture of Jesus our "high priest forever, in the order of Melchizedek" (Heb 6:20). The reference to Melchizedek recalls the pastor's earlier reference (Heb 5:10) and transitions to the sermon's longest expository section, in which he makes the case for the better priesthood, the better covenant, the better tabernacle, and the better sacrifice.

Since Our Great High Priest, Christ Jesus[36]

Since our great high priest, Christ Jesus, bears the name above all names,
  Reigning Son of God, surpassing other titles, powers, and claims;
    Since to heaven our Lord has passed, let us hold our witness fast!

Since we have a priest who suffered, knowing weakness, tears, and pain,
  Who, like us, was tried and tempted, unlike us, without a stain;
    Since he shared our lowly place, let us boldly speak his grace.

Sacrifice and suffering over, now he sits at God's right hand,
  Crowned with praise, no more an outcast, his preeminence long planned;
    Such a great high priest we have, strong to help, supreme to save.

Love's example, hope's attraction, faith's beginning and its end,
  Pioneer of our salvation, mighty advocate and friend:
    Jesus, high in glory raised, our ascended Lord, be praised!

CHRISTOPHER M. IDLE, 1973

35. Ibid., 155.
36. Borger, Tel, and Witvliet, eds., *Lift Up Your Hearts*, 210.

8

The Better Priesthood
(Hebrews 7:1–10:18)

"Religion compels us to the perception that God is not to be found in religion."

KARL BARTH [1]

THE PASTOR BUILDS HIS case for the superiority of Jesus' high priestly ministry by making a series of comparisons. He compares Christ's sacrifice to the Levitical priesthood, to the old covenant, to Tabernacle religion, and to the sacrificial system. My sense is that the pastor never meant to interrupt the flow of his exposition with a detailed analysis of the Aaronic priesthood and the sacrificial system. He never would have envisioned an extended exposition of the book of Leviticus. We honor the original meaning and method of Hebrews by recognizing the momentum of the pastor's argument. We want to track his fast-paced exposition to his equally powerful exhortation. Faithful exposition avoids getting bogged down in such details. This expository section is largely illustrative, culminating in the exhortation to "hold unswervingly to the hope we profess, for he who promised is faithful" (Heb 10:23).

Biblical scholars analyze the technical details of the text but often shy away from identifying its impact on today's church. It is easier for them to talk about the syncretistic threat of the Jewish tradition facing first-century believers than to confront the corrupting impact of religious

---

1. Barth, *Romans*, 242.

practices facing contemporary Christians. If we want to preach Hebrews effectively we need to apply the pastor's sustained argument against religion to the popular forces and traditions that threaten to subvert the supremacy of Christ, distort the character of the church, and reject the mission of God.

The accumulative impact of the pastor's oral argument builds to a pastoral climax. It is apparent that the pastor is in search of shadows, not the Platonic variety that frame the real world as a pale illusion, but the literary types that foreshadow the progressive revelation of God. The pastor is in search of the better hope (Heb 7:19), the permanent priesthood (7:24), the true tabernacle (8:2), the better promises (8:6), the mediator of a new covenant (9:15), the heavenly sanctuary (9:24), and the once-for-all perfect sacrifice (10:12–14). The pastor's exhortation to faithfulness to the end is not rooted in the long history of prophetic rebuke but in the fulfillment of the sacrificial system. He might have called on Isaiah or Jeremiah to make his case, but instead he called on Moses and Aaron to prove the supremacy of Christ.

The Order of Melchizedek

The pastor begins with an obscure and mysterious person named Melchizedek, whose brief story is cited in Genesis 14:14–27 and Psalm 110:4. Earlier references to Psalm 110:4 (5:5–6, 10; 6:10) have prepared the listener for a fuller exposition of the psalm. But it would have been difficult for anyone to have anticipated the pastor's argument. He finds in Melchizedek an ancient precedent for a perfect, permanent priesthood. Melchizedek lived in the time of Abraham and foreshadowed Jesus' high priestly ministry. Aaron's Levitical priesthood followed Melchizedek by several hundred years and was based on the Mosaic law and ancestry. The Aaronic priesthood was eventually judged to be "weak and useless" and was "set aside" because Jesus became "the guarantor of a better covenant" (Heb 7:18, 22).

Melchizedek symbolizes a flesh and blood type for the incarnate One. His name meant the "king of righteousness" and he was the King of Salem, which means the "king of peace." He was a priest of God Most High, described in four poetic lines:

> Without father, without mother, without genealogy;
> having neither beginning of days nor end of life;

made like the Son of God;

he remains a priest forever. [2]

Melchizedek was an historical person who played a cameo role in salvation history. He offered Abraham bread and wine and blessed Abraham, saying, "Blessed be Abram by God Most High, Creator of heaven and earth. And praise be to God Most High, who delivered your enemies into your hand" (Gen 14:18–20). Abraham honored Melchizedek and acknowledged his priestly role with a special tithe. Our knowledge about Melchizedek ends here, but the pastor is about to use him to underscore the better hope and the better promises and the better priesthood found in Jesus. We know nothing about Melchizedek's parents, his birth, his ancestry, and his death. But the pastor sees bold truth in the silence and finds wisdom in our ignorance. He embraces Melchizedek as the ancient type that foreshadows the new and permanent priesthood of Jesus. Looking forward, Abraham never could have foreseen it, but looking back, the Psalmist is led by the Spirit to give a messianic significance to Melchizedek.

Psalm 110 is the most popular psalm in the New Testament. It is quoted seven times and alluded to fifteen times.[3] There are two stanzas in Psalm 110, and the lead verse of both stanzas is quoted in Hebrews. Psalm 110:1 concludes the seven affirmations given in the introduction (Heb 1:13) and Psalm 110:4 declares the christological importance of Melchizedek. Both verses emphasize that God has spoken (Heb 1:1). Stanza one honors the King: "The Lord says, 'Sit at my right hand until I make your enemies a footstool for your feet.'" Stanza two swears in the priest: "The Lord has sworn and will not change his mind: 'You are a priest forever, in the order of Melchizedek.'" "God spoke the king-priest Messiah into being, just as he had spoken creation into being. . . . God ruled and saved, the two acts were the same thing. All the parts of the universe and history fell into place and made sense; all the longings and appetites of the spirit found a terminus. The life without and the life within were demonstrated to be a single life: the life of God in Jesus Christ, Lord and Savior."[4]

Inspired, the pastor develops the Melchizedek theme and builds his case "for another priest to come, one in the order of Melchizedek, not in

2. Cockerill, *Hebrews*, 298,

3. Kirkpatrick, *Commentary on the Psalms*, 665.

4. Peterson, *Earth & Altar*, 45, 47.

the order of Aaron" (Heb 7:11). But there is a strategic twist to his interpretation. Instead of Jesus resembling Melchizedek, it is Melchizedek who
resembles the Son of God (7:3). What we don't know about Melchizedek
is used figuratively to illustrate the new and better priesthood of Jesus
Christ. In this case, as F. F. Bruce wrote, "It is not the type which determines the antitype, but the antitype which determines the type: Jesus is
not portrayed after the pattern of Melchizedek, but Melchizedek is 'made
conformable to the Son of God.'"[5]

The pastor does not press the correspondence between the Messiah
and Melchizedek on all points. Melchizedek is a type of Christ, but "there
is no suggestion that the bread and wine he shared with Abraham was a
type of the Lord's Supper."[6] The truth the pastor seeks to drive home is
that Jesus forms a permanent priesthood, not on the basis of human ancestry from the tribe of Levi, not on the basis of the Mosaic law, and not
on the basis of human weakness and sin, but on the "basis of the power
of an indestructible life," and the sworn testimony of God himself (Heb
7:16, 20). Jesus has become the guarantor of a better covenant, because
he lives forever, saves completely, and "always lives to intercede for them"
(Heb 7:25). F. F. Bruce writes, "The new priesthood is better because
the new priest is Jesus. Jesus, who endured sore temptations; Jesus, who
poured out his heart in earnest prayer to God; Jesus, who learned by suffering how hard the way of obedience could be; Jesus, who interceded for
his disciples that their faith might not fail when the hour of testing came;
Jesus, who offered up his life to God as a sin offering on their behalf—
this same Jesus is the unchanging priest and helper of all who come to
God through him."[7]

"Such a high priest truly meets our need—one who is holy, blame-
less, pure, set apart from sinners, exalted above the heavens" (Heb 7:26).
The pastor finds in Jesus what T. S. Eliot called the objective correlative,
that is, the true correlation between type and antitype.[8] Melchizedek
foreshadows Jesus Christ, the King of righteousness and the King of
peace and our great high priest, "who has been made perfect forever"
(Heb 7:28). The pastor makes sure we grasp his big idea: "Now the main
point of what we are saying is this: We do have such a high priest, who sat

5. Bruce, *Hebrews*, 160.

6. Old, *The Reading and Preaching of the Scriptures*, vol. 2, 324.

7. Ibid., 176.

8. Sire, *Praying the Psalms of Jesus*, 31.

down at the right hand of the throne of the Majesty in heaven, and who serves in the sanctuary, the true tabernacle set up by the Lord, not by a mere human being" (Heb 8:1–2). The pastor has not finished comparing the old covenant and the new covenant, but his main point is clear. His exposition has been building on what he said in the first paragraph of his sermon (Heb 1:3).

In terms of practical pastoral application, there is an implicit challenge in Hebrews against modeling pastoral ministry after the stipulations and rules of the old covenant. Hebrews challenges any notion of retrofitting the Levitical priesthood in any form or fashion for Christian use. A first-person plural dependency on Jesus Christ as our great high priest seems difficult to sustain and the temptation to default to a priestly class is real. Well meaning but misguided believers want to experience what it is to follow Christ vicariously through their pastor. Instead of living by faith, they want to see their pastor live by faith. They want to look to their pastor for the feeling of reassurance that the Christ-life is being lived out. The pastor becomes a symbol for living the life they are either unable or unwilling to live themselves. Instead of taking up the cross and following Jesus, they want to listen to their pastor talk about the cross. Instead of using their spiritual gifts for God's kingdom work, they want to watch the pastor use his or her gifts. We need not belabor this point, but Hebrews, along with the rest of the New Testament, assumes the immediacy of the believer's personal relationship with the living God. The notion of a spiritual elite exercising oversight over passive religious admirers is never entertained by the pastor.

Better, Better, Better

The order of Melchizedek precedes the old Levitical priesthood and is used by the pastor to introduce "a better hope" by which "we draw near to God" (Heb 7:19). This better hope is rooted in Jesus who offered the better sacrifice "once for all when he offered himself" (Heb 7:27). Jesus provides the *better* ministry established on *better* promises in a *better* sanctuary. The pastor's extended illustration sets up an in-depth comparison between the old order and the new covenant. The old order, prescribed by the Mosaic law, with its ceremonial rituals and external regulations, is contained in an earthly tabernacle and presided over by priests who were required to offer daily sacrifices for their sins and the sins of the people. The new covenant is meditated by Christ on our behalf before the very presence of God. Jesus "is able to save completely those who come to God through him, because he always lives to intercede for them" (Heb 7:25). "He has appeared once for all at the culmination of the ages to do away with sin by the sacrifice of himself" (Heb 9:26). "For by one sacrifice he has made perfect forever those who are being made holy" (Heb 10:14).

The pastor's spiraling exposition was intended to be heard not read. The themes are played out rhythmically like a symphony rather than read linearly like a lecture. He is preaching to the ear, not the eye. His lengthy quote from Jeremiah 31 and Psalm 40, and his references to Exodus 24 and 25, are not meant to be studied in detail as much as remembered in delight. The tension between type and antitype generates a momentum that carries the logic and the pathos of the message forward.

We should pay attention to the pastor's advice when he says, "But we cannot discuss these things in detail now" (Heb 9:5). The force of the sermon should not be interrupted by distracting digressions into tabernacle furniture, priestly offerings, the location of the golden altar of incense, and legal technicalities surrounding wills. When preachers yield to the temptation to preach the text like this, they interrupt the synergy of exposition and exhortation and the thrust of the message suffers. It is like watching a movie with a lot of commercial interruptions or listening to a soundtrack at a slower speed. One commentary divides this section (Heb 8:1–10:19) into ten expository sections, each with its own points of application. Preaching ten sermons on this section would distort the pastor's intended impact. To become fascinated with the details of the tabernacle and the sacrificial system is to miss the message he intended. We want to remain true to the sermon's expository momentum and preach the pastor's exhortation (Heb 10:19–39). To do that we have to keep up with the pastor's fast-paced tempo.

The High Priest's Perfect Sacrifice

At every turn the pastor insists on the inadequacy of the old order. The Aaronic high priest was obligated by the Mosaic law to offer both gifts and sacrifices at the tabernacle. Once a year the high priest entered the inner room, the Most Holy Place, with the sacrificial blood of calves, but all these "external regulations" (Heb 9:10) did was to prove "that the gifts and sacrifices being offered were not able to clear the conscience of the worshiper" (Heb 9:9). These sacrifices "repeated endlessly year after year," could never "make perfect those who draw near to worship" (Heb 10:1). The pastor reasons that "the Holy Spirit was showing by this that the way into the Most Holy Place had not yet been disclosed as long as the first tabernacle was still functioning" (Heb 9:8). This earthly sanctuary was a shadowy copy of the heavenly reality of the presence of God. Moses built the tabernacle to the divine specifications revealed to him on Mount Sinai (Exodus 25:40). But it was only a prototype of the real thing. The wilderness tabernacle was a theological object lesson for the heavenly presence of God, "the greater and more perfect tabernacle that is not made with human hands, that is to say, is not part of this creation" (Heb 9:11).

The pastor does not envision a heavenly tabernacle with an inner room, a new Most Holy Place, but Christ sitting down at the right hand of the throne of the Majesty in heaven (Heb 1:3; 8:1). Christ serves in this new sanctuary, "the true tabernacle set up by the Lord, not by a mere human being" (Heb 8:2).[9] The real drama of the atoning sacrifice of Christ on the cross is played out not just "outside the city gate" (Heb 13:12), but in the very presence of the Father. The pastor's focus is not on the earthly scene of Jesus' death on the cross but on the high priestly sacrifice of Christ's blood, "who through the eternal Spirit offered himself unblemished to God" (Heb 9:14).

We tend to dwell on the crucifixion, but the pastor turns our attention to Christ's new covenant mediation before the Majesty in heaven through his atoning sacrifice for our sins. His exposition of the old order reveals the extensive preparations that have gone into the atonement throughout salvation history by means of illustrations and types. God's actions and theological object lessons have been building to the climax celebrated in Hebrews. He did not give Cain and Abel a theology lesson before choosing Abel's sacrifice and disqualifying Cain's offering of fruit. He did not explain to Abraham how the command to sacrifice his son Isaac was a picture of the will of the Father in giving up his one and only Son. Nor did God explain to Job that he would take the world's unjust suffering and nail it to the cross. By divine design King David and the

9. Cockerill, *Hebrews*, 391: "Thus any suggestion that 'the greater and more perfect Tent' represents a heavenly 'Holy Place' is nothing more than a vestigial remnant from the parallel the pastor has drawn between the Old Tent and the New . . . . By thus stressing the heavenly location of Christ's ministry, the pastor affirms its unique effectiveness in bringing God's people into his presence."

prophets discovered that a broken and contrite heart meant more than sacrifices.

The pastor helps us to see that there is more going on within the communion of the triune God than we could begin to imagine. In 1897 the British theologian P. T. Forsyth observed that Christ's "revelation was more action than instruction. He revealed by redeeming." Christ came not to declare forgiveness or explain forgiveness but to effect forgiveness. Forsyth wrote, "The great mass of Christ's work was like a stable iceberg. It was hidden. It was His dealing with God, not man. The great thing was done with God. It was independent of our knowledge of it. The greatest thing ever done in the world was done out of sight."[10] Hebrews pulls the curtain back and offers a glimpse into the profound meaning and cost of the atonement.

Psalm 40 draws the pastor's expository spiral to a conclusion. He explains the enduring efficaciousness of Christ's sacrifice by finding "a prophetic utterance which he recognizes as appropriate to the Son of God at the time of his incarnation."[11] He paraphrases the line "my ears you have dug for me" to fit the incarnation, "a body you prepared for me," and to underscore the offering of Christ himself. The external obligation to offer animal sacrifices is compared to the perfect sacrifice made possible by the incarnate One: "Here I am—it is written about me in the scroll—I have come to do your will, my God" (Heb 10:7). "His incarnation itself is viewed as an act of submission to God's will and, as such, an anticipation of his supreme submission to that will in death."[12] "Hebrews goes beyond Psalm 40; the perpetual sacrifices of the past have become obsolete in terms of the permanent sacrifice of Christ."[13] But in another sense the pastor captures the original essence of the psalm calling for the king's "obedience and profound spirituality" because "sacrifices in and of themselves achieved nothing."[14] Only this time, Jesus Christ is the King-Priest who is perfect in his obedience and perfect in his sacrifice. In him Psalm 40 realizes its true objective correlative. The pastor underscores the christological interpretation explicitly, when he says, "By that will, we have been made holy through the sacrifice of the body of Jesus Christ once for

10. Forsyth, *God*, 19.

11. Bruce, *Hebrews*, 239.

12. Ibid., 242.

13. Craigie, *Psalms 1–50*, 317.

14. Ibid.

all" (Heb 10:10). James Denny wrote, "It is the Atonement which explains the Incarnation: the Incarnation takes place in order that the sin of the world may be put away by the offering of the body of Jesus Christ."[15]

The law, with all of its ceremonial procedures and external regulations, including the priesthood, the tabernacle, and the sacrifices, was designed by God to point exclusively to Jesus Christ, who "was sacrificed once to take away the sins of many; and he will appear a second time, not to bear sin, but to bring salvation to those who are waiting for him" (Heb 9:28).

The pastor begins and ends this section with the prophet Jeremiah's description of the new covenant, and in both cases he underscores two important truths.[16] First, he stresses the internal transformation wrought by the grace and mercy of God: "I will put my laws in their hearts, and I will write them on their minds" (Heb 8:10; 10:16). And second, he emphasizes God's everlasting forgiveness: "For I will forgive their wickedness and will remember their sins no more" (Heb 8:12; 9:17). He then sums up the whole section with a single line: "And where these have been forgiven, sacrifice for sin is no longer necessary" (Heb 10:18).

Good Religion

Hebrews must have had an enormous impact on believers who were tempted to reappropriate the sacred practices required by the Mosaic law and honored by centuries of religious observance. The pastor is about to exhort believers to hold unswervingly to the hope they have in Christ and not to give up meeting together (Heb 10:23, 25). The cultural impact of what they were giving up was enormous. Sincere believers must have wondered what they were supposed to do when they assembled for worship because their traditional religious practices were transcended in Christ.

15. Denny, *The Death of Christ*, 234.

16. The new covenant was by no means new to God. Everything in the Mosaic covenant pointed forward to this new covenant. The essence of being God's covenant people was never a matter of external religion, ethnic identity, ritual conformity, and legalistic duty. The new covenant was not new in the sense that over time God came up with a better plan. Jeremiah was not introducing a new improved program that promised to work better. God's promises through Adam, Noah, Abraham, Moses, and David, all pointed forward to a personal relationship with God based on God's love and mercy. What was new was that God was making the means and the power of his redemptive purposes more fully known.

Jesus fulfilled and removed the Levitical priesthood, the earthly sanctuary, the sacrificial system, and the liturgical year. What they were accustomed to seeing and doing was no longer required. The prescribed religious habits of sincere people had been rendered obsolete. The radical freedom of meeting without these special days, sacred buildings, liturgical rituals, and prescribed sacrifices was meant to be liberating, but for many it was threatening.

Jesus effectively put good religion out of business, in fact the very best religion, the religion instituted and prescribed by God. And if Jesus rendered this very good religion obsolete, what does that say about the end of good religion gone bad? The message of Hebrews is in keeping with Jesus' final departure from the Jerusalem temple. Matthew describes Jesus as being especially agitated. His prophetic rebuke was fierce in tone and temper. He burned with anger against the teachers of the law and the Pharisees for their hypocrisy, showy piety, and hostility to the revelation of God. Like the prophet Isaiah, Jesus pronounced seven woes (Isa 5:8–6:5). He called them names: "You hypocrites! You snakes! You brood of vipers!" He blamed them for the blood of the prophets from the blood of righteous Abel to the blood of Zechariah. His parting words were, "For I tell you, you will not see me again until you say, 'Blessed is he who comes in the name of the Lord'" (Matt 23:39).

The disciples understood that Jesus was angry at bad religion, but at the time they never dreamed that Jesus was bringing the whole system down, the good religion along with the bad. Jesus was bringing an end not just to bad priests but to the whole priesthood, not just to corrupt practices surrounding the sacrificial system, but to the whole sacrificial system. The disciples did not understand the fuller implications of Jesus' blistering prophetic rebuke. If they did, they never would have come "up to him to call his attention to its buildings." When Jesus walked out of the temple for the last time he turned his back on good religion. The old sacrificial, Levitical priestly temple system was about to be rendered obsolete.

The disciples were trying to get Jesus to notice "how the temple was adorned with beautiful stones and with gifts dedicated to God," but Luke reports that Jesus noticed the poor widow giving her offering of two very small copper coins. Jesus made an example of her. He used her act of worship to drive the message of the gospel home. "Truly I tell you," he said, "this poor widow has put in more than all the others. All these people gave their gifts out of their wealth; but she out of her poverty put in all she had to live on" (Luke 23:3–5).

Following Pentecost, Peter and John were about to enter the temple when a lame man asked them for money. Peter said to the man, "Look at us! Silver and gold I do not have, but what I do have I give you. In the name of Jesus Christ of Nazareth, walk!"(Acts 3:4–6). Luke reports, "He jumped to his feet and began to walk. Then he went with them into the temple courts, walking and jumping and praising God." People recognized that this was the lame man who had sat at the temple gate called Beautiful, and they were filled with wonder and amazement at what had happened to him. What could be more beautiful than the temple? What could be more amazing than the gate called Beautiful? The answer: A poor lame beggar on his feet walking, jumping, and dancing—praising God. After Pentecost, Peter preached a second message and he along with John was hauled before the Sanhedrin. Then Peter, filled with the Holy Spirit, said, "It is by the name of Jesus Christ of Nazareth, whom you crucified but whom God raised from the dead, that this man stands before you healed. Jesus is the 'stone you builders rejected, which has become the cornerstone.' Salvation is found in no one else, for there is no other name given under heaven by which you must be saved"(Acts 4:10–12). These two events converge: Jesus leaving the temple and praising the poor widow and Peter and John dragged from the temple, after healing the lame man, to stand trial before the Sanhedrin. Peter's Spirit-filled message confirms that Jesus has replaced the temple. The temple has been eclipsed by the beauty of the gospel of Jesus Christ. Needy people like us are transformed and that is good news.

Zambian New Testament scholar Joe Kapolyo emphasizes the significance of Jesus turning his back on institutional Judaism and abandoning the whole sacrificial system.[17] What Jesus refuses to do is turn his back on the Jewish people! The destruction of the temple prophesied in Jesus' Sermon on the End of the World (Matt 24) signifies not only the end of Judaism as a religion but the end of all religions, including Christendom. Only Christ fulfills the human need for salvation and the longing of the soul. If the temple is done away with, how much more will all religious traditions be eclipsed by the presence of Jesus? Jesus is Lord. He is the one who is greater than Judaism, Islam, Hinduism, Confucianism, ancestral

17. Kapolyo, "Matthew," 1161.

worship, tribal animism, existential selfism, and all forms of Christless Christianity.

Hebrews is always a timely message because of the persistent and pervasive danger of substituting religious habits rooted in the biblical tradition for Christ and his Church. Vital Christianity can devolve quickly into religious practices and rituals derived more from the culture than the New Testament. This temptation can come in the form of ancient traditions or trendy innovations. We have left behind the sacrificial system of the Levitical priesthood but we have adopted a professional clergy to practice the Christian faith in our place. Pastors do for us what disciples were originally meant to do for themselves—read the Bible, pray, witness, worship, and make disciples. We no longer have a great high priest who once a year enters the Most Holy Place, but we have our celebrity pastors whom the Apostle Paul called super-apostles who cater to our felt needs. We don't have a tabernacle in the wilderness but we have impressive sanctuaries that take on the aura of a holy place.

In *The Lost History of Christianity,* historian Philip Jenkins argues that "control of the landscape" by impressive sacred edifices is an important way to secure a religion in the minds of the people and in the traditions of a culture.[18] He claims that one of the reasons Christianity declined in central Asia was because Christians did not have landmark church buildings. In 1450 as he lay dying, Pope Nicholas shared his dream with his cardinals of a Vatican that would be greater than any emperor's palace: "A popular faith, sustained only on doctrines, will never be anything but feeble and vacillating. But if the authority of the Holy See were visibly displayed in majestic buildings, imperishable memorials, and witnesses seemingly planted by the Hand of God Himself, belief would grow and strengthen like a tradition from one generation to another, and all the world would accept and revere it. Noble edifices, combining taste and beauty with imposing proportions, would immediately conduce to the exaltation of the Chair of St. Peter . . . ."[19]

Pope Nicholas was discerning enough to know that doctrinal statements would never sustain the body of Christ, but he was wrong to think that the solution was to be found in impressive buildings. Christendom has managed to construct a parasitic religious system that drains the energy out of the body of Christ and competes with the mission of God. By

18. Jenkins, *The Lost History of Christianity*, 216.

19. Scotti, *Basilica*, 21.

the time well-meaning Christians manage all the externals (the committees, the programs, the budgets, the facilities, the staff, the denomination, the marketing, the public relations, the special events, the wedding chapel, the funeral home, the youth organization, the community service, etc.) we have nothing left for real worship, costly discipleship, and global missions. Although God replaced the good religion prescribed by Mosaic law with its types and illustrations pointing to Christ, many still cling to bad religion in the name of Christendom.

Blessed Assurance, Jesus Is Mine![20]

Blessed assurance, Jesus is mine! O what a foretaste of glory divine
Heir of salvation, purchase of God, born of his Spirit, washed in his blood.
This is my story, this is my song, praising my Savior all the day long.
This is my story, this is my song, praising my Savior all the day long.

FANNY JANE CROSBY, 1873

All Glory Be To Christ[21]

Should nothing of our efforts stand
No legacy survive
Unless the Lord does raise the house
In vain its builders strive
To you who boast tomorrow's gain
Tell me what is your life
A mist that vanishes at dawn
All glory be to Christ!

Chorus:
All glory be to Christ our king!
All glory be to Christ!
His rule and reign we'll ever sing,
All glory to Christ!

His will be done, his kingdom come

20. McKim, ed., *The Presbyterian Hymnal*, 341.
21. From the album, *Joy Has Dawned*, released 27 November 2012. Words by Dustin Kensrue. Arrangement by Kings Kaleidoscope. © Dead Bird Theology (ASCAP), It's All About Jesus Music (ASCAP).

On earth as is above
Who is himself our daily bread
Praise him the Lord of love
Let living water satisfy
The thirsty without price
We'll take a cup of kindness yet
All glory be to Christ! (*chorus*)

When on the day the great I Am
The faithful and the true
The Lamb who was for sinners slain
Is making all things new.
Behold our God shall live with us
And be our steadfast light
And we shall ere his people be
All glory be to Christ! (*chorus*)

DUSTIN KENSRUE

9

Perseverance of the Saints
(Hebrews 10:19–39)

*"Doctrine is not an affair of the tongue, but of the life; it is not ap-
prehended by the intellect and memory merely . . . but is received
only when it possesses the whole soul."*

JOHN CALVIN[1]

THE PASTOR EMPHASIZES THAT "we have been made holy through the
sacrifice of the body of Jesus Christ once for all" (Heb 10:10; see 2:11).
To be made holy in this way is to be given full assurance of our salvation (Heb 7:25). Jesus' entrance into the Most Holy Place on our behalf
encompasses the whole of justification by faith through grace alone and
the entire sanctifying work of the Holy Spirit. "For by one sacrifice he
has made perfect forever those who are being made holy" (Heb 10:14).
The pastor's exposition boldly asserts the work of Christ, the once-for-all
sacrifice of himself (Heb 7:25).

This is the redemptive pilgrimage from death to life, from sin's depravity to salvation's deliverance, that causes us to fix our eyes on Jesus.
We are not following a religious tour guide or spiritual director, exploring
religious sites and sharing spiritual experiences. This is not a pilgrimage
from birth to death, nor a quest for spiritual enlightenment. This is not

1. Calvin, *Institutes of the Christian Religion*, vol 2., III, VI, 4.

the faith journey that many talk about in vague, existential terms. Hebrews is about the pilgrimage that follows on the heels of Jesus Christ as he heads to the cross. Jesus is our trailblazer, the pioneer of our salvation (Heb 2:10), our forerunner (6:20), who "enters the inner sanctuary behind the curtain" on our behalf (6:19-20). We fix our eyes on Jesus, "the pioneer and perfecter of faith, who for the joy set before him endured the cross, scorning its shame, and sat down at the right hand of the throne of God" (12:2). Jesus is not our mystical mascot, but our mediator before God, who saves completely and "lives to intercede" for us (7:25).

The pastor's exposition on redemption climaxes in an extended pastoral exhortation. This carefully crafted sentence flows uninterrupted. It builds an aural momentum that comes through even in its written form (Heb 10:19-25). The compelling refrain, "Let us," is repeated three times and focuses on our shared body-life commitment in Christ to faith, hope, and love. The entire exhortation is marked by a relational inclusion that emphasizes our life together in Christ. *We* have "confidence to enter the Most Holy Place by the blood of Jesus, by a new and living way opened for us through the curtain, that is, his body, and since we have a great priest over the house of God, let us draw near to God with a sincere heart with the full assurance that faith brings, having our hearts sprinkled to cleanse us from a guilty conscience and having our bodies washed with pure water" (Heb 10:19-22).

The reason we have confidence to go where no person has gone before rests exclusively on Jesus Christ. Our text (Heb 10:19-25) forms a symphonic parallel to the opening prelude (Heb 4:14-16), climaxing in the pastor's extended exposition on Jesus our Great High Priest (4:14-10:39).

> Therefore, since we have a great high priest who has ascended into heaven, Jesus the Son of God, let us hold firmly to the faith we profess. For we do not have a high priest who is unable to empathize with our weaknesses, but we have one who has been tempted in every way, just as we are—yet he did not sin. Let us then approach the throne of grace with confidence, so that we may receive mercy and find grace to help us in our time of need (Heb 4:14-16).

We are confident not in ourselves but in Christ alone. The Apostle Paul gave the flip side of confidence when he emphatically declared his "no confidence in the flesh." He listed all the religious reasons he had previously claimed for his self confidence: "circumcised on the eighth day, of the people of Israel, of the tribe of Benjamin, a Hebrew of Hebrews; in regard to the law, a Pharisee; as for zeal, persecuting the church; as for righteousness based on the law, faultless" (Phil 3:5–6). But now he considered all of these things garbage compared to knowing Christ, not having a righteousness based on the law, but a righteousness based on faith in Christ.

The subtlety with which religious self-justification creeps back into the picture in Christian garb is a constant threat. Like Paul, we may have an impressive list of spiritual credentials that threaten to bolster the ego and endanger the soul. Misplaced confidence is one of our greatest dangers. Even if you were raised in a solid Christian home by loving parents, baptized in a Bible-believing church, educated in a respected Christian college, and ordained as a minister of the Word and Sacrament, all of this is "inferior stuff," call it "garbage", compared to knowing Jesus Christ personally, experiencing his resurrection power, and partnering with him in his suffering (Phil 3:8–11, *The Message*). Our confidence cannot rest in our family heritage or in our denominational affiliation or in our personality or in our ability to preach the gospel. Our confidence for this life and the next is in Christ alone.

By the Blood of Jesus

Up until now all of our attention has been drawn to Jesus who enters the inner sanctuary, the Most Holy Place, "the greater and more perfect tabernacle that is not made with human hands" (Heb 9:11). But now the focus shifts to our bold access on the basis of the sacrificial death of Jesus, which is expressed in two graphic images, "the blood of Jesus" and "the curtain, that is, his body."

When we think of blood most of us don't associate it with sacrifices. We identity blood with life. Bleeding is the surgeon's worst enemy. When an artery is cut the doctor's first priority is to stop the bleeding. Dr. Paul Brand tells of a famous surgeon who used to ask his new students, "In case of massive bleeding, what is your most useful instrument?" Most young doctors guessed wrong. There was only one correct answer: "Your thumb, sir." Why? Dr. Brand explains, "The thumb is readily available—every doctor has one—and it offers a perfect blend of strong pressure and gentle compliancy."[2]

2. Brand and Yancey, "Blood," 39.

When I had surgery a number of years ago, I required six units of blood. There was a blood shortage at the time and the doctors asked my parents if they knew people who would be willing to give blood. The need for blood was announced in a faculty meeting at the college where my father taught. Immediately six men left the faculty meeting and went to the hospital to give blood. I don't think my father ever told that story without tearing up.

Modern medicine has made us aware of the preciousness of blood. Without it we die. Every one of the one hundred trillion cells in our body needs the resources transported by blood. But as valuable as blood is to sustain physical life, the blood of the Lamb is infinitely more valuable. We are redeemed by "the precious blood of Christ, a lamb without blemish or defect" (1 Pet 1:19). Although we may shy away from the imagery of Christ's blood, the apostles embraced it as essential for understanding the cross and our salvation. Through "faith in his blood" we are able to draw near to the holy God (Rom 3:25; Eph 2:13). In Christ, we are "justified" (Rom 5:9), "redeemed" (Eph 1:7), and have "peace through his blood, shed on the cross" (Col 1:20). In the book of Revelation, all praise is given "to him who loves us and has freed us from our sins by his blood" (Rev 1:5).

The apostles emphasize the cleansing power of Christ's blood. The blood of Christ cleanses our consciences (Heb 9:14) and "purifies us from all sin" (1 Jn 1:7). Those who are saved "have washed their robes and made them white in the blood of the Lamb" (Rev 7:14). Normally we think of blood staining rather than cleansing. We scrub blood out, we don't wash with it. Yet the Bible is insistent on associating blood with cleansing and Christian hymns celebrate it.

Nothing but the Blood of Jesus[3]

What can wash away my sin?
Nothing but the blood of Jesus . . .
O precious is the flow
That makes me white as snow;
No other fount I know,
Nothing but the blood of Jesus.

ROBERT LOWRY

3. Forbis, ed. *The Baptist Hymnal*, 135.

There is a Fountain Filled with Blood[4]
There is a fountain filled with blood
Drawn from Immanuel's veins,
And sinners plunged beneath that flood
Lose all their guilty stains . . .

WILLIAM COWPER

It is remarkable that the theological meaning of blood corresponds so closely to the physiological use of blood. Biology helps to explain the theology of the cross. The circulatory system illuminates the sacrificial system. The role that blood plays in our bodies is absolutely astounding. Every cell in the body has to be tied into the capillary system if it is to survive. Individual red blood cells deliver oxygen through a chemical process of gas diffusion and transfusion and absorb the waste products such as carbon dioxide and uric acid. These hazardous chemicals are then filtered out by the kidneys. The red blood cells are cleaned up and prepared for another payload of oxygen. Without blood constantly fueling the body with nutrients and cleansing our system of toxic chemicals, we couldn't survive. God chose an amazing analogy to illustrate our spiritual cleansing. The biblical symbolism of the blood of Jesus takes on fresh meaning for those who are familiar with modern medicine and unfamiliar with animal sacrifices. What blood does for the body, Christ's blood does for our souls.

By the New and Living Way

Jesus opened up a new way into the presence of God never before experienced. This new way of redemption corresponds to the promise of the new covenant (Heb 8:8) and leads to the end of external religious regulations inaugurated in "the time of the new order" (Heb 9:10). This new way resonates with the new song sung in Revelation: "Worthy is the Lamb, who was slain, to receive power and wealth and wisdom and strength and honor and glory and praise!" (Rev 5:12). This is the new way that has been anticipated from the beginning and is now fulfilled.

This is what the Lord says—he who made a way through the sea,
a path through the mighty waters. . . . Forget the former things;

4. Shorney, Shorney, Schraeder, Weck, Holstein, eds., *Worship and Rejoice*, 256.

do not dwell on the past. See, I am doing a new thing! Now it springs up; do you not perceive it? I am making a way in the wilderness and streams in the wasteland" (Isa 43:16–19).

"He who was seated on the throne said, 'I am making everything new!'" (Rev 21:5).

This is the pastor's "counterpart to the affirmation of John 14:6: 'I am the way, and the truth, and the life; no one comes to the Father, but by me.'"[5] Jesus is both high priest and sacrifice; he is both the great shepherd and the lamb. He sacrifices his body once for all for the sins of many, permitting open access "through the curtain." The image of the curtain does triple duty, looking at the death of Jesus from three key perspectives: his body, the temple in Jerusalem, and the heavenly presence of God. The pastor uses the image of the curtain to symbolize Jesus' flesh. At his death on the cross Jesus used his body to tear down the curtain separating physical death and eternal life. This "incarnate curtain" required the shedding of blood and the tearing of skin (John 19:34).[6]

The second curtain is the "temple curtain" representing the inner curtain separating the Holy Place from the Most Holy Place. This is the "temple curtain" that was torn in two from top to bottom when Jesus breathed his last (Mark 15:38; cf. Matt 27:51, Luke 23:45). "The tearing of the curtain is a sign that Christ's once-for-all sacrifice of his body makes obsolete the law's provisions for dealing with sin. The torn curtain represents both the passing of the old covenant and the new opening into the heavenly temple made possible through the blood of Jesus. The tearing of the physical curtain signifies that God's majestic presence is no longer distant but rather shines forth from the crucified and risen Christ."[7]

The third use of the figure is the "heavenly curtain." Jesus' sacrificial death overcomes the divide between earth and heaven. The pastor couples the historical crucifixion of Jesus on earth with the efficacy of his atoning sacrifice in heaven. "He entered the Most Holy Place once

---

5. Bruce, *Hebrews*, 250.

6. Vanhoozer, *Faith Speaking Understanding*, 210. I would have quickly passed over Vanhoozer's point if I had not experienced this sensation of tearing flesh personally. When I was a teenager the tops of my feet were cut about two inches across in order for doctors to inject dye throughout my lymph glands in preparation for cancer surgery. I was awake through the surgery and although my feet had been numbed to reduce pain I still remember a vivid sense of tearing as they opened the cut wider to find the lymph glands.

7. Ibid., 211.

for all by his own blood, thus obtaining eternal redemption" (Heb 9:12). The figure of the curtain reveals the efficacy of Christ's death over three spheres of separation from God: the temporal, the religious, and the earthly. "The climax of the drama is the moment when all three curtains are torn simultaneously. Hebrews 10:19–25 describes this climactic moment when Jesus' death opens up a new and better access to life in God's presence (it also stands at the climax of the book of Hebrews). It is the capstone of the author's exposition of the person and work of Jesus Christ as definitive sacrifice and superior high priest . . . ."[8]

Let Us Draw Near to God

The pastor roots our confidence in three blessings: the blood of Jesus, the new and living way opened up for us through his body, and Jesus' superlative priesthood. Jesus is the greatest great high priest ever. He is the Son over God's house (Heb 3:6). No one compares to Jesus. "Christ is faithful as the Son over God's house. And we are his house, if indeed we hold firmly to our confidence and the hope in which we glory" (3:6). Each blessing represents the total gift of grace. Each part represents the whole, rendering a powerful threefold testimony to the supremacy of Jesus Christ. Therefore, given all that God has done to free us from our sins and make us holy, the pastor "urges his listeners (as well as himself) to respond wholeheartedly to the present blessings they have through Christ."[9] These three blessings are followed by three exhortations. Like the blessings each exhortation represents the whole, so that whether grasped singularly or together the listener receives a complete picture of saving faith.

In Handel's *Messiah*, the phrase "unto us," from Isaiah 9:6, "For unto us a child is born," is repeated fourteen times. The pastor's threefold exhortation, "Let us . . . Let us . . . Let us . . . , " is made possible by the gift of Christ. Handel drove that truth home by emphasizing "unto us" over and over again, until the phrase sings in our souls. Only when the force of "unto us" is truly grasped by us personally can we respond to the "let us" exhortations.

The pastor's confident call to discipleship based on what Christ has done resonates with other New Testament texts. These "let us"

8. Ibid., 210.

9. O'Brien, *Hebrews*, 366.

exhortations are best understood in concert with these other vivid descriptions of discipleship. Jesus' promise of the easy yoke, "Take my yoke upon you and learn from me" (Matt 11:29) finds its fulfillment alongside the pastor's exhortation to draw near to God. If we grasp the great commandment, "Love the Lord your God with all you heart and with all your soul and with all your mind . . . and your neighbor as yourself" (Matt 22:37), we will pay attention to the pastor's admonition to spur one another on to love and good deeds. If we embrace the great commission, "Go and make disciples of all nations, baptizing them in the name of the Father and of the Son and of the Holy Spirit, teaching them to obey everything I have commanded you" (Matt 28:19-20), we will respond to the force of his encouragement to hold unswervingly to the hope we profess. Everything said here is the sum and substance of the Jesus' way. These exhortations fit with Jesus' promise of the abundant life (John 10:10) and with the Apostle Paul's call to present our bodies as living sacrifices (Romans 12:1-2). The pastor's positive appeal is rooted in the faith, hope, and love of Christ.

> *Let us* draw near to God with a sincere heart and with the full assurance that *faith* brings, having our hearts sprinkled to cleanse us from a guilty conscience and having our bodies washed with pure water.

> *Let us* hold unswervingly to the *hope* we profess, for he who promised is faithful.

> And *let us* consider how we may spur one another on toward *love* and good deeds, not giving up meeting together, as some are in the habit of doing, but encouraging one another—and all the more as you see the Day approaching. (Heb 10:22-25)

As we have said, Hebrews seeks to revitalize and renew believers who are in danger of drifting away and letting go of their confidence in Christ. The pastor warns against apostasy based on apathy. He challenges believers to grow beyond recycled entry-level evangelism. He is concerned that they could become as sluggish and hard-hearted as the Israelites in the wilderness if they are not intent on imitating "those who through faith and patience inherit what has been promised" (Heb 6:12). He has much more to say about imitating the faithful saints who have gone before (Heb 11:4-12:3). But only after his powerful exposition on Jesus our great high priest, he lays out the true path to spiritual renewal through vital worship

(Heb 10:22–25), fear-of-God accountability (10:26–31), and a long obedience in the same direction (10:32–39).

Vital Worship

The pastor weaves together the *manner* and the *means* in which we draw near to God. We are to "approach God's throne of grace" (Heb 4:16) and "draw near to worship" (10:1) by means of the gospel of grace, with a sincere heart and in full assurance of faith. This is the heartfelt assurance promised in the new covenant, when God says, "I will put my laws in their minds and write them on their hearts. I will be their God and they will be my people" (Heb 8:10; see also Jer 31:33; Ezek 36:26–27).

The power of this indwelling principle—God inscribing his will on our hearts—is a pictorial metaphor flexible in form found throughout the New Testament from Jesus' conversation with Nicodemus on the new birth, to the last supper when Jesus raised the cup and said, "This cup is the new covenant in my blood, which is poured out for you." We are reminded that new life in Christ depends upon a sacrificial spiritual transformation (John 3:7; Luke 22:20). Jesus preached the necessity of the new covenant in his Sermon on the Mount, when he said, "For I tell you unless your righteousness surpasses that of the Pharisees and the teachers of the law, you will certainly not enter the kingdom of heaven" (Matt 5:20). He pictured the power of the new covenant when he used the imagery of the vine and branches. "Remain in me, and I will remain in you. No branch can bear fruit by itself; it must remain in the vine. Neither can you bear fruit unless you remain in me . . . . If you remain in me and my words remain in you, ask whatever you wish, and it will be given you" (John 15:4, 7). The Apostle Paul equated the indwelling principle of the new covenant with being in Christ: "If anyone is in Christ, he is a new creation; the old has gone, the new has come!" (2 Cor 5:17). Instead of being conformed to the world, Christ's followers are to "be transformed by the renewing of [their] mind" (Rom 12:2).

Having described the *manner* in which we draw near to God, the pastor reiterates the *means* by which we draw near. How God goes about inscribing his will on our hearts has two sides and both sides are important. On God's side we have all the initiative, all the grace, all the redemption. In other words, all "the heavy lifting" belongs to God. On our side we have openness, repentance, acceptance, submission, trust, and faith. God's revelation and our receptivity are the two sides of heart-scripted theology. God inscribes his will on our hearts through the Word of creation and the Word made flesh. Divine inscription comes through creation and redemption. The way to this faith is costly and complex. It involves incarnation, crucifixion, resurrection, and glorification. All this and more inscribes God's will on our hearts and gives us full assurance, for we must include Pentecost, the body of Christ, and the mission of God. The Holy Spirit's gifts and the Holy Spirit's fruit inscribe God's will on our hearts. On our side, we have receptive hearts, real confession, deep repentance, willed passivity, and cross-bearing. We are open to the new birth, to the new creation, and to the renewing of our minds. We say with Paul, "For me to live is Christ and to die is gain" (Phil 1:21).

The pastor builds on the image of the blood of Jesus by reminding his hearers of "Moses' sprinkling the people with blood at the inauguration of the first covenant at Sinai (Exod 24:3–8)."[10] Our confident new covenant access to the very presence of God is made possible by the blood of Christ, by "having our hearts sprinkled to cleanse us from a guilty conscience . . ." (Heb 10:22). The people of the Exodus, after hearing Moses explain the word of the Law, answered Moses, "Everything the Lord has said we will do" (Exod 24:3). Early the next morning Moses built an altar at the foot of the mount. He took the blood of the sacrificial animals and splashed it against the altar and then sprinkled it on the people. He said, "This is the blood of the covenant that the Lord has made with you in accordance with all these words" (Exod 24:8). This solemn act united covenantal obedience and sacrificial redemption in the mind of the people. The sprinkling of the blood reminded the people of the Passover and the instructions given to each family to sprinkle the blood of the Passover lamb on the three sides of the doorframe (Exod 12:5–7).

The image of sprinkled blood is a vivid image. I remember sitting in a crowded New York restaurant with a young lawyer discussing the significance of the Passover and Christ's atoning sacrifice. "Do you know what happens when you take the blood of the lamb and sprinkle it with a hyssop branch against the door frame?" my lawyer friend asked. In a gesture that caught the attention of others in the restaurant, he jumped up from his seat and swung his imaginary hyssop branch dipped in blood to one side and then to the other and finally straight up and down. "Do

10. O'Brien, *Hebrews*, 367.

you see?" he said. "There in the doorway the sprinkled blood makes the sign of the cross!"

"Having our hearts sprinkled to cleanse us from a guilty conscience," corresponds to the outward means, "having our bodies washed with pure water." The pastor draws attention to the inner transformation of the heart, "not merely a forgiven heart," but a heart freed from dead works, and the outward transformation of the conduct of the body.[11] Old Testament imagery of priestly cleansing rites is clearly in view, but the New Covenant realities of baptism and Eucharist are perfectly reasonable pastoral applications. F. F. Bruce suggests that "the present reality which [the pastor] has in mind is probably Christian baptism—consisting, of course, not merely in the outward application of water, but in the outward application of water as the visible sign of the inward and spiritual cleansing wrought by God in those who come to him through Christ."[12]

"Let us hold unswervingly to the hope we profess, for he who promised is faithful." We are exhorted to keep a tight grip on the objective content of our hope, the unfailing promise of salvation through Jesus Christ. We must not look to religion or humanitarian effort to maintain our "faith" when we loosen our grip on the faith, hope, and love of Christ. Everything good in the Christian life comes from an unswerving commitment, an unwavering confession, and unbendable resolve to honor our friendship with our Lord and Savior Jesus Christ.

The pastor's call to vital worship strips everything away so that only the faith, hope, and love of Christ remains. Everything that might fill the void left by the obsolescence of religion is avoided. Left to ourselves, religion evolves into something we create. Human initiative distorts obedience and worship into something complex and confusing, but true spirituality involves an immediate and personal *sacrificial* encounter with the living God who redeems us from sin and death. Our human tendency is to make life more complicated and confused than it need be.

11. Cockerill, *Hebrews*, 474.

12. Bruce, *Hebrews*, 255. G. Guthrie, *Hebrews*, 344, disagrees: "Commentators have been too quick to find in 'having our bodies washed' a reference to Christian baptism; who can deny that the phrase may have been intended to draw such a connection? Yet the author gives no overt signals that he has the Christian rite in mind. What we do have in Hebrews are uses of the washing imagery in connection with the purification rites found in the Pentateuch (e.g. Heb 9:13). Thus, the writer continues the use of Old Testament imagery to communicate that the work of Christ has prepared believers to enter the presence of God. To suggest any more moves the interpreter into the realm of speculation."

The Spirit's direction is clear. God has commanded us to fix our eyes on Jesus. We invariably turn away from the worship and mission of God and focus on our felt needs.

The human response to a personal saving encounter with the living God ought to be intuitively simple, inherently sacrificial, and lovingly obedient. The unadorned quality of worship prescribed in the Old Testament (Exod 20:22-26) is fulfilled in the New Covenant. Our vision of God is by faith, not by sight. Instead of a physical representation of God there is a spiritual understanding of God. God is defined linguistically, not visually. In a visual and visceral sense God remains hidden. God refuses to be reduced to a "thing" that can be worshiped or a "program" that can be implemented. God reveals himself as the living subject, who is rationally, spiritually, and emotionally comprehensible. The hidden God is present among his people personally, by his Holy Spirit, but not materially, in the form of surrogates. Instead of projecting himself in a shrine or a memorial, God insists on a conversation with his people. The Word and Spirit of God make the hidden God real in the body of Christ.

We are given no hint in the New Testament that the tabernacle serves as a guide for constructing church buildings and sanctuaries, but we persist in trying to use glass and stone to inspire transcendence. Everything the tabernacle represented and stood for pointed forward to Christ and was fulfilled in Christ. By design, the household of God focuses people's attention on the Lord by honoring and obeying Christ in everyday living, not by building a building or marketing appealing programs. It is the body of Christ, not the church building, that points true worshipers to the living God. Jesus shifted the emphasis from architecture to relationships.

"And let us consider how we may spur one another on toward love and good deeds, not giving up meeting together, as some are in the habit of doing, but encouraging one another—and all the more as you see the Day approaching." Vital worship and real mission are a consequence of our life together in Christ. The motivational challenge of our faith develops organically from a sincere heart, a cleansed conscience, and an unwavering hope. These are the qualities God uses to accomplish his work. The pastor's focus is personal. He is directing us to our brothers and sisters in Christ. He is not interested in motivational strategies or techniques. Nor is he concerned with raising volunteers to complete a task. His aim is to deepen the sincerity of heart and the assurance of faith so that believers will be inspired to love and do good works. The pastor uses a strong word to focus in on the impact and influence we have on one another. We are to "stimulate," "stir up," and "arouse" one another.[13] But perhaps the best word is the more literal translation, to "provoke" one another. The pastor uses "intentional irony" to underscore his spiritual direction: "as forcefully as some 'provoke' others to anger, God's people should 'provoke' one another to 'love and good works.'"[14] Or to put it another way, lovingly we get in one another's faces, not just for the sake of good works, but to "be filled to the measure of the fullness of God" (Eph 3:19). The pastor seeks an environment in which the gospel is understood and brothers and sisters are discovering the joy of living out their commitment to the gospel. The spiritual life of individual believers is held in positive tension with the body life of the whole community. The transformation of the community of believers is never sacrificed for the sake of the individual nor is the individual sacrificed for the sake of community. What is good for the individual is good for the body and what is good for the body is good for the individual.

The pastor's method of "provocation" depends on "not giving up meeting together, as some are in the habit of doing . . . ." The Greek word for "meeting together" literally means "epi-synagogue" which may imply a unique assembly of Jewish Christians meeting separately from the synagogue. Or it may simply mean that the pastor does not want believers to forsake the meeting of the church.[15] Presumably some believers reasoned that since they were free from the ceremonial law, the ritual practices, the feast days, the sacrificial system, and the rabbinical leadership, they no longer needed to meet together. There may also have been a social stigma attached to assembling together that was easily avoided by not meeting. It is not difficult to imagine some believers using the argument that "justification by faith in Christ alone" made church attendance optional. We hear similar arguments from believers today. Many Christians look upon the church as optional, as one of many weekend possibilities. If they're caught up with their work and sleep, and have nothing more pressing to do, they may attend church. Going to church is something optional for many and they feel no compelling reason to really belong to a church.

The pastor does not stop here to develop a theology of the church, partly because he cannot conceive of faith in Christ apart from the body

13. Bruce, *Hebrews*, 256.

14. Cockerill, *Hebrews*, 478.

15. Bruce, *Hebrews*, 258.

of Christ. The obsolescence of Old Testament liturgical and priestly customs does not in any way diminish the importance of vital worship and fellowship among Christ's followers. The Apostle Paul may have worked out these truths more explicitly, but the pastor gives every indication of being in wholehearted agreement. As he said, "We are his house, if indeed we hold firmly to our confidence and the hope in which we glory" (3:6). The relational and spiritual character of this "house," built by God of people, is no less material, temporal, spatial, and concrete, than if it had been built with stone and steel. The essence of Christ's power is made manifest in and through the church, the body of Christ. Spirit-led enlightenment and empowerment focuses on the church rather than the individual believer. The supremacy of Christ over all things creates a special identity and purpose for the church. Jesus is not only Lord of the universe but the head of the church and his presence fills not only the cosmos, but the church. This high view of the church and its impact in the world echoes Jesus' authoritative pronouncement in the Sermon on the Mount, when he declared to his disciples, "You are the salt of the earth," and "You are the light of the world" (Matt 5: 13, 14). The pastor may not spell out in detail what he means by provoking one another to love and good deeds, but he undoubtedly encouraged believers to consider how best to build-up the household of faith.[16]

The pastor leaves us with one final thought before emphasizing moral purity and accountability. He exhorts believers to develop a sense of urgency. We are to live as if the once distant future is now immanent. We are exhorted to encourage one another, "all the more as you see the Day approaching."[17] This prevailing sense of immediacy belongs to the believer even though the generations may come and go. "Each successive Christian generation is called upon to live as the generation of the end time, if it is to live as a Christian generation."[18] "But do not forget this one thing, dear friends," wrote the Apostle Peter. "With the Lord a day is like a thousand years, and a thousand years are like a day" (2 Pet 3:8).

16. There are twenty practical suggestions listed in the appendix that are designed to encourage spiritual growth in the household of God and strengthen the church's gospel impact.

17. Douthat, *Bad Religion*, 49. Douthat observes that Martin Luther King, Jr. used eschatological language to encourage social justice whereas Billy Graham used eschatology to limit social change. Douthat quotes Graham as saying after the 1963 March on Washington, "Only when Christ comes again will the lion lie down with the lamb and the little white children of Alabama walk hand in hand with little black children."

18. Bruce, *Hebrews*, 259.

Fear-of-the-Lord accountability

The pastor follows up his encouraging exhortations with a dire warning: "If we deliberately keep on sinning after we have received the knowledge of the truth, no sacrifice for sins is left, but only a fearful expectation of judgment and of raging fire that will consume the enemies of God" (Heb 10:26–27). Flagrant disobedience amounts to a rejection of the means of grace and a defiant repudiation of Christ's atoning sacrifice. This is the fourth and most severe warning passage (Heb 2:1–4; 3:7–4:11; 6:4–8). In all of these warning passages the principle sin in view appears to be the grave sin of outright apostasy, that is, the intentional, willful desertion of the living God.[19] Faithfulness affirms that "the only absolutely essential thing in life is Jesus himself."[20] To deny that Jesus is enough can be as respectful as the rich young ruler or as deceitful as Judas or as expeditious as Pilate. We can even be enthusiastic admirers of Jesus but if we "deliberately keep on sinning after we have received the knowledge of the truth, no sacrifice for sin is left" (Heb 10:26). Denial may be subtle or defiant, but if anyone elevates their own will over the revelation of God they are flirting with apostasy. "A church that attempts to supplant a consistently and strongly held norm in Scripture is a church that has given up hope that Jesus is Answer enough."[21]

The pastor began with a rhetorical question—"How shall we escape if we ignore so great a salvation?" (Heb 2:3)—followed by a direct warning: "See to it, brothers and sisters, that none of you has a sinful, unbelieving heart that turns away from the living God" (Heb 3:12). He further intensifies his prophetic message by describing the worst case scenario: "It is impossible for those who have once been enlightened, who have tasted the heavenly gift, who have shared in the Holy Spirit, who have tasted the goodness of the word of God and the powers of the coming age and who have fallen, to be brought back to repentance. To their loss they are crucifying the Son of God all over again and subjecting him to public disgrace"(Heb 6:4–6). In this fourth and final warning, the pastor emphasizes the consequences for repudiating "Jesus' magnificent priestly and sacrificial work."[22] He stresses "a fearful expectation of judgment" and a "raging fire that will consume the enemies of God" (Heb 10:27).

---

19. Ibid., 261.

20. Gagnon, "The Bible and Homosexual Practice," 3.

21. Ibid.

22. O'Brien, *Hebrews*, 373.

He argues from the lesser to the great by comparing the law of Moses to the sacrifice of Christ. "Anyone who rejected the law of Moses died, without mercy on the testimony of two or three witnesses. How much more severely do you think someone deserves to be punished who has trampled the Son of God underfoot, who has treated as an unholy thing the blood of the covenant that sanctified them, and who has insulted the Spirit of grace?" (Heb 10:28–29).

The pastor targets professing believers, who through apathy and neglect, are in danger of repudiating the grace of Christ. Such defiance may appear outwardly polite, intellectually sophisticated, and religiously respectable, but the consequences for defying the holy God will be dreadful. If they have concluded that Jesus Christ is not the Savior he claimed to be, that his atoning sacrifice is unnecessary, and that he is not coming again, they are guilty of despising their salvation. They would be trampling the Son of God underfoot by denying that "God has promised to make all Christ's enemies a footstool for his feet" (Heb 1:13; 10:13).[23] They would be profaning the blood of the covenant by denying the reality of Christ's atoning sacrifice on the cross. And they would be insulting the Spirit of grace by holding in contempt what they once embraced with thanksgiving. The pastor quotes from Deuteronomy 32:35, "It is mine to avenge; I will repay," to underscore that those who turn against God and his mercy are worse than the Israelites who proved hardhearted and unfaithful. Then, for emphasis he repeats the next line in Moses' song, "The Lord will judge his people" (Deut 32:36). To underscore the tragic state of apostasy the pastor uses the word *fearful* or *terrifying* twice (Heb 10:27, 31). He wants his hearers to recoil at the very possibility of apostasy and say to themselves, "We are never, ever going there!" He wants to convince them that to fall into the hands of the living God after willfully rejecting his mercy and despising his salvation is something that they will never ever do!

The pastor proves that vital worship calls for fear-of-the-Lord accountability. Saving faith is consistent with a way of life that is lived responsively and authentically before the triune God.[24] Scholars describe the "fear of the Lord" as a "bound phrase," meaning that the four words cannot be defined separately but bear a singular meaning. Bruce Waltke calls it "the quintessential rubric, which expresses in a nutshell the basic

23. Ibid., 378.

24. Peterson, *Christ Plays in Ten Thousand Places*, 40.

grammar that holds the covenant community together."[25] "Fear of the Lord" marks the way of life consistent with those who pay attention to their great salvation (Heb 2:3), who hold firmly to their confidence in the Son (Heb 3:6), who make every effort to enter into God's rest (Heb 4:11), who let themselves be taken forward to maturity (Heb 6:2), and who refuse to shrink back (Heb 10:39). This is what the Apostle Paul meant when he said to "work out your salvation with fear and trembling, for it is God who works in you to will and to act in order to fulfill his good purpose" (Phil 2:12–13). And this is what Jesus meant when he said, "For I tell you that unless your righteousness surpasses that of the Pharisees and the teachers of the law, you will certainly not enter the kingdom of heaven" (Matt 5:20).

There is a form of compassion advocated in the Christian community that compounds the problem of sin. It is a reactionary compassion, often derived from personal experience with moral rigidity and legalism. Its advocates do not want to appear negative and insensitive. They rightly seek to offer the gospel of grace to everyone, no matter how sinful, but they wrongly abuse that grace when they use it to minimize the problem of sin. They forget that to be justified by the grace of Christ is not to be excused but to be forgiven and sanctified. God's grace does not condone, it atones. Compassion minus God's "No" to ungodliness boils down to "I'm OK, you're OK" acceptance. When "grace" overlooks the commands of God there is little appreciation for the negative impact that ongoing tolerance of sinful lifestyles has on the household of faith. The danger we ought to fear is unwittingly distorting the gospel by emphasizing grace at the expense of obedience. H. Richard Niebuhr described liberalism "as consisting in a God without wrath bringing people without sin into a kingdom without judgment through a Christ without a cross."[26] If we equate grace with acceptance and obedience with legalism we fall into the danger of apostasy.

Dietrich Bonhoeffer warned that the very grace of Christ, which is so essential for healing, is often used as a poison. Repeated exposure to the Word of God may render the hearer impenitent and callous. "One hears and yet does not hear. One receives and yet is not helped. God's forgiveness is not accepted but the person learns how to deal with himself gracefully. Forgiveness is taken into one's own hands." When a person

25. Ibid., 42.
26. Niebuhr, *The Kingdom of God*, 191–92.

lives in "unrecognized and undisclosed sin," "the word of grace becomes a poison." Bonhoeffer concluded that "countless Christians hear the word of grace only in this way. For them it has become a sleeping pill. The person is cheated out of a salutary life in awe of God."[27] Such a place is far from the throne of grace. Kierkegaard expressed his longing this way: "that I might learn not only to take refuge in grace, but to take refuge in such a way as to make use of grace."[28]

A Long Obedience in the Same Direction

Once again the pastor follows up hard truth and a dire warning with encouragement. He builds on their past testimony of real faithfulness. "Remember those earlier days after you received the light . . ." (Heb 10:32). His dire warning is matched by his warm sympathy and genuine respect. Having spoken against the potential danger of apostasy, he now reassures them by remembering their courageous endurance and steadfast faithfulness. Like a soldier who stands his ground on the field of battle, they have "endured in a great conflict full of suffering" (Heb 10:32). Whatever concern the pastor felt toward his hearers—the concern that prompted the severe warning—it was not allowed to color his deep appreciation for their record of sacrificial faithfulness. Their personal experience of insult and shaming as well as physical abuse and persecution had earned his unqualified respect. They had "stood side by side with those who were so treated" (Heb 10:33). He commends them, "You suffered along with those in prison and joyfully accepted the confiscation of your property, because you knew that you yourselves had better and lasting possessions" (10:34).

This raises a question for us. What happens when there is no testimony of tested faithfulness to build upon? The warning against apostasy is received more seriously when believers know something of the practical and personal cost of discipleship. Can a disciple truly practice New Testament Christianity and not experience some form of "push-back" from the world? If culture at its core is antithetical to God's will and hostile to the Jesus way, it is difficult to imagine faithful Christians not being marginalized or insulted. The subtleties of social hostility may be difficult to identify and articulate, but they can be real and felt deeply. If we cannot

27. Bonhoeffer, *Spiritual Care*, 31.
28. Kierkegaard, *Training in Christianity*, 7.

identify with the social alienation and social hostility experienced by the first hearers of Hebrews, is it because our Christianity is held hostage to the spirit of the times?

The believer's intentional decision to act according to God's will, even though it means suffering the world's hostility, underscores a marked behavioral change. We choose to enter through the narrow gate, because the broad way leads to disobedience and destruction (Matt 7:13–14). We make it our decision "to look after orphans and widows in their distress and to keep [ourselves] from being polluted by the world" (Jas 1:27). We no longer love the world or "anything in the world," because "everything in the world—the lust of the flesh, the lust of the eyes, and the pride of life—comes not from the Father but from the world" (1 John 2:15–16).

Suffering serves as a discipline, strengthening the believer's moral and ethical actions. We become like Jesus learning obedience by what we suffer (Heb 5:8). We face a choice. We either take "the path of least resistance—going along with the values, norms, and practices" acceptable to society—or we obey the will of God and suffer "the consequences of criticism and condemnation by unbelieving family and friends."[29]

Faith and Faithfulness

The pastor concludes this section with a clear admonition restated in parallel lines and directed to his hearers. Then he includes himself in this shared commitment to faithfulness to the end: "We're not quitters who lose out. Oh, no! We'll stay with it and survive, trusting all the way" (Heb 10:39 *The Message*). The pastor's spiritual direction is bold and blunt,

> "So *do not throw away your confidence*; it will be richly rewarded.
>
> *You need to persevere* so that when you have done the will of God, you will receive what he has promised. For,
>> 'In just a little while, he who is coming will come and will not delay'" (Isa 26:20; Hab 2:3).
> And,
>> "But my righteous one will live by faith. And I take no pleasure in the one who shrinks back" (Hab 2:4).
> But *we do not belong to those who shrink back* and are destroyed, but to those who have faith and are saved" (Heb 10:35–39).

29. Jobes, *1 Peter*, 265.

The pastor's warning against throwing away their *confidence* has nothing to do with a negative mood swing. He's not worried about them being discouraged, as much as he is concerned that they might throw away their faith in Christ altogether. The word "confidence" (Gk. *parrhēsia*) was used earlier to describe how we are to approach God's throne of grace. We are exhorted to approach "with *confidence*, so that we may receive mercy and find grace to help us in our time of need" (Heb 4:16). And at the start of this exhortative section, he says, "Therefore, brothers and sisters, since we have *confidence* to enter the Most Holy Place by the blood of Jesus . . . [L]et us draw near to God" (Heb 10:19-22). The pastor's focus here is not on self-confidence or a winning attitude. The confidence he calls for is a confidence in Christ that spreads across all personality types and emotional ranges. To "hold firmly to our confidence" (Heb 3:6) means embracing wholeheartedly "the hope in which we glory" (Heb 3:6); it means holding "our original conviction firmly to the end" (Heb 3:14); it means holding "firmly to the faith we profess" (Heb 4:14); and it means showing "diligence to the very end" (Heb 6:11). Confidence is not just an attitude but a way of life lived in anticipation of God's great reward in heaven (Luke 6:23).

The pastor draws out the meaning of this God-centered confidence by calling for perseverance. Obedience to the will of God is not optional. God expects wholehearted righteousness and holy living. Jesus gives us back the life we have lost in the living. Step by step he brings order out of the chaos of our old way of living. He brings clarity out of the clutter and confusion of our old agenda. Christ establishes a rhythm between worship and work, prayer and play, rest and restlessness. We are called to new priorities, perspectives, and preferences. Jesus' strategy for living is not packaged for easy consumption. Today's laid-back, easygoing, connect-the-dots, paint-by-number Christianity, on sale everywhere, is not what the pastor had in mind when he called for patient endurance. The cost of discipleship is real.

The pastor supports his call to patient endurance by quoting from the Septuagint version of Isaiah 26:20-21 and Habakkuk 2:3-4. The Old Testament context sets up a sharp contrast between those who live sinful lives and the righteous who live by faith. Believers are admonished to wait patiently for God's judgment and to live by faith. The emphasis in the Hebrew text is on the certainty of God's coming judgment, but in the Septuagint it is on the one who is coming. The pastor applies the Septuagint version of Habakkuk 2:3 to the second coming of Christ. He

places the definite article before the participle "coming," which yields the
messianic title "The Coming One."[30] Then the pastor applies Habakkuk
2:4, "my righteous one shall live by faith," not to "the coming one," but to
the believer. Therefore the believer who lives by faith will not shrink back,
because God takes "no pleasure in the one who shrinks back" (10:38).[31]
The pastor is appalled at the thought of shrinking back. He doesn't want
any believer to go there. "We do not belong to those who shrink back and
are destroyed, but to those who have faith and are saved" (10:39). "We're
not quitters who lose out. Oh, no! We'll stay with it and survive, trusting
all the way" (10:39, *The Message*).

Shrinkage

The pastor warns against sluggish learners who are too spiritually im-
mature to grasp the meaning and impact of the gospel.[32] His admonition not to shrink back is suggestive of a gradual withdrawal and a timid
response to subtle societal pressures against faith in Christ. The pastor is
concerned that his hearers are vulnerable to the cultural pressures that
threaten to undermine their faith in Christ and their participation in the
body of Christ.

In *Death by Suburb: How to keep the Suburbs from Killing your
Soul*, David Goetz translates the pastor's deep concerns into the practical

30. Bruce, *Hebrews*, 274. (Note the use of "the coming one" in Matt 3:11; 11:3; 21:9;
Luke 7:19; 19:38; John 1:15, 27; Rev 1:4.)

31. The Apostle Paul quoted Habakkuk 2:4 in Romans to capture the essence of
the gospel of Jesus Christ. He wrote, "For in the gospel a righteousness from God
is revealed, a righteousness that is by faith from first to last, just as it is written: 'The
righteous will live by faith'" (Rom 1:17; see Gal 3:11). In Romans, Paul's concern is
not how righteous people live, but how sinful people become righteous. John Stott
concludes, "Those who are righteous by faith also live by faith. Having begun in faith,
they continue in the same path" (Stott, *Romans*, 65). James Dunn sees Paul's quotation
as deliberately ambiguous. Paul does not seek to give 2:4 a new meaning, but rather
the fullest possible meaning (Dunn, *Romans*, 48). We live by faith in dependence
upon the faithfulness of God. Thus, to live by faith is to abandon every pretension
to self-sufficiency and put all of our confidence in the all-sufficiency of Christ. F. F.
Bruce writes, "There is no fundamental difference in this respect between Paul and
the author of Hebrews; but our author, reproducing the clause together with part of
its context, emphasizes the forward-looking character of saving faith, and in fact includes in 'faith' not only what Paul means by the word but also what Paul more often
expresses by the companion word 'hope'" (*Hebrews*, 274–75).

32. O'Brien, *Hebrews*, 204.

cultural issues that undermine the faith and faithfulness of many believers today. We are easily seduced by the toxic good life and the spirit of the times. Goetz warns, "Too much of the good life ends up being toxic, deforming us spiritually. The drive to succeed, to make one's children succeed, overpowers the best intentions to live more reflectively, no matter the piety. Should it be any surprise that the true life in Christ never germinates?"[33] Suburbia has the effect of co-opting our best intentions and turning our spirituality into a list of activities: "Bible studies, small group meetings, reading yet another best-selling book on the key to the victorious Christian living, even serving at the local homeless shelter."[34] But instead of these activities strengthening our faith they often leave us burnt out and empty. Instead of deepening our faith and leading us into mission these things turn us in upon ourselves. They don't enlarge our world, they shrink our world. We look for a sense of glory and transcendence in our "immortality symbols," our bank balance, home, car, child, job, vacations, etc. "It's about the glory that the thing bestows on me."[35]

The question is this: how do we live for Christ in a culture that caters to "the cravings of my gluttonous, overindulged self"? "There's no greater bondage," Goetz writes, "than living only for what I don't yet have and for the evasive approval of people, who, frankly, I don't really know or care about who will always have just a little more than I."[36] Our quest for ease and entertainment is destroying our souls. "Religion in the 'burbs tends to be more a program to join than it is an experience that changes your life. The more I participate in the programs, the further I remove myself from the deep suffering of the world. That's too bad. The entrance to the thicker, deeper life in Christ goes directly through the suffering of others."[37]

Our inability to overcome Perpetual Spiritual Adolescence (PSA) comes from our refusal to stay rooted in Christian community and to develop the spiritual friendships that call for self-denial and love. For the good of our own souls we need friendships that challenge us to give and to grow. "I live in spiritual poverty if my 'starter castle' envy is so great

33. Goetz, *Death by Suburb*, 9.

34. Ibid., 14.

35. Ibid., 42.

36. Ibid., 71.

37. Ibid., 108–9.

that my friends possess only the immortality symbols that I feel good about."[38]

You can almost hear the pastor's response. "Let us draw near to God with a sincere heart and with the full assurance that faith brings. . . . Let us hold unswervingly to the hope we profess, for he who promised is faithful. And let us consider how we may spur one another on toward love and good deeds, not giving up meeting together . . ." (Heb 10:22–25). Against the negative narrative of drifting away and shrinking back, the pastor offers a compelling counter narrative. He launches into the personal stories of salvation history so that we might identify with the saints who have gone before and live "by faith." He wants us to add our names to those "whose weakness was turned to strength," "so that [we] will not grow weary and lose heart" (11:34; 12:3).

Rejoice, the Lord Is King![39]

Rejoice, the Lord is King! Your Lord and King adore!
Rejoice, give thanks, and sing, and triumph evermore.
Lift up your heart; lift up your voice! Rejoice, again I say rejoice!

Our Savior, Jesus, reigns, the God of truth and love;
When he had purged our stains, *he took his seat above.*
Lift up your heart; lift up your voice! Rejoice, again I say rejoice!

His kingdom cannot fail; he rules o'er earth and heav'n;
The keys of death and hell are to our Jesus giv'n.
Lift up your heart; lift up your voice! Rejoice, again I say rejoice!

Rejoice in glorious hope! For Christ, the Judge shall come
And *gather all the saints* to their eternal home.
Lift up your heart; lift up your voice! Rejoice, again I say rejoice!

CHARLES WESLEY, 1746

38. Ibid., 163.

39. Shorney, Shorney, Schraeder, Weck, and Holstein, eds., *Worship and Rejoice*, 342.

10

Life of Faith and Faithfulness
(Hebrews 11:1–12:3)

"No Christian, thinking Christianly, divesting himself of the easy self-deceptions of secularist thinking, will pretend that Christianity is an easy faith—easy to accept, easy to explore, easy to rest in, easy to explain. It isn't. We must outdo the unbelievers in agreeing with them on that subject."

HARRY BLAMIRES[1]

FAITH AND FAITHFULNESS ARE the pulsating themes that build momentum and draw the sermon to its theological and rhetorical climax. The pastor's fast-paced highlight reel of the righteous who live and die by faith (Heb 11:4–39) drives the powerful thrust of his message to a Jesus-focused crescendo (Heb 12:1–3). Hebrews 11 seems to lend itself to a modern-day sermon series on the heroes of the faith, but that is not what the pastor envisioned. He crafted a five-minute recap of salvation history designed to show in real world terms how the righteous live by faith. If we slow down the "by faith" cadence and pause to examine the narrative details of these illustrative characters, we unwittingly interrupt the pastor's high-impact message. He's on a roll. Let's let him bring it home and make his case: faithfulness to the end proves faith from the beginning.

1. Blamires, *The Christian Mind*, 119–20.

The pastor has explained the negative example of the hardhearted Israelites in the wilderness (Heb 3:7–4:11). He has explored the multifaceted superiority of Christ and the new covenant over the old covenant's priesthood and sacrificial system (Heb 4:14–10:18). And now in chapter eleven he examines key Old Testament examples set in their redemptive historical sequence.[2] The climax to this exemplary list is Jesus, the pioneer and perfecter of faith, who "for the joy set before him endured the cross, scorning its shame, and sat down at the right hand of the throne of God" (Heb 12:2). He concludes the body of his sermon right where he began with Jesus seated at the right hand of the throne of God (Heb 1:3,13; 8:1; 10:12). This is the fifth and final reference to Psalm 110:1. It offers the ultimate reason and highest incentive to fix our eyes on Jesus and to "consider him who endured such opposition from sinners, so that [we] will not grow weary and lose heart."

Faith Defined

The pastor frames the "by faith" biographies with a definition of faith that sees personal hope and the creation of the universe as essential realities that are bound together and begotten at the command of God. The pastor moves deftly from the personal to the cosmic in a concise summary. Everything depends upon the God who "has spoken to us by his Son, whom he appointed heir of all things, and through whom also he made the universe" (Heb 1:2).

"Now faith is confidence (*hypostasis*) in what we hope for and assurance (*elenchos*) about what we do not see" (Heb 11:1, NIV). The choice of the word *hypostasis* to describe the believer's state of faith may represent the objective and essential reality of hope as well as the subjective and emotive assurance of hope in Christ. We may not have to choose between the objective and the subjective meanings of the word, because the double meaning may have been intended by the pastor.[3] Faith is defined

2. O'Brien, *Hebrews*, 395.

3. Bruce, *Hebrews*, 277: "There is something to be said for the objective meaning ("faith is the substance of things hoped for" KJV) . . . . But on the whole the subjective 'assurance' is the more probable, especially as this meaning chimes in well with the companion word 'conviction.'" O'Brien, *Hebrews*, 399: "We prefer to take hypostasis as signifying 'realty' or 'substance' (AV, REB) . . . . This objective understanding of hypostasis is consistent with the forward-looking aspect of faith that is repeatedly demonstrated in Hebrews 11." Cockerill, *Hebrews*, 520: "'Now faith is the reality of

here as a way of life, meaning we live "as if the things hoped for are real."[4] Therefore, the substantive reality of faith and the deep subjective assurance of faith are distinguishable but inseparable in the mind and heart of the righteous who live by faith.

The pastor may also have intended a double meaning when he used the term *elenchos* to describe faith's *assurance* (subjective) or faith's *proof* or *evidence* (objective) "about what we do not see." Scholars may want to choose between faith as "the assurance of things not seen" and faith as "the evidence of things not seen," but the ambiguity plays to the pastor's purpose of testifying to faith's subjective conviction and objective demonstration. The ancients were commended for their faith in the invisible reality of God. Their lives tell the story of deep assurance in the truth of God, even as their lives confidently demonstrate and prove its reality.

The "proof" that the pastor has in mind is not a scientific proof, the kind that can be replicated in the laboratory through repeatable experiments. He means a more relational confirmation based on trust and a shared understanding of God's acts in history. This evidence consists of the relational bond that exists between God and his creation. This "proof" lies outside of science but it is for science. It is in history, but not explainable by historical forces. The Apostle Paul uses the resurrection of Jesus Christ as the ultimate relational proof to verify God's intentions for creation and humanity. The resurrection is a historical event that proves God's faithfulness to his Word. The resurrection validates and verifies that life is meaningful and that meaning itself is rooted in the unseen God. Faith did not create the resurrection of Jesus; the resurrection created faith.

Faith does not operate in a different realm from sight. Faith is the earnest expectation of sight. In the most real world the two are inseparably linked and inherent in objective reality. "Without faith," wrote the author of Hebrews, "it is impossible to please him, for whoever would draw near to God must believe that he exists and that he rewards those who seek him" (Heb 11:6). Sight does not create that which is seen, nor does faith create that which is believed. If seeing meant believing for the first disciples, then believing means seeing for today's disciples. The

things hoped for, the evidence of things not seen.' Faith is oriented toward the future, hoped-for realization of God's promised existence, providence (v.6), fidelity (v.11) and power (v.19). . . . The philosophers used this term [hypostasis] to distinguish 'reality' from mere 'appearance.'"

4. Cockerill, *Hebrews,* 521.

resurrection of Christ is a fact of science and history that is believed by faith. If the resurrection of Christ did not actually happen in real time and real history, the Apostle Paul spelled out the verdict: our faith is useless and we are guilty of bearing false witness. We are still in our sins and we are lost, without hope in the world. "If only for this life we have hope in Christ, we are of all people most to be pitied" (1 Cor 15:19).

The essential ground for our faith lies not in ourselves but in God, and where that faith is present it cannot help but manifest itself in the believer's genuine confidence and resilient steadfastness. "For the Christian, the efficacy of one's faith lies not in faith itself but in the faithfulness of the One who is the object of that faith. In other words, our faith is only as good as the One we're trusting. If God is not faithful to his Word, then our faith can accomplish nothing at all."[5]

Calvin wrote, "We shall now have a full definition of faith if we say that it is a firm and sure knowledge of the divine favor toward us, founded on the truth of a free promise in Christ, and revealed to our minds, and sealed on our hearts, by the Holy Spirit."[6] "No one can well perceive the power of faith," Calvin held, "without at the same time feeling it in his heart."[7]

Since faith is the reality of things hoped for, it has to be more than a mental assent to a set of intellectual propositions. Certainly not less than a creedal confession and a conceptual understanding, but by virtue of the subject believed in, faith calls for holistic understanding fused with passion. We were meant to live and work in anticipation of the faith-held vision of the coming kingdom of God and the new heaven and the new earth. Like Abraham we are "looking forward to the city with foundations, whose architect and builder is God" (Heb 11:10). For John Wesley faith was a matter of personal trust and intellectual conviction. Faith is more than a cognitive decision; it is full surrender. P. T. Forsyth put it this way: "Faith is not simply surrender, but adoring surrender, not a mere sense of dependence, but an act of intelligent committal, and the confession of holiness which is able to save, keep, and bless for ever."[8] For Martin Luther faith was more than just believing that what God said was true.

5. Litfin, *Conceiving The Christian College*, 190.

6. Calvin, *Institutes*, III, 2, 7, 475.

7. Ibid., III, 20, 12, 157.

8. Forsyth, *The Soul of Prayer*, 68.

Saving faith meant throwing yourself on God.[9] So, before we embark on the pastor's sweep of salvation history and the description of how the righteous live by faith, it is helpful to remember Luther's discovery of the objective and essential ground for righteousness:

> Though I lived as a monk without reproach, I felt that I was a sinner before God with an extremely disturbed conscience. I could not believe that God was placated by my satisfaction. I did not love, indeed I hated the righteous God who punishes sinners . . . . At last by the mercy of God, meditating day and night, I turned to the context of the following words: "In it (the Gospel) the righteousness of God is revealed, as it is written, 'He who through faith is righteous shall live.'" There I began to understand the righteousness of God, namely by faith. And this is the meaning: The righteousness of God which is revealed by the gospel, is a passive righteousness with which the merciful God justifies us by faith, as it is written, "He who through faith is righteous shall live." Here I felt that I was altogether born again and had entered paradise itself through open gates. There a totally other face of the entire Scripture showed itself to me. So then I ran through the Scriptures from memory. I found analogies in other phrases as: the work of God, that is what God does in us; the power of God, with which he makes us strong; the wisdom of God, with which he makes us wise; the strength of God, the salvation of God, the glory of God. And I extolled my sweetest word with a love as great as the hatred with which I had before hated the word "righteousness of God."[10]

The Righteous Live By Faith

The pastor's fast-paced rendition of salvation history recalls pivotal portraits of faith. He edits down the details to a single act or course of action that captures the essence of faith. Each of these faith-inspired scenarios portrays the drama of salvation in the real world. Ordinary people are commended for their faith, and this faith defines them inwardly and outwardly. They believe in the living God who continues to speak in specific, concrete ways, and they respond in life-changing obedience. Faith involves discernment, devotion, trust, conviction, insight, and surrender.

9. Bloesch, *Essentials of Evangelical Theology*, vol. 1, 224.
10. Todd, *Luther*, 77–78.

Hebrews 11 teaches us that righteousness is not whatever we wish it to be; it is what God declares it to be. The righteous live by faith, because they take God at his word and trust him with their lives. They demonstrate this real-world faith in practical ways. These acts of faith include Abel's better offering, Enoch's devotion, Noah's building of the ark, Abraham's obedience, Isaac's blessing, Jacob's worship, and Joseph's faithfulness to the end. The pastor flies through these examples, building his case for the necessity and practicality of faith.

In the middle of his description of Abraham's faith the pastor breaks up the flow of his argument with a meditation on the eschatological motivation for faith and faithful service (Heb 11:13–16). When we hear him say "All these people were still living by faith when they died," we know that he means for us to live by faith until we die or Christ comes again. His point being, that if they could live by faith so should we. He expects us to embrace their longing and expectation for a better country: "They did not receive the things promised; they saw them and welcomed them from a distance, admitting that they were foreigners and strangers on earth. People who say such things show that they are looking for a country of their own. If they had been thinking of the country they had left, they would have had opportunity to return. Instead they were longing for a better country—a heavenly one" (Heb 11:13–16).

The life of faith has profound theological and sociological implications. The pastor insists that those who live by faith live as "foreigners and strangers on earth." The followers of Jesus Christ become strangers in their own homeland. To be looking for a country of their own renders them de facto foreigners in the land of our birth. Without moving from one country to another, and without crossing any political or regional boundaries, Christ's followers become resident aliens, by virtue of their newfound faith in Christ. This is what the psalmist meant when he prayed, "Blessed are those whose strength is in you, whose hearts are set on pilgrimage" (Ps 84:5).

The pastor warns us not to interpret the search for a heavenly home as an ethereal, spiritual quest, with the result that our lives reflect the priorities, passions, values, ambitions, and goals of a worldly, faithless culture. He challenges us to work out the life of faith in our jobs and in our families. We want the concrete practicality of Abel's sacrifice and Noah's ark. We want to see ourselves the way Abraham saw himself: "a stranger in a foreign country."

What we must not do is turn a living, passionate faith in Christ into another religion alongside other religions, just another option among contemporary spiritualities. The pastor's emphasis is on the inheritance to come, the believer's eschatological hope, the culmination of our salvation when Christ comes again. On this side of eternity he envisions a sacrificial life of holy obedience, rather than the fulfillment of the American dream, personal success, and the material good life. We may have to undergo some soul-searching and repentance before we can confidently apply the pastor's concluding thought to ourselves: "Therefore God is not ashamed to be called their God, for he has prepared a city for them" (Heb 11:16; see 2:11).

The Abraham Story

The pastor's foremost example of faith is Abraham. In spite of his weaknesses and self-serving strategies, we know that God was not ashamed to be called Abraham's God. The incident the pastor highlights in Abraham's life is especially relevant for those of us who have turned our children into immortality symbols. God told Abraham that his promise to him and to future generations was all wrapped up in the birth of his son Isaac and Abraham believed him. But "God tested him" (Heb 11:17).

Everything in the story of Abraham builds to this point and everything after is an epilogue. Abraham's faith was tested in many ways but the previous tests paled in comparison to this ultimate test. Abraham learned to trust in God. He was vitally aware of God's intense interest in his life and future. So when the shattering Word of God came, it hit like a hammer blow, but Abraham accepted it and obeyed. "Take your son, your only son, whom you love—Isaac—and go to the region of Moriah. Sacrifice him there as a burnt offering on a mountain I will show you" (Gen 22:2).

> By faith Abraham, when God tested him, offered Isaac as a sacrifice. He who had embraced the promises was about to sacrifice his one and only son, even though God had said to him, "It is through Isaac that your offspring will be reckoned." Abraham reasoned that God could even raise the dead, and so in a manner of speaking he did receive Isaac back from death (Heb 11:17–19).

The weight of Abraham's story and passion shifts from birth to sacrifice. The patriarch was willing to follow the Word of God to the grave and back again. He had to walk by faith. What else could he do? The drama of faith is real. Genesis reads, "He reached out his hand and took the knife to slay his son. But the angel of the Lord called out to him from heaven, "Abraham! Abraham!"

"Here I am," he replied.

"Do not lay a hand on the boy. Do not do anything to him. Now I know that you fear God, because you have not withheld from me your son, your only son" (Gen 22:10–12). In Genesis the focus of the story is on God's response. The divine perspective was what mattered and God's verdict on Abraham's actions was crucial. We cannot hear this story without picturing the cross of Christ. Abraham demonstrated his faithfulness to God, but more importantly he shows us the faithfulness of God. Abraham is a picture of God giving up his one and only Son for our salvation. We meditate on the kindred spirit and the shared passion that the Lord God felt with and for Abraham. "Now I know that you fear God, *because you have not withheld from me your son, your only son*" (Heb 22:12). Abraham's ultimate test revealed God's ultimate provision.

No Heroes

There are no heroes among God's people, only saints who have gone before. The testimony of God's first sacrificial lamb remains true: "By faith Abel still speaks, even though he is dead" (Heb 11:4). The Bible remembers resilient saints. There is a difference between idolizing and remembering. Abraham lived 175 years before he was "gathered to his people." His effort to buy a burial plot from the Hittites near Mamre in order to bury his wife Sarah receives detailed attention. Nomadic wanderers like Abraham who were "looking forward to the city with foundations, whose architect and builder is God" had to make special arrangements to bury their dead (Gen 23; Heb 11:10). Abraham died "at a good old age" and Isaac buried him next to Sarah, but I doubt that there was much of a eulogy that day, at least not a eulogy commensurate with his stature in salvation history. Did Isaac recall that defining moment when by faith his father Abraham offered him up as a sacrifice? That moment of faithfulness became a movement of divine promise, because "Abraham reasoned that God could even raise the dead, and so in a manner of speaking he did receive Isaac back from death" (Heb 11:19).

The pastor celebrated Isaac, Jacob, and Joseph's faithfulness to the end by highlighting their last act of faithfulness. Our attention is focused on their faith and trust in God's promise right up to the end. Jacob, "when he was dying, blessed each of Joseph's sons, and worshiped as he leaned on the top of his staff" (Heb 11:21). By faith, Joseph spoke about the exodus. Their "death-bed" faithfulness pointed forward, because they were "longing for a better country—a heavenly one" (Heb 11:16).

If anyone qualified for hero status, it was Moses. He was a model of faithfulness because "he regarded disgrace for the sake of Christ as of greater value than the treasures of Egypt" (Heb 11:26). But Moses died unheroically and in one sense prematurely (Deut 34:7). He was buried by God in an unmarked grave in Moab outside of the promised land. God made sure that there was no possibility of erecting a shrine or creating a memorial. Even though Moses was faithful to the end, preaching God's Word, warning the people of their sinful propensity to rebellion and disobedience, and establishing Joshua's leadership, God held Moses accountable for his wilful act of disobedience. Obedience was never optional and God's verdict was certain, "because you broke faith with me in the presence of the Israelites . . . and because you did not uphold my holiness among the Israelites . . . you will see the land only from a distance; you will not enter the land I am giving to the people of Israel" (Deut 32:51–52).

The pastor's selection of Rahab the Canaanite prostitute, who welcomed the spies (Heb 11:31), as a model of faithfulness challenges the elite status of these "heroes" of the faith. Everyone in this chapter was a sinner, with stories of shame and violence. The pastor wants us to see ourselves in these ordinary people who put their trust in God. He wants us to identify with Abel's repentance and Noah's holy fear. He wants us to join Abraham in "longing for a better country—a heavenly one" (Heb 11:16). He wants us to determine that we will be a blessing to our children right up to our dying breath and that like Jacob we will worship on our death bed. He wants us to be like Rahab countering our home culture and grasping the testimony of God against all the odds. We have to rethink our understanding of God and remember that to God there are no nameless masses. God intends to relate to each one of us in the way he related to Moses. The Lord knows us as well as he knew Noah or Abraham. Our lives are no less important to God than their lives. As a child of Abraham through faith in Christ, our lives are as important to the Lord as the life of Abraham.

The by-faith bios are about ordinary saints who were faithful to the end. Their uniqueness lies not in their abilities and achievements, but in God's empowering presence. Mercy, not merit, governed the call of God in their lives. Noah was the son of an arrogant father. Abraham was a nobody. Moses was a fugitive. Yet all them were unique image-bearers of God, and all of them were ordinary sinners saved by grace. To know this about them helps us to stand with them, and to see ourselves in their experiences. Their story becomes our story.

Shortly after graduation from Tyndale Theological Seminary in Toronto, Hernando Hernandez and Laura Binkley were killed. Laura was stabbed to death in her apartment. She was serving in an orphanage in Moscow and the police suspected that one of her assailants was a girl she had befriended and shared Christ with. Hernando was coming home from a student conference in Colombia with a car full of young Christian leaders. Their car was struck on a narrow mountain road by a speeding bus and sent careening over a cliff into a deep ravine. Everybody in the car was killed. Both Hernando and Laura came from solid, supportive, Christ-centered families that had offered them up to the Lord. It was a crushing blow. They were two of the seminary's best students, marked by selfless love and kingdom focus. No sooner had they graduated, than they were gone.

Laura was a home-grown Canadian. Hernando was a Colombian. They both had a profound impact on me. I was a young seminary teacher and they were my teaching assistants in Theology 101. Their passion for Christ, coupled with their compassion for the poor and their global sensitivity, raised the excitement level exponentially for our introductory theology class. Their tutorials went way beyond processing information. Laura embraced theology with tears of compassion for the lost and needy. Hernando, dressed in green fatigues and a black T-shirt, was a bold and fiery, yet friendly prophet. He was determined to unsettle our bland complacency and focus our attention on Christ's social justice. Hernando accomplished this the Jesus way—with humility.

These two young disciples taught me that there are no heroes in Christ, only saints who have gone before. Sometimes our time is short, and without much notice we join that "great cloud of witnesses" who have run the race with their eyes fixed on Jesus, the pioneer and perfecter of faith. The emphasis in Hebrews 11 is on momentum, not memorials; on faithfulness, not heroics. The race continues. The saints cheer us on. What is important is that we remain faithful to the end.

We never outgrow our need to trust and grow in the grace and knowledge of the Lord Jesus Christ. We may expect life to get easier and more put-together, but it doesn't. Our life and testimony in our twenties are just as important to God as they are in our fifties. When the psalmist says "Teach us to number our days so we may gain a heart of wisdom," we know two things: our days are valuable and our time is limited (Ps 90:12). Our worth is not measured by what we achieve, but by what we receive in Christ. Our joy is measured by how faithful and obedient we have been to what we have received. We were never meant to become less dependent upon the Lord, only more dependent. "As for mortals, their days are like grass, they flourish like a flower of the field; the wind blows over it and it is gone, and its place remembers it no more" (Ps 103:15). Life is short and often hard. The goal is being faithful, not making a name for ourselves or building a reputation. We haven't arrived, but we press on to take hold of that for which Christ Jesus took hold of us (Phil 3:12).

The pastor weans us away from our preoccupation with the start of the Christian life and focuses our attention on the perseverance of faith. Life is not a sprint but a marathon. It's not over until it's over. Faithfulness to the end affirms our faith from the beginning. And the end in faithfulness to the end may be a long way off, but it is the only end worth pursuing. The pastor ends his by-faith bios the way so many preachers do: "I could go and on, but I've run out of time. There are so many more—Gideon, Barak, Samson, Jephthah, David, Samuel, the prophets . . ." (11:32 *The Message*). These six names are paired in reverse chronological order and span the period from the judges to the monarchy.[11] They represent the faithful multitude, this "great cloud of witnesses," who through the centuries have testified to the real-world impact of faith in God. The faithful have achieved much, not in their own strength but in God's, and they have suffered much, not for their own glory, but for God's glory.

The pastor's fast-paced recital of events spans salvation history up to the time of Christ. He piles up the staccato phrases describing the triumph and the tragedy of living by faith. Undoubtedly we would all prefer to be on the victorious side, conquering kingdoms, administering justice, gaining what was promised, shutting the mouths of lions, and escaping the edge of the sword, but that is not for us to decide. We would like to rout armies and experience miraculous healings, but we don't get to choose between triumph and tragedy, that's up to God. The

11. Gideon (Judg 7:1–25; Isa 9:4; 10:26; Ps 83:9); Barak (Judg 4–5); Samson (Judg 13:1–16:31); Jephthah (Judg 11); David (1 Sam 16–2 Sam 24); Samuel (1 Sam 1–16).

tortured, abused, flogged, and jailed are just as faithful as the victorious. Any illusion that the measure of our faith determines positive or negative outcomes is dispelled by the pastor's description of the high cost of faithfulness. He paints a picture of extreme suffering: "They were put to death by stoning; they were sawed in two; they were killed by the sword. They went about in sheepskins and goatskins, destitute, persecuted and mistreated—the world was not worthy of them. They wandered in deserts and mountains, living in caves and holes in the ground" (Heb 11:37–38).

This rapid-fire sequence of personalities and stories is brought to an end by repeating two important themes: the ancients were commended for their faith (Heb 1:1–2; 11:39) and "none of them received what had been promised" (Heb 11:39; 11:13). They longed to see the fulfillment that only Christ could bring (1 Pet 1:10–12), because "God had planned something better for us so that only together with us would they be made perfect" (Heb 11:40). This better plan is a theme that has run through the pastor's entire sermon. In Christ we have a "better hope" (Heb 7:19), a "better covenant" (7:22), "better promises" (8:6), a "better sacrifice" (9:23), "better possessions" (10:34), a "better country" (11:16), and a "better resurrection" (11:35). "In God's gracious purpose the perfection of the Old Testament faithful was only possible together with us. . . . They died without having received the ultimate promise until the advent of Christ, his sacrificial death, and the enacting of the new covenant."[12]

Running the Race

The pastor shifts his key metaphor from pilgrimage to running a marathon. He moves from the long obedience in the same direction to an athletic contest in the "crowded tiers of the an amphitheater."[13] He has picked up the pace from the nomadic trek of faith in search of a better country to a race to the finish. There is a heightened sense of urgency and anticipation. The pastor includes himself. We are running in the company of the committed, "surrounded by such a great cloud of witnesses." We are not alone. We are in this race together. The pastor adds to his heartening "Let us" challenges:

"Let us draw near to God with a sincere heart . . ."

"Let us hold unswervingly to the hope we profess . . ."

12. O'Brien, *Hebrews*, 447.
13. Hughes, *Hebrews*, 518.

"Let us consider how we may spur one another on toward love . . ."

"Let us throw off everything that hinders and the sin that so easily entangles."

"Let us run with perseverance the race marked out for us . . ."

"[Let us fix] our eyes on Jesus, the pioneer and perfecter of faith" (Heb 10:22–23; 12:1–2).

The imagery of a great cloud of witnesses stands for the all-encompassing host of saints who have gone before. These are the believers who have been faithful to the end. They are like Abel, even though dead they still speak (Heb 11:4). They are not passive spectators but active witnesses to the power of the resurrection and the hope of glory. Their stories help us to interpret our stories. Their legacy of faith and faithfulness inspire our own. Paul pictures them "absent from the body and present with the Lord" (2 Cor 5:8). John describes "a great multitude that no one can count, from every nation, tribe, people and language, standing before the throne and before the Lamb" (Rev 7:9). Since the pastor delivered this sermon the throng has gotten considerably larger and the prayers of a suffering church have remained intense. The souls of those who have been slain because of the Word of God and the testimony of Jesus call out, "How long, Sovereign Lord, holy and true, until the inhabitants of the earth avenge our blood?" (Rev 6:9–10). We picture our loved ones and dear friends in this great company saying with all the saints, "Amen. Come, Lord Jesus" (Rev 22:20). The impressive image of the great cloud of witnesses is meant to encourage and inspire us. The "cloud" signifies the magnitude and unanimity of the testimony of these stalwart witnesses. "The pastor would have his hearers feel that they can reach out and touch these heroes who lived by faith. It is these faithful from the past whose approval is worth courting despite the sneer of the unbelieving world."[14]

The competitive race is a favorite image for the apostles. The popularity of games in the Roman Empire provided a compelling image for the very different kind of competition the New Testament writers had in mind. "Run in such a way as to get the prize," challenged the Apostle Paul. "Everyone who competes in the games goes into strict training." But Paul was clear on the difference between athletics and faithfulness. "They do it to get a crown that will not last, but we do it to get a crown that will last forever" (1 Cor 9:24–25). These references to sports and competition

---

14. Cockerill, *Hebrews*, 602.

were not intended to justify our modern fascination with sports, but to challenge us in a radically different kind of race.

Like a good runner who strips down for the race, the pastor encourages believers to "throw off everything that hinders and the sin that so easily entangles." The hindrances he has in mind are the sins "of whatever kind" that interfere with running the race.[15] He addressed this issue earlier when he spoke of the dangers of unbelief and the hardening of our hearts (Heb 3:19; 4:7). He warned against a sluggishness that would make it difficult to distinguish good from evil (5:14). Throughout the sermon he has exhorted us to "pay careful attention" (Heb 2:1), to "hold firmly to our confidence" (Heb 3:6), to "hold our original conviction firmly to the end" (Heb 3:14), and to "hold firmly to the faith we profess" (Heb 4:14).

Throwing off the sin that so easily entangles is easier said than done (Heb 12:2). When we lived in Bloomington, Indiana, the land our home was on had once been part of a farm. The backyard was surrounded by a chain-link fence running along the property line. About ten feet inside the fence was a dense growth of bushes, vines, and trees. When I attempted to clear a path through the growth, I discovered the farm's old barbed wire fence. The trees had grown up around it and through it and in some instances the barbed wire was deeply embedded in the trees. From a few feet away you could hardly see it, but it was there and had to come out so our children would not run into the barbed wire when they played. Removing the rusty steel wire took longer than I anticipated. The fence was so intertwined with the brush and trees that I had to spend hours cutting through the barbed wire with a hacksaw, slowly extracting it from its nearly invisible stranglehold on the trees. That barbed-wire fence is a picture to me of the evil in my life—in our lives and in our society—that is deeply embedded in and wrapped around the way we work, how we think about ourselves, how we use money and relate sexually, and how we act toward our enemies. Life has grown up and around and through this evil, which has a grip on how our lives are lived. The evil does not come down by cutting into it at one point. We require continuous self-examination in order to detect the complex strategies of self-deception.

Sprint or Marathon?

San Diego has a "Rock 'n' Roll" marathon that can be run in two hours, ten minutes and eight seconds, but the race described in Hebrews takes

15. Hughes, *Hebrews*, 520.

a lifetime to run. Paul Szymanski ran the marathon with his ten-year-old daughter Grace. Grace suffers from severe autism and Paul pushed her all 26.2 miles in a jogging stroller. Their race is a metaphor for the marathon Paul and Laura have been running with Grace. They have cared for their daughter with the love of Christ—a daily, sacrificial love. This is the commitment the Apostle Paul commended when he said, "I press on to take hold of that for which Christ Jesus took hold of me" (Phil 3:13).

When David Mensah spoke at the graduation service of the Tamale Baptist College in northern Ghana, his text was Hebrews 12. His wife, Brenda, reminded me that I had spoken from that same text at David's graduation from Tyndale University in Toronto twenty-five years earlier. Brenda said that as the first student in his cap and gown passed across the stage for his diploma, she recalled that David had been in that same place twenty-five years ago. Then she started to think about all that she and David had seen God do in their little corner of the globe where the Lord had placed them. She reflected on how meaningful their lives had been because the Lord had kept them in his race. Memory after memory flooded back and she just couldn't stop weeping. Brenda said, "I wondered what it would be like to meet with all the graduates who had walked across that stage twenty-five years ago and to hear their stories of God's grace over the years. And then I wondered what great plans God has for these young pastors that are running up behind us to take the baton."

At David's graduation, I illustrated the metaphor of the race by comparing two runners. In the movie *Chariots of Fire*, which was popular at the time, Eric Liddell expressed his reason for entering the 1924 Olympics with the famous line, "God made me fast, and when I run I feel his favor." The movie captured that moment of exhilaration when Liddell crossed the finish line, winning gold. He had committed several years of his life to preparing for the Paris games. All of his time and energy were poured into running the Olympic race and when he won, the race was over. Eric Liddell knew what he had to do, and he did it. He achieved his goal. In life we long for that moment of exhilarating release when we have accomplished the long-sought-after goal—when we can finally say it is finished. But Christ's followers face the challenge of a long obedience in the same direction, not a 400-meter race. Discipleship requires more than a quick burst of spiritual energy for a few years. The race God has called us to is not a sprint but a marathon.

The second image that I used to illustrate the metaphor of the race came closer to capturing the essence of the Christian race. Terry Fox died from cancer in the early eighties, but not before inspiring a nation with his personal courage. Setting out to jog across Canada on an artificial limb, he became a symbol of hope and perseverance. His quest came to be called the Marathon of Hope. His trek across Canada received nightly news coverage and he captured the attention of the nation. Terry Fox succeeded in raising millions of dollars for cancer research but even more importantly, and impossible to measure, was the impact of his courage and determination on millions of Canadians. Terry Fox's marathon was not over until his life was over. This is how it is for those who "run with perseverance the race marked out for us, fixing our eyes on Jesus."

Although Terry Fox's Marathon of Hope may be a better analogy of the Christian life than Eric Liddell's 400-meter Olympic race, Liddell's life was an outstanding example of spiritual stamina and Christ-centered endurance. He obeyed the call of God to go to China as a missionary, where he served until his death. His life did not peak at the 1924 Olympics. He saw Jesus leading him to China for a life of service and hardship far more demanding than the Olympics. Eric Liddell put behind him the events that made him famous, and ran the marathon of faith with his eyes fixed on Jesus. A friend of mine, David Michell, remembered Eric Liddell from his experience as a young boy when he, along with 174 other children of missionary parents, was imprisoned in a Japanese Internment Camp in China during the Second World War. Eric Liddell was a prisoner at the same camp and became known for his Christlike presence and his selfless devotion to helping the children in the camp. Liddell died of a brain tumor three days before the Allies arrived, but right up to the end, Liddell's reputation as a follower of Jesus was evident to all.

The pastor insists that we are to run the race that is clearly "marked out for us" with determination and perseverance. Yet if the path of discipleship is clear and straightforward, why do we make it so difficult? "A mind cluttered by excuses," writes Dallas Willard, "may make a mystery of discipleship, or it may see it as something to be dreaded. But there is no mystery about desiring and intending to be like someone that is a very common thing. And if we intend to be like Christ, that will be obvious to every thoughtful person around us, as well as to ourselves."[16] The "secret" to running the race is simple. "It is the intelligent, informed, unyielding resolve to live as Jesus lived in all aspects of life."[17] A refusal to run the race is tantamount to apostasy even as our commitment to run is evident

16. Willard, "Discipleship," 25.
17. Willard, *The Spirit of the Disciplines*, 10.

to all. Everyone will know if we have counted the cost and entered the race with our eyes fixed on Jesus. And make no mistake, all eyes are on Jesus, both for those who have proven their faithfulness to the end and those who desire to do so.

The Pioneer and Perfecter of the Faith

> Let us run looking unto the Pioneer and Perfecter of the faith, Jesus, who for the joy set before him endured a cross, despising the shame, and has taken his seat at the right hand of the throne of God (Heb 12:2).[18]

The pastor returns to the description of Jesus used at the outset. "In bringing many sons and daughters to glory, it was fitting that God, for whom and through whom everything exists, should make the pioneer (*archēgos*) of their salvation perfect (*teleiōtes*) through what he suffered" (Heb 2:10). In between these two parallel descriptions (Heb 2:9–10; 12:1–2), the pastor exhorts us to fix our thoughts on Jesus our apostle and high priest (Heb 3:1). Jesus finishes what he began. He is our leader and founder. He is not only the pioneer who blazed the trail but he is also the one who perfected salvation and will bring it to completion. "By the single offering of himself to God, Christ was perfected through suffering and obtained perfection for all who believe and obey him (Heb 2:10; 5:9; 7:28; 9:14; 10:5–10, 14).[19] The pairing of these descriptive titles cover the full range of who Jesus is and what he has done. His essential being and his historical becoming are held in tension.[20]

The pastor exhorts us to focus on Jesus by turning away from distractions. The verb translated "fixing" is an unusual word and "implies a definite looking away from others and directing one's gaze towards Jesus.

---

18. Cockerill, *Hebrews*, 600.

19. O'Brien, *Hebrews*, 454.

20. Cockerill, *Hebrews*, 607: "The work of Christ that opens the way for approaching God in the present is, as we have seen, the same work necessary for final entrance into the divine presence. 'Pioneer and Perfecter of the faith,' then, encompasses all that the Son of God has done as both Pioneer and High Priest. As 'Pioneer and Perfecter' of the way 'of faith' he is able to do everything necessary to succor the people of God in their daily pilgrimage, and thus to bring them into their ultimate destiny. The pastor has reserved this comprehensive term for 12:1–3, the high point of his appeal, and used it to invoke all that he has said about the full sufficiency of the Son of God as the Savior of his people."

It suggests the impossibility of looking in two directions at once."[21] Like a marksman eyeing the target or an equestrian rider viewing the jump or a runner focusing on the finish, the believer's eyes are fixed on Jesus. Just as ocean lifeguards have to keep their eyes on the swimmers, believers must be trained to keep their eyes on Jesus. Like a surgeon, who will not divert her eyes from the patient, but calls for scalpel without ever glancing away, the follower of Jesus keeps her eyes on the pioneer and perfecter of her faith. We all need the exhortation to keep looking to Jesus. For many of us our vision of Christ has become blurred. We need the spiritual equivalent of laser surgery to correct our vision. Just as a laser light is used to reshape the inner layers of the cornea we need the light of God's Word, illumined by the Holy Spirit, to reshape our inner self and restore a 20/20 vision of Christ.

One of the important ways we do this is by seeing Jesus everywhere we look in salvation history. Every covenant and promise depends upon him. Every deliverance story finds its fulfillment in him. Every leading character points to him. The story has always been about him from beginning to end. The praying imagination works in us the way it worked in Moses causing us to see him who is invisible. We see Christ implicitly in Abraham's call to sacrifice his one and only son, and in Isaiah's Suffering Servant, and in Zechariah's mourned and martyred messiah. We see the hidden Christ in Bethlehem's manger and on the Sea of Galilee and in Jerusalem's temple.

Everywhere we look from Genesis to Revelation we see the pioneer and perfecter of our faith. Every genre, theme, image, figure, and plot point to Christ.[22]

Faith

The faith that is pioneered and perfected by Jesus is the same faith anticipated by those described in chapter 11 as living by faith. This is the particular faith that procures salvation for the people of God. This is the faith that is defined by Christ and is not to be confused with popular notions of faith. Ecumenical services are described as interfaith gatherings. "Faith is knowing that no matter what you'll be okay." Community centers "welcome people of all faiths, or no faith at all." When questioned

21. D. Guthrie, *Hebrews*, 251.
22. Keller, *Preaching*, 70ff.

about religion Prince Charles has said that when he becomes king, he would rather inherit the title "Defender of Faith," instead of "Defender of the Faith" and so represent all his subjects.

The single most difficult issue confronting Christians today may be the specific and definitive meaning of the Christian faith. Modern objections to biblical miracles and the problem of pain and suffering seem to pale in significance when compared to the bold claim made by Jesus, "I am the way, the truth, and the life, no one comes to the Father except through me" (John 14:6). Celebrity Oprah Winfrey appears to speak for many when she says, "One of the biggest mistakes humans make is to believe there is only one way. Actually, there are many diverse paths leading to what you call God."[23]

When the Lausanne committee, sponsored by the World Evangelical Fellowship, met and drafted a two-page theological document on evangelization, Rabbi A. James Rudin of the American Jewish Committee called it a "blueprint of spiritual genocide." Missiologist Arthur Glasser of the Fuller Seminary School of World Missions remembers when the seminary released a statement identifying Fuller Seminary with efforts to evangelize Jews. When this became known, a group of prominent rabbis protested to David Hubbard, who was president of Fuller Seminary at the time. The rabbis, whom David Hubbard knew personally, asked him to dissociate the seminary from "proselytizing." In the face of these objections, President Hubbard encouraged the faculty to persevere, saying, "If Jesus is not the Messiah of the Jewish people, he can hardly be the Christ of the Christian faith."[24]

Joy

The radical nature and unique character of the Christian faith is beautifully set forth in a single sentence. "For the joy set before him he endured the cross, scorning the shame, and sat down at the right hand of the throne of God" (Heb 12:2). It is striking that "joy" and "shame," "cross" and "throne" should be spoken of in the same breath. For the joy of securing our salvation, Jesus endured the cross, despised the disgrace, scorned the shame, and then took his seat at the right hand of the throne of God. The contrast here between joy and shame could not be greater. Philip

23. Taylor, "The Church of O," 45.
24. Smedes, "A Man After God's Own Heart," 11.

Hughes writes, "The shame of the cross, where Christ bore the sins of the world, is something infinitely more intense than the pain of the cross. Others have suffered the pain of crucifixion, but he alone has endured the shame of human depravity in all its foulness and degradation. But the cross is the gateway to joy, his joy and ours . . . ."[25]

This is the unique joy, often juxtaposed with grief and sorrow, that runs through salvation history. Job spoke of his one consolation, "My joy in unrelenting pain—that I had not denied the words of the Holy One" (Job 6:10). The psalmist promised, "Those who sow with tears will reap with songs of joy" (Ps 126:5). And Nehemiah encouraged, "Do not grieve, for the joy of the Lord is your strength" (Neh 8:10). On the eve of his crucifixion, as Jesus walked from the upper room to Gethsemane, he made repeated references to joy. He told his disciples that the key to real joy was to remain in him, to keep his commands, and to abide in his love. "I have told you this so that my joy may be in you and that your joy may be complete" (John 15:11). Jesus distinguishes his joy from every other form of worldly happiness with the simplest of all possessive pronouns, "my." Jesus warned the disciples that they will face great grief in all kinds of trials. "Very truly I tell you, you will weep and mourn while the world rejoices. You will grieve, but your grief will turn to joy" (John 16:20).

The promise of joy rising out of the grief corresponds with the pastor's description of Jesus: "for the joy set before him he endured the cross." The transition from grief to joy describes Good Friday sorrow and Easter Sunday joy. Jesus compares the joy that is greater than grief to a woman giving birth to a child: "when her baby is born she forgets her anguish because of her joy that a child is born into the world" (John 16:21; Isa 26:16–21). The disciples are like this woman in labor, in "a little while" (Isa 26:20) their grief will turn to joy because they have been given "new birth into a living hope through the resurrection of Jesus Christ from the dead and into an inheritance that can never perish, spoil or fade" (1 Pet 1:3). The joy of Easter is so powerful that "no one will take away your joy" (John 16:22), because nothing "will be able to separate us from the love of God that is in Christ Jesus our Lord" (Rom 8:39).

Once more the pastor sounds the refrain from Psalm 110:1 (Heb 1:3, 13; 8:1; 10:12; 12:2) when he says that Jesus "is seated at the right hand of God." Only this time "he focuses on the continued session of Christ."[26] "He has taken his seat" and his rule and reign "is completely

25. Hughes, *Hebrews*, 525.

26. O'Brien, *Hebrews*, 458; Bruce, *Hebrews*, 339. In this final reference (12:2) the

and permanently effective."[27] The believer's resilience lies primarily in the vertical authority of the risen and triumphant Savior. We may turn to mentors and friends, pastors and parents, to sustain us, but ultimately we have to focus on Christ.

Resilience

It is imperative that we fix our eyes on Jesus and consider him who suffered "such opposition from sinners." When we compare the magnitude of Jesus' suffering to our own it helps put our own suffering in perspective and it inspires our gratitude for the greatness of salvation. A broader and deeper reverence for Jesus' redemptive accomplishment and his sovereign authority helps to assure that we will not grow weary and lose heart. Thus the goal of fixing our eyes on Jesus and following his example of faithfulness in the midst of hardship is that we not give out and quit the race. The repetition of Psalm 110 and the exalted status of Christ is in sync with the constant reminder throughout the sermon for believers not to "drift away," or become sluggish and lazy (Heb 2:1; 5:11; 6:12) or give up on their confidence (Heb 3:6, 14; 5:11). The risen and reigning Christ can supply the strength and fortitude believers need in order to run the race. "The pastor helps his hearers feel what he is saying by likening spiritual fatigue to a deep sense of physical exhaustion in order that they might draw upon the One who has endured."[28]

In Christ, we find more than enough strength and joy for this race. Faithfulness to the end authenticates faith from the beginning. And the end in faithfulness to the end may seem like a long way off, but it is the only end worth pursuing if we are serious about following Jesus. Søren Kierkegaard, the nineteenth-century Danish Christian prophet, reminds Christ's followers, "Don't finish with life until it's finished with you."[29] Life is not like a school exam that we can finish ahead of time if we are especially clever. We can't retire early from a life of faith in Christ any more than we can retire early from life itself. As Yankee baseball legend Yogi Berra said, "It's not over until it's over."

---

author uses the perfect tense, instead of the imperative (1:13) or the aorist indicative (1:3; 8:1; 10:12; 12:2), to show the permanent and sustained authority of Jesus.

27. Cockerill, *Hebrews*, 610.

28. Ibid., 613.

29. Kierkegaard, *Parables*, 85.

Awake, My Soul, Stretch Every Nerve[30]

Awake, my soul, stretch every nerve, and press with vigor on;
A heav'nly race demands thy zeal, and an immortal crown.

A cloud of witnesses around hold thee in full survey;
Forget the steps already trod and onward urge thy way.

'Tis God's all-animating voice that calls thee from on high;
'tis his own hand presents the prize to thine aspiring eye.

That prize, with peerless glories bright, shall e'er new luster boast,
While victor's wreaths and monarch's gems shall blend in common dust.

Blest Savior, introduced by thee, have I my race begun,
And, crowned with vict'ry, at thy feet I'll lay my honors down.

PHILIP DODDRIDGE, 1740

30. Roff, ed., *The Trinity Hymnal*, 576.

11

The Lord's Discipline
(Hebrews 12:4–29)

"In all this you greatly rejoice, though now for a little while you may have had to suffer grief in all kinds of trials. These have come so that the proven genuineness of your faith—of greater worth than gold, which perishes even though refined by fire—may result in praise, glory and honor when Jesus Christ is revealed."

1 PETER 1:6–7

THE BEST WAY NOT to give up and lose heart is to keep our eyes fixed on Jesus. If we do that we will never forget that our heavenly Father loves us enough to discipline us. If the Son, the radiance of God's glory, was made "perfect through suffering," we should expect to suffer. If the Son helps those who are being tempted, because he himself was tempted, we should expect to face trials and temptations. If the Son of God, our great high priest, is "able to deal gently with those who are ignorant and are going astray, since he himself is subject to weakness," we too ought to share in his weakness (Heb 5:2). If Jesus "learned obedience from what he suffered" (Heb 5:8), we should expect his pedagogy to become our pedagogy. His learning curve is our learning curve, because the way to know Christ is to become like Jesus. "Both the one who makes [people] holy and those who are made holy are of the same family. So Jesus is not ashamed to call them brothers and sisters" (Heb 2:11). In "bringing many

161

sons and daughters to glory," Jesus brought us into a relationship with the Father that parallels his own (Heb 2:10). With our eyes fixed on Jesus we begin to understand the high cost of perseverance. Faithfulness to the end doesn't come without a true focus and a real fight.

The pastor has crafted his hour-long sermon with a thematic symmetry that weaves his tapestry of truth into a inspiring pattern. If he were a composer scoring a symphony we would hear similar themes resounding through the entire work. If he were an architect we would see in the design a flow in which each part is true to the whole. Professor Cockerill sees in our section (Heb 12:4–9) a close parallel to the sermon's overture (Heb 1:1–2:18). Since the pioneer of our salvation was made perfect through what he suffered (Heb 2:10), we now join him in a "struggle against sin" and in the experience of hardship so that we might produce a harvest of righteousness (Heb 12:4, 7, 11). The warning against falling short of the grace of God (Heb 12:14–17) corresponds to the warning against drifting away and neglecting so great a salvation (Heb 2:1–4). And the contrast between the mountain of fear and the mountain of joy (12:18–24) is anticipated in the contrast between the word spoken through the angels (Heb 2:2) and the revelation of the Son (Heb 1:5–13). Finally, Cockerill sees a parallel between "God's earth-shaking word spoken at the Judgment" (12:25–29) and God's final revelation through his Son (1:1–4).[1]

Our heavenly Father disciplines us in order to train us in holiness. God uses the hardships and disappointments of life "for our good, that we may share in his holiness" (Heb 12:10). The pastor asks, "Have you forgotten how good parents treat children, and that God regards you as his children?" He quotes from Proverbs, "My dear child, don't shrug off God's discipline, but don't be crushed by it either. It's the child he loves that he disciplines; the child he embraces, he also corrects." The pastor quotes two verses from the Septuagint version of Proverbs 3 (Prov 3:11–12), but he probably had the entire chapter in mind. The loving discipline of the Lord cultivates wisdom and understanding and leads to genuine organic spiritual growth that impacts all of life: "She is a tree of life to those who take hold of her; those who hold her fast will be blessed" (Prov 3:18). He builds on this organic imagery as he contrasts "a harvest of righteousness and peace" (Heb 12:11) with a "bitter root" that "grows up to cause trouble an defile many" (12:15). Proverbs 3 contrasts wisdom's

---

1. Cockerill, *Hebrews*, 614.

"pleasant ways" and "paths of peace" with the shameful schemes of the wicked. The pastor develops this contrast by comparing resilient saints who pursue peace and holiness to godless Esau who sold his inheritance for a single meal.

The spiritual struggle encountered by Christ's followers is not intended to shake their faith but to strengthen their faith. In the providence of God, suffering serves as a discipline fostering spiritual maturity and holiness. The pastor distinguishes between the stoic ideal of self-sufficiency and the true objective of deeper dependence upon God. "God is educating you; that's why you must never drop out. He's treating you as dear children. This trouble you're in isn't punishment; it's *training*, the normal experience of children" (Heb 12:5-7, *The Message*).

At a time when so many people feel their parents have been either abusive or permissive the pastor's parental analogy may impress us as a risky analogy. But even those who have experienced abusive parenting or permissive parenting often have a definite sense of what good parenting should be like, or at the very least they know what it is not. Selfless love may be foreign to our sinful selves, but it is still deeply rooted in our creatureliness. We are made in God's image so that no matter how broken and twisted our lives may become some part of us continues to resonate with the will of God. To come to that realization through negative experiences is disturbing, but these tragic experiences only serve to highlight the importance of loving parents and sacrificial love. The author of Hebrews was well aware of the difference between human fathers and the heavenly Father. The logic of his illustration moves from the lesser to the greater: "Moreover, we have all had human fathers who disciplined us and we respected them for it. How much more should we submit to the Father of our spirits and live! Our fathers disciplined us for a little while as they thought best; but God disciplines us for our good, that we may share in his holiness" (Heb 12:9-10). Those who have been parented well will readily see the value of the metaphor, but all believers can learn to appreciate its significance. In fact, those who have been deprived of good parenting can now rejoice in the nurture and discipline of their heavenly Father.

Holiness Training

The pastor follows up his exhortation to "consider him who endured such opposition from sinful [people], so that you will not grow weary and lose heart" with a challenge to remember that God disciplines his sons and daughters. Looking to Jesus and his cross is consistent with looking to our heavenly Father who disciplines us. God uses the struggle against sin and the hardships of life to train his children in holiness. Suffering is more than an endurance test, it is holiness training. Resistance means more than mere survival, it results in our sanctification. What is intended by the world, the flesh, and the devil, to destroy the follower of Jesus, God uses to strengthen the believer. The pastor links Christ's suffering for our salvation with our suffering for Christ's sake. It is the will of our heavenly Father for us to learn obedience by the things that we suffer. As the Apostle Paul said, "We know that in all things God works for the good of those who love him, who have been called according his purpose" (Rom 8:28). There is no effort here to distinguish between evil that comes from the devil and discipline that comes from God. We are to see it all as essential training in holiness. All the hardship, all the disappointment, all the opposition, can be considered part of the discipline God can use to make us stronger! If we try to distinguish bad suffering from good discipline we will end up bitter and resentful. "The person who accepts discipline at the hand of God as something designed by his heavenly Father for his good will cease to feel resentful and rebellious; he has 'calmed and quieted' his soul (Ps 131:2), which thus provides fertile soil for the cultivation of a righteous life, responsive to the will of God."[2]

If there ever was a person who had grounds for bitterness it was the great Old Testament patriarch Joseph. Sold into slavery by his brothers, Joseph had reason enough to hate, but because of God he refused to hate. He chose instead to see his life in terms of the providence of God. "Don't be afraid," Joseph reassured his brothers. "Am I in the place of God? You intended to harm me, but God intended it for good to accomplish what is now being done, the saving of many lives" (Gen 50:19–20).

I remember an occasion when I especially needed the pastor's applied wisdom in my life. After months of criticism and power plays in our church congregation in Bloomington, Indiana, I felt like escaping as far as I could from pastoral ministry. The pressure seemed unrelenting and was taking its toll. I had never experienced such hate and animosity,

2. Bruce, *Hebrews*, 346.

much of it directed toward me personally. To gain some perspective my wife Virginia and I traveled to Baltimore one weekend to visit Eugene and Jan Peterson. I had been so impressed and helped by Peterson's perspective on pastoral ministry that I had called him to ask if we could meet together over dinner. The Petersons received us warmly and listened to our sharing. We began in Eugene's study and ended six hours later at a restaurant. They listened, asked questions, shared a few experiences of their own, and offered encouragement. Neither Eugene nor Jan was quick to say what we should do, but they helped us understand the meaning of what we were going through. We left feeling reaffirmed, knowing that the ugly opposition at church did not mean we were displeasing to God or that our ministry was a failure. Their simple counsel—that good work often takes place in the midst of struggle—reassured us.

A few days after our visit I received a letter from Eugene. He wrote,

> As I have continued to think and pray I want to urge you to not be too eager to solve the problems and get rid of the suffering that is coming from a murmuring congregation. And to believe that God knew what kind of congregation it was when he called you there—that perhaps the pain they inflict is being used to the purposes of holiness in you.
>
> Among the early church fathers there was a saying to the effect, "The best bishop is a bad bishop." Meaning: The purpose, spiritually, of a bishop is that pastors learn obedience; if the bishop always gives reasonable and just commands, it is easy to obey, but if unreasonable and unjust then we really learn obedience and humility. Substitute "congregation" for "bishop" and we are in a strenuous school of vocational holiness . . . .

I struggle over Peterson's advice, but I know it is true and the pastor writing Hebrews would certainly agree with it. I find it difficult to consider it beneficial, let alone "pure joy" (Jas 1:2). I don't like trials, any trials, let alone the wild assortment the world manages to dish out. The impulse to escape is strong. The temptation to meet evil with evil is constant. At times I vacillate between anger and depression, but the counsel of Eugene and the pastor in Hebrews focuses me again on the spiritual benefit of the struggle.

The "no-excuse" Christian life advocated by the pastor offers us a rationale for engaging in the race. Our actions are eagerly observed and inspired by a great cloud of witnesses. Our personal stories are part of God's great salvation history story. We have entered an arena far greater than the Roman Coliseum or the 110,000 seat Olympic Centre in Sydney,

Australia. The competition is a matter of life and death—eternal life and eternal death—and we can ill afford to lose our focus. We keep our eyes on Jesus the pioneer and perfecter of our faith. Like a marksman eyeing the target or a sprinter focused on the finish, we fix our eyes on Jesus. In his cross we see our cross. We are not admirers of Jesus but followers of Jesus, facing our griefs and loses with the determination not to give in to sin, but to throw off the sin that so easily entangles and to run the race flat out with Jesus. How can anyone who is serious about following Jesus put in a lackluster, half-hearted effort? In the Christian life it is only a matter of time before posers get exposed as impostors.

Two Weaknesses

There are two kinds of weakness addressed by the pastor in his spiritual direction. There is the carnal weakness that succumbs to sin. We know that kind of weakness all too well. Then, there is the sacrificial weakness of the cross that resists sin. One form of weakness must be overcome while the other must be embraced. There is the weakness that causes us to "drift away" and give up and there is the weakness that learns obedience from what is suffered. The apostles resonated with the Apostle Paul's description of this cruciform weakness: "I will boast all the more gladly about my weaknesses, so that Christ's power may rest on me. That is why, for Christ's sake, I delight in weaknesses, in insults, in hardships, in persecutions, in difficulties. For when I am weak, then I am strong" (2 Cor 12:9–11).

Joni Eareckson Tada has spent over forty-four years in a wheelchair. She broke her neck in a diving accident that left her quadriplegic. She has used her entire adult life to testify to the fact that God can use the horror of tragedy and the deep anguish of suffering, for his glory. In one of her many books, Joni imagines arriving in heaven with her wheelchair. In her new glorified body and standing on resurrected legs, she will say, "Lord Jesus, do you see that wheelchair over there? Well, you were right. When you put me in it, it was a lot of trouble. But the weaker I was in that thing, the harder I leaned on you. And the harder I leaned on you, the stronger I discovered you to be. I do not think I would have ever known the glory of your grace were it not for the weakness of that wheelchair. So thank you, Lord Jesus for that. Now, if you like, you can send that thing off to hell."[3]

3. Waters and Zuck, eds., *Why O God?*, 324.

Not every believer sees life the way Joni does, but we should. We have a tendency to cling to worldly weakness and we try to leverage God's grace as an excuse. We are tempted to confuse faith in Christ with faith in ourselves. Karl Barth challenged this misplaced trust. He wrote, "This most profound effort of man to trust in himself, to see himself as in the right, has become pointless. I believe—not in myself—I believe in God the Father, the Son and the Holy Ghost."[4] "The greatest hindrance to faith is again and again just the pride and anxiety of our human hearts. We would rather not live by grace . . . . We do not wish to receive grace; at best we prefer to give ourselves grace. This swing to and fro between pride and anxiety is man's life."[5]

Dietrich Bonhoeffer warned the church against catering to worldly weakness: "An escapist church can be certain that it will immediately win over all the weaklings, all those who are only too glad to be lied to and deceived, all the starry-eye dreamers, all the unborn sons of the earth."[6] Bonhoeffer did not mean that the church should not care for the weak. The answer to his rhetorical question is obvious. "What church would be so merciless, so inhuman, as not to deal compassionately with this weakness of suffering people and thereby save souls for the kingdom of heaven? . . . Should the weakling remain without help? Would that be in the spirit of Jesus Christ? No, the weak should receive help. We do in fact receive help, from Christ. However, Christ does not will or intend this weakness; instead, he makes us strong. He does not lead us in a religious flight from this world to other worlds beyond; rather, he gives us back to the earth as its loyal children."[7]

The followers of Christ who are serious about maturity learn to distinguish between a weakness that begs for pity and a weakness that prays for strength. Weakness can foster a false dependency on others or a true dependency on God. Although it may seem harsh to say, some people cling to their weakness as their own personal claim to significance, a merit badge inviting attention and sympathy. Their affliction provides them with a convenient excuse for remaining as they are instead of a compelling reason for becoming what God calls them to be. A good church not only attracts people who are weak, broken, confused, and hurt, but offers

---

4. Barth, *Dogmatics in Outline*, 18.

5. Ibid., 20.

6. Huntemann, *The Other Bonhoeffer*, 101.

7. Bonhoeffer, *A Testament To Freedom*, 89.

Christ to heal their wounds, restore their souls, and lead them in paths of righteousness.

No one can read the Bible honestly and come up with the notion that its okay for the people of God to be slothful, complacent, fearful, permissive, and indulgent. This is the bondage to sin that we have been liberated from in Christ. We are no longer trapped in an endless cycle of good intentions, followed by sin and guilt, and another stab at good intentions.

When the Apostle Paul said, "the Spirit helps us in our weakness," he was not implying that the Spirit is sympathetic to our carnal desires and condones our sin. He was not referring to the weakness due to our sin, but to the weakness that comes from entering into solidarity with God and his redemptive purposes. This is the weakness that all creation feels as it waits for liberation from its bondage to decay. This is the weakness that groans inwardly "as we wait eagerly for our adoption, the redemption of our bodies" (Rom 8:23). This is the weakness that intercedes on behalf of others with the help of the Holy Spirit. This is the cross-bearing weakness that knows that nothing can separate us from the love of Christ. This is the weakness that knows we are more than conquerors through him who loved us, and knows this without any hint of pride. This new vulnerability is not the result of sin, but of obedience.

Given the pastor's serious concerns with apathy and apostasy (Heb 2:1; 5:11; 6:1–12; 10:26–39), we are motivated to ask whether we are guilty of cultivating a passive spectator mentality in our churches. Cross-bearing weakness empowers the church, but worldly weakness drains the church of its gospel power. Jesus warned his disciples to "be as shrewd as snakes and as innocent as doves," because he was sending them out "like sheep among wolves" (Matt 10:16). In the story of Little Red Riding Hood the big bad wolf pretends to be the little girl's bedridden sickly grandmother. Little Red knows something is strange. She says to the disguised wolf,

> "What a deep voice you have!"
> The wolf responds, "The better to greet you with."
> "Goodness, what big eyes you have!"
> "The better to see you with."
> "And what big hands you have!"
> "The better to hug you with."
> "What a big mouth you have."

"The better to eat you with!" And with this the wolf jumps out of bed, and eats her up.

Wolves in disguise have always been a threat to the church (Acts 5:1–11), making it necessary for the church to remain vigilant. The church that entertains the admirers of Jesus and caters to their felt needs tends to attract self-absorbed weaklings who have no intention of changing their egocentric ways. In fact they use their many weaknesses to bully the church into paying attention to them. They can be narcissistic, hungry for attention, eager to have their opinion heard, and totally absorbed in their own story. What better place to try to satisfy their insatiable needs than the church where people are supposed to pay attention to them? Such weaklings may have escaped from the world and retreated to the church, but they will only bring the world into the church if they do not confront their sin and turn to Christ for transformation. Frequently they have left a trail of relational destruction in their path, but they have no intention of setting things right. When they attempt to serve others they are usually more trouble than they're worth, because they serve according to their whim and preference, always expecting to receive high praise for their efforts. Christ did not call his followers to this kind of weakness. This is the sin-nursing, blame-casting weakness that he came to overcome. Real evangelism involves discipleship and true confession results in commitment. Richard Lovelace writes: "We may need to challenge more, and comfort less, in our evangelism and discipleship. We need to make it harder for people to retain assurance of salvation when they move into serious sin. . . . We need to tell some persons who think they have gotten saved to get lost. The Puritans were biblically realistic about this; we have become sloppy and sentimental in promoting assurance under any circumstances."[8]

The Nature / Nature Debate

Genetics plays a big role in becoming a gifted athlete. Swedish physiologist Per-Olof Astrand came down humorously on the side of nature, when he said, "To become an Olympic athlete, choose your parents well."[9] Nevertheless, considerable attention is given to nutrition, training, technique, and attitude in developing top-notch athletes. Training is strenuous for

8. Lovelace, "Evangelicalism," 25.
9. Shoeller, "Perfect Form," 120.

even the most gifted athlete. Through constant and rigorous practice elite athletes force their minds and bodies to memorize complex body movements so that amazing feats become almost second nature. The athlete's determination to improve and excel through physical and mental conditioning is a great example for everyone who follows Jesus, not just for an elite few, but for all believers.

The pastor leaves no doubt that the life of conversion calls for serious effort. But when our evangelism implies that all it takes to become a follower of Christ is a quick decision for Jesus, we end up undermining the biblical message. If we teach that the gifts of the Spirit produce an automatic predisposition and enthusiasm for ministry, we are seriously misrepresenting the hard work involved in discipleship. Thus, when we fail to feel motivated to show hospitality or befriend a stranger or help guide our children, we conveniently conclude that we don't have that particular spiritual gift.

If we divide believers into two camps with the average, ordinary believer in one camp and the exceptional, elite believer in another, we make an artificial and unbiblical distinction. We are suggesting that the majority of believers are admirers of Jesus who never get in the race, while a minority of believers are really serious about their faith. There is no biblical basis for accepting Jesus as Savior without accepting him as Lord. In many churches, considerable time and energy is dedicated by sincere followers of Jesus to placating the admirers of Jesus—the high-maintenance majority.

The pastor insists that we all have it in us, in our new nature, to be nurtured and challenged in the faith. We come to Christ just as we are, poor sinners in need of grace, but we do not remain as we were. Our weakness is turned to strength (11:34). "Both the one who makes people holy and those who are made holy are of the same family. So Jesus is not ashamed to call them brothers and sisters" (Heb 2:11).

Resistance Training

In *The Trellis and the Vine*, Colin Marshall and Tony Payne, call for a ministry mind-set shift from focusing on church structures (running programs, organizing events, managing people, and marketing the church) to making and maturing genuine disciples of Christ. We have been spending too much time on the *trellis* to the neglect of the *vine*.

Instead of calling all Christians to live into their calling as disciples we have been preoccupied with institutional growth. The authors admit that "this is not hard to understand, nor even hard to do—unless, of course, you happen to be a sinful person living in a sinful world. The deceptively simple task of disciple-making is made demanding, frustrating and difficult in our world, not because it is so hard to grasp but because it is hard to persevere in."[10]

Our earthly parents tried to discipline us as they thought best, "but God disciplines us for our good, in order that we may share in his holiness" (Heb 12:10). Moral transformation does not happen automatically. Nothing required here becomes "second nature" without tremendous spiritual, intellectual, and emotional effort. The pastor calls for total engagement. There is no divorce between salvation and sanctification. To be saved is to be sanctified. To be a child of God involves becoming subject to the discipline of our heavenly Father's holiness training. If we are going to strengthen our feeble arms and weak knees, we better start working out and getting in shape.

Everyone is noticing how much bigger and stronger athletes are than they were just a few decades ago. Today, runners and swimmers have developed considerably more upper body strength and muscle tone than in the past. Nearly all competing athletes are lifting weights and undergoing resistance training. Weight training machines are aptly named, such as, back extension, tricep press, ab crunch, and the leg press. There's a lot of pulling, pressing, curling, lifting, and extending in order to get in shape. No one can exercise for us, either physically or spiritually. If we don't strengthen our feeble arms and weak knees no one can do it for us. What is required is not a quick burst of enthusiasm, but a steady, disciplined effort. Getting in shape spiritually is doable, but we have to take responsibility. We have to make the effort. The costly grace of Christ does not eliminate the effort on our part.

Returning to the metaphor of the race, the pastor pictures the believer removing any obstacles that may get in the way. He quotes a single phrase from Proverbs, "Make level paths for your feet" (Prov 4:26), but he has the whole context in mind. The previous verse, "Let your eyes look straight ahead; fix your gaze directly before you" (Heb 4:25), recalls his exhortation to fix our eyes on Jesus, the pioneer and perfecter of the faith. All along he has insisted on removing the distractions and speculations

10. Marshall and Payne, *The Trellis and the Vine*, 151.

that interfere with following Jesus. "Make level paths for your feet and take only ways that are firm. Do not swerve to the right or the left; keep your foot from evil" (Prov 4:26–27). Before we can ever hope to be a help to others we have to personally assume responsibility for our own spiritual growth. If we don't keep our eyes on Jesus we are not only of little help to others, but in danger of leading them astray. "So don't sit around on your hands! No more dragging your feet! Clear the path for long-distance runners so no one will trip and fall, so no one will step in a hole and sprain an ankle. Help each other out. And run for it!" (Heb 12:12 *The Message*). Think of Amen! as the Christian equivalent to "on your mark, get set, go!"

The Esau Factor

The pastor admonishes everyone to assume responsibility for the peace and holiness of the believing community. "Make every effort to live in peace with everyone and to be holy; without holiness no one will see the Lord" (Heb 12:14; Ps 34:15). The challenge to pursue peace and holiness has been the driving impulse of the entire sermon. It is expressed here with a marked sense of intensity and urgency. If we expect to be "outposts of heaven," God's gifts of peace and holiness need to "be worked out concretely in our lives as believers."[11] The entire biblical community is challenged to remain vigilant against the insidious roots of bitterness and godlessness. "While the leaders may have particular pastoral and teaching responsibilities, this activity of watchful care is incumbent on everyone, regardless of their particular gifts."[12]

We might like to keep everything positive and upbeat, but the pastor's "See to it" exhortations require the whole church to be on the alert against falling short of the grace of God, by practicing sexual immorality, becoming godless, and refusing "him who speaks" (Heb 12:15, 16, 25). The stakes are high. The pastor's warning against falling short of the grace of God recalls the wilderness generation (Heb 3:7–4:11). In view of their apostasy, he warns believers against falling short of God's promised rest (4:1). A bitter root that is allowed to grow up will not only cause "trouble and defile many" but will have an eternal impact (Heb 12:15, 25). The bitter root metaphor is drawn from the Septuagint version of Deuteronomy

11. O'Brien, *Hebrews*, 472.

12. Ibid., 473.

THE LORD'S DISCIPLINE (HEBREWS 12:4-29)   173

29 and the biblical case against idolatry, "detestable images and idols of wood and stone, of silver and gold" (Deut 29:17). A heart that is turned away from the Lord produces a "bitter poison" (Deut 29:18) an apt metaphor for a stubborn resistance to the will of God. The pastor holds out little hope that a sinful, unbelieving heart can "be brought back to repentance" (6:6). Those who turn against God in this way "are crucifying the Son of God all over again and subjecting him to public disgrace" (Heb 6:6). They are trampling "the Son of God underfoot" and insulting "the Spirit of grace" (Heb 10:29).

The pastor uses Esau as "the ultimate example of apostasy."[13] He is a type, representing those who throw away their rich inheritance in Christ for immediate, physical pleasure. Idolatry willfully abandons the will of God and adultery becomes a metaphor for apostasy; sexual immorality stands for spiritual idolatry. The idolater fixates on a physical, tangible, and material reality in lieu of the invisible, everlasting reality of God. Esau did this blatantly, unapologetically, inexcusably. He showed contempt for God's covenant of salvation by handing over his inheritance rights for a simple meal (Gen 25:29–34). He sold his soul for a bowl of soup. Tragically, his impulse to satisfy his immediate bodily desire took precedence over everything that truly mattered. He prostituted his relationship with God.[14] Consequently, even though he came to regret his whimsical yet devastating decision, and "he sought the blessing with tears, he could not change what he had done" (Heb 12:17). Worldly grief, rather than true repentance, led Esau to plot his brother Jacob's murder (2 Cor 7:10; Gen 27:41).

The greater tragedy today are the many "Esaus" in the church who want their version of Christianity without having to follow the Lord Jesus. They remind us of those false disciples described by Jesus in the Sermon on the Mount. They say, "Lord, Lord, did we not prophesy in your name and in your name drive out demons and in your name perform many miracles?" But Jesus says, "I will tell them plainly, 'I never knew you. Away from me, you evildoers!'" (Matt 7:22–23). They practice a form of external religion and selective obedience that is compatible with the culture. By all worldly accounts they are members in "good standing" but like Esau they have given themselves over to their willful passions. Their identity is found either in their sexual freedom or their material

13. Cockerill, *Hebrews*, 633.

14. O'Brien, *Hebrews*, 475; Cockerill, *Hebrews*, 639; Bruce, *Hebrews*, 350.

lifestyle or their vocational pride or their religious effort or their physical health or even something as mundane as golf, fashion, or food. They are defined by their "immortality symbols," the physical, tangible objects of glory that give their lives temporal meaning. But as soon as their idols prove worthless, their health deteriorates, their children disappoint, their wealth becomes pointless, and their dreams are dashed, they are filled with sorrow and remorse. "Godly sorrow brings repentance that leads to salvation and leaves no regret," wrote the Apostle Paul, "but worldly sorrow brings death" (2 Cor 7:10).

Sadly, the church is left with the task of presiding over the funerals of many "Esaus" who have long since drifted away from the faith. They have retained their affiliation with Christianity, but they no longer believe in "the elementary truths of God's word" (Heb 5:12). Nevertheless, their often broken and pagan families expect the church to eulogize their departed loved one even though they themselves have grown cold and indifferent to the faith. If the pastor had used Judas as his example of "worldly sorrow" he would have curtailed the power of his application, but by using Esau he drove his point home. "Esau continues as a cautionary example of the impossibility of restoring again to repentance those who have rebelliously sinned against the light."[15] "The application is plain," writes F. F. Bruce. "It is a reinforcement of the warning given at an earlier stage in the argument, that after apostasy no second repentance is possible."[16] "Therefore, since the promise of entering his rest still stands, let us be careful that none of you be found to have fallen short of it" (Heb 4:1).

Two Mountains

The pastor builds the momentum of his message to a peak by picturing two mountains, the mountain of fear and the mountain of joy. He alluded to this contrasting picture earlier when he referred to the giving of the Law on Mount Sinai: "the message spoken through angels was binding, and every violation and disobedience received its just punishment" (Heb 2:2). He compared the Sinai experience to the great salvation of Jesus Christ "which was first announced by the Lord," confirmed by the apostles, and testified to by signs, wonders, miracles, and the gifts of the

15. Hughes, *Hebrews*, 541.
16. Bruce, *Hebrews*, 352.

Holy Spirit (Heb 2:3-4). As we have seen, the thrust of the sermon argues persuasively for the complete sufficiency of Christ's once-and-for-all atoning sacrifice. Everything Mount Sinai anticipated and foreshadowed has been accomplished in Christ perfectly. So as we near the end of the sermon we come full circle.

This vision of the two mountains, one of doom and the other of deliverance, does not set up a crisis of decision. The pastor intends the comparison to convey the believer's long-established conviction and confidence in Christ. He is convinced that his brothers and sisters are beyond indecision and doubt. "But we do not belong to those who shrink back and are destroyed, but to those who have faith and are saved" (Heb 10:39). His vision anticipates reverent, awe-inspiring worship and joyful celebration. He asserts with conviction, "We are convinced of better things in your case" (Heb 6:9). Therefore he declares with confidence, "You have not come to a mountain that can be touched. . . . But you have come to Mount Zion" (Heb 12:18, 22).

The contrast between the two comings (*proselēlyhate*) leads to a parallel seven-point description of Sinai and Zion. The comparative symmetry of the two lists can be found only in the number of features, yet there is no correspondence between the seven terrors of Sinai and the seven triumphs of Zion.[17] One list is all dread; the other is all joy. "By careful selection, addition, and omission the pastor has presented Sinai as the dreadful place of judgment and of exclusion from God's presence."[18] He is not arguing here for the inestimable importance of the Law of God and the strategic significance of God's revelation at Sinai for salvation history. The value of the Law, the sacrificial system, and the Levitical priesthood, is beyond dispute. But what the pastor declares emphatically is that no one can cling to the religion of Sinai, the best designed religion of all time, and live. The Law's purpose has been fulfilled in Christ, that's what the whole sermon has been about from beginning to end. The religion of Mount Sinai has been replaced categorically by something absolutely better.

> You have not come to a mountain that can be touched / and that is burning with fire; / and to darkness, / and to gloom, / and to storm; / and to a trumpet blast, / and to a voice speaking words that those who heard it begged that no further word be spoken

17. Hughes, *Hebrews*, 545.
18. Cockerill, *Hebrews*, 646.

to them, because they could not bear what was commanded: "If even an animal touches the mountain, it must be stoned to death." The sight was so terrifying that Moses said, "I am trembling with fear" (Heb 12:18–21).

"The recital of these terms in measured cadence" would have created "a verbal impression of the awesome majesty of God who made his presence known at Sinai."[19] The physical, tangible, and visceral experience of God at Sinai served the divine purpose, but now the pastor sees that purpose fulfilled and eclipsed by the gospel of Mount Zion. The weight of this dreadful depiction of holy awe does not in any way play into the hands of the second-century heretic Marcion of Sinope at Rome (ca. 144) who rejected the Old Testament revelation of God. Far from rejecting Sinai as invalid, the pastor encourages us to embrace Sinai as the necessary ground for the better way of Christ. But what he does reject categorically is a reliance on Sinai religion. The gospel of Christ cannot be brought back into the old traditions of rituals and ceremonies and priestly orders and sacred edifices. That day has passed decisively. Any harkening back to the religious system instituted at Sinai violates the way of the cross.

The practical application of the message of Hebrews for believers today is this: any form of Christianity that competes like other religions for the attention of its adherents through its rituals, practices, priests, traditions, and sacred spaces, has fallen back into an obsolete and worldly strategy. "Christians had none of the visible apparatus which in those days was habitually associated with religion and worship—no sacred buildings, no altars, no sacrificing priest. Their pagan neighbors thought they had no God, and called them atheists; their Jewish neighbors, too, might criticize them for having no visible means of spiritual support."[20] Like Jesus in the Gospels, Hebrews sees the fundamental difference between apostasy and faithfulness in the tension between a religion about God and a Christ-centered relationship with God. The pastor calls for a decisive end to religion, even the best religion ever conceived and strategically designed by God for our salvation. Hebrews demonstrates the Sinai Covenant's inability to atone for sins in the face of God's judgment.[21]

The contrast between the two descriptions could not be greater. All the identifying qualities of Mount Zion are relationally God-centered and

19. Lane, *Hebrews*, vol. 2, 462.

20. Bruce, *Hebrews*, 379.

21. O'Brien, *Hebrews*, 482.

culminate in Jesus the mediator of the new covenant, whose sprinkled, sacrificial blood is powerful to save.

> "But you have come to Mount Zion, / and to the city of the living God, the heavenly Jerusalem, / and you have come to thousands upon thousands of angels in joyful assembly, / and to the church of the firstborn, whose names are written in heaven, / and you have come to God, the Judge of all, / and to the spirits of the righteous made perfect, / and to Jesus the mediator of a new covenant, / and to the sprinkled blood that speaks a better word than the blood of Abel" (Heb 12:22–24).

Instead of Sinai's awful terror, darkness, and gloom, Zion is pulsating with awe-inspiring worship, joy, and love. There are "thousands upon thousands of angels in joyful assembly" and all the righteous are the firstborn children of God, living by faith, known by name, and perfected by Jesus. In the parallel descriptions of Sinai and Zion, God is actively speaking and judging. At Sinai, the voice of God strikes terror and the people plead for relief. No one can bear the holy presence of God. But on Mount Zion, the saints are exhorted to hear the voice of God: "See to it that you do not refuse him who speaks" (Heb 12:25). The pastor's description of the city of the living God recalls John's description of the throne of God and the heavenly city in the book of Revelation.

Although there is a vivid contrast between the mountain of fear and the mountain of joy, the pastor emphasizes the similarities between the two descriptions. The God of Mount Sinai is the same God as the God of Mount Zion, and this holy and just God is the judge of all. The pastor's final less-to-greater argument drives home his faithfulness-to-the-end exhortation. At Sinai, the people of God could not bear to listen to God, because of their sinfulness. Even Moses was trembling with fear. But in Jesus we have the mediator of the new covenant whose sprinkled blood takes away the sins of many, "and he will appear a second time, not to bear sin, but to bring salvation to those who are waiting for him" (Heb 9:28). Because of Jesus we have no excuse not to listen to God. The good news of the gospel of grace removes our fear and dread of the living God, but it does not remove the consequences of judgment for turning away from God. "See to it that you do not refuse him who speaks," declares the pastor. "If they did not escape when they refused him who warned them on earth, how much less will we, if we turn away from him who warns us from heaven." He references his earlier less-to-greater argument (Heb 2:2–3) to show how God's judgment on the disobedient at Sinai anticipates God's final judgment.[22] This is the judgment that will fall on those who "drift away" from "so great a salvation" (2:2–3), who "have once been enlightened, who have tasted the heavenly gift, who have shared in the Holy Spirit, who have tasted the goodness of the word of God and the powers of the coming age," but "who have fallen away . . ." (Heb 6:4–6).

If the Israelites were terrified of God at Mount Sinai, the terror will only be greater when God comes at the final judgment. "At that time his voice shook the earth, but now he has promised, 'Once more I will shake not only the earth but also the heavens.' The words 'once more' indicate the removing of what can be shaken—that is, created things—so that what cannot be shaken may remain" (Heb 12:26–27). The pastor paraphrases the prophet Haggai (Hag 2:6) to describe the final judgment as a violent shaking of heaven and earth. "To disobey the gospel incurs judgment more certain and terrible even than that incurred by disobedience to the law."[23] This final, ultimate shakedown pictures the end of evil. And this end will be the cataclysmic end of everything that does not belong to the kingdom of God. This part of God's character and this part of the story do not receive much attention these days in religious circles. Judgment gets poor reviews among those who admire Jesus and practice consumer religion. One wonders if the inability to believe in hell is not matched by the inability to believe in heaven. Much of popular spirituality seems to believe only in the present moment.

Haggai's prophecy of the coming judgment and the violent shaking of the cosmos was not meant to shake the confidence of those who have come to Mount Zion, who belong to the church of the firstborn, and who are made righteous by Jesus the mediator of the new covenant. The pastor includes himself among the unshaken saints, who are destined for everlasting rest (Heb 4:3), in "the City with foundations, whose architect and builder is God" (Heb 11:10).

> Therefore, since we are receiving a kingdom that cannot be shaken, let us be thankful, and so worship God acceptably with reverence and awe, for our "God is a consuming fire" (Heb 12:28–29).

Imagine what it would be like to live our lives from the conviction that we are receiving a kingdom that cannot be shaken, ruled by the Son

22. Cockerill, *Hebrews*, 664.

23. Bruce, *Hebrews*, 363.

who "sat down at the right hand of the Majesty in heaven" (Heb 1:3). No wonder the pastor exhorts himself along with all his hearers to live into this salvation-shaped reality. "Let us be thankful and let us worship God acceptably with reverence and awe . . . ." The accumulation of these hortatory subjunctives continues to build: "Let us draw near to God with a sincere heart and full assurance of faith . . ." (Heb 10:22); "Let us hold unswervingly to the hope we profess, for he who promised is faithful" (Heb 10:23); "Let us consider how we may spur one another on toward love and good deeds . . ." (Heb 10:24); "Let us throw off everything that hinders and the sin that so easily entangles" (Heb 12:1); "Let us run with perseverance the race marked out for us, fixing our eyes on Jesus, the pioneer and perfecter of faith" (12:1–2); and now the pastor adds to his spiritual direction, "Let us be thankful . . . ." When we truly believe that the overarching reality that envelops all pain and suffering is the grace and goodness of God, gratitude is our response. Heaven awaits saved sinners, those who have turned to Christ for their salvation. Hell awaits unsaved sinners, those who have refused to turn to Christ for salvation. Everything is bracketed by God's grace. Even the dark night of the soul awaits the dawn of God's renewing grace.

If God's promise permeates everything—even pain and suffering, grief and loss—then what the Apostle Paul writes is true: "In all things God works for the good of those who love him, who have been called according to his purpose" (Rom 8:28). Then we whose hope is in God can "consider it pure joy" when we face "trials of many kinds, because [we] know that the testing of [our] faith develops perseverance" (Jas 1:2). Gratitude enables us to bracket the brevity of life, with its pain and sorrow, with the words "Praise the Lord, O my soul, all my inmost being, praise his holy name" (Ps 103:1). Worship is both the first word and the last word for those who have put their confidence in Christ. For "we have this hope as an anchor for the soul, firm and secure" (Heb 6:19).

The final appeal, to worship and serve God acceptably, requires believers to "regard every aspect of their lives as an expression of their devotion to him."[24] In his concluding exhortation (Heb 13:1–19) the pastor translates his call for "reverence" and "awe" into daily faith and practice. But before that he cannot resist concluding his comparison of the two mountains with one last striking phrase drawn from Israel's experience at Sinai. The pastor quotes a line from Deuteronomy, where Yahweh warns

24. O'Brien, Hebrews, 500.

the people of Israel not to make for themselves idols, because "our 'God is a consuming fire'" (Deut 4:24 LXX). He ends on a note of judgment, reminding us that the God of Sinai and the God of Mount Zion are one in the same. Fire burns up what is worthless and cursed (Heb 6:8). Anyone who deliberately keeps on sinning can count on the "raging fire" of judgment that consumes God's enemies (Heb 10:27). Our pastor never retreats from reminding us of the dreadful consequences of apostasy. His persistence ought to be matched by our perseverance. Faithfulness to the end affirms true faith from the beginning.

Fight the Good Fight[25]

Fight the good fight with all thy might, Christ is thy strength and Christ thy right.
Lay hold on life, and it shall be thy joy and crown eternally.

Run the straight race through God's good grace; lift up thine eyes and seek Christ's face;
Life with its way before us lies; Christ is the path, and Christ the prize.

Cast care aside; lean on thy guide. God's boundless mercy will provide.
Trust, and thy trusting soul shall prove Christ is its life, and Christ its love.

Faint not nor fear: God's arms are near. God changeth not, and thou art dear.
Only believe, and thou shalt see that Christ is all in all to thee.

JOHN SAMUEL BEWLEY MONSELL, 1863

---

25. McKim, ed., *The Presbyterian Hymnal*, 307.

12

A Faithful Family of Faith
(Hebrews 13:1–25)

"We belong to one another only through and in Jesus Christ."

Dietrich Bonhoeffer[1]

SINCERE BELIEVERS ARE BOUND to ask what it means to be "receiving a kingdom that cannot be shaken," and to worship God in gratitude "with reverence and awe." The pastor anticipates these concerns in his closing exhortations and offers practical spiritual direction for the daily life of the household of faith. If the congregation has embraced his encouragement to pay attention to "so great a salvation" and to fix their eyes on Jesus, all that is needed to conclude is a brief sketch of kingdom ethics (Heb 13:1–6), a perspective on leadership (Heb 13:7–19), and a benediction (Heb 13:20–21). And this is what they receive in the characteristic style of our pastor who integrates his closing exhortation with his prevailing themes of resilient confidence in the finality and ultimacy of the revelation of Jesus Christ. Even now he cannot resist emphasizing the end of religion and the radical cross-bearing strategy of joining Jesus in the social ostracism and scorn that comes from living outside the religious camp.

We sense that the pastor is satisfied that his grave warnings against apostasy have been heard and that he can relax now. His prophetic

1. Bonhoeffer, *Life Together*, 21.

intensity gives way to a parental love and nurture that is brief and to the point. It is difficult to capture "the brevity, balance, and pungency" of the original in our translations.[2] His carefully crafted four pairs of exhortations continue the imperative force of the passive middle voice,

> *Let brotherly love endure.*
>
> *Do not forget to practice hospitality:* by practicing hospitality some people have entertained angels without realizing it.
>
> *Remember those who are imprisoned,* as though you shared their imprisonment; remember those who are ill-treated because you yourselves are also in the body.
>
> *Let marriage be honorably esteemed among all;* let the marriage bed be kept unpolluted, for God will judge fornicators and adulterers.
>
> *Let your way of life be free from love of money.* Be content with the things which are available, for God himself has said, "I will never abandon you; I will never forsake you." So we in turn have courage and say, "The Lord is my helper; I will not be afraid; what can man do to me?" (Heb 13:1–6).[3]

The pastor's quick imperatives exhort believers to continue what they have already been doing. To do otherwise works against the grain of the household of faith. Need-meeting love and genuine hospitality are the natural Spirit-led impulse of the people of God. This calls for nothing unusual or heroic. His spiritual direction is simple, easy to understand, and undebatable. By the Word and Spirit of Christ the church practices "a distinctive kind of existence—with unique ways of birthing and dying, of becoming youthful and growing old, of marrying and remaining single, of celebrating and sacrificing, of thinking and imagining, of worshiping the true God and protesting against false gods—and that these distinctive beliefs and practices constitute the church's own culture."[4] Clearly the kingdom ethic for Christian disciples is much more than an intellectual challenge. It involves our moral consistency, our spiritual discipline, and our whole devotion to Christ. This down-to-earth, bottom-line spiritual direction is in contrast to the intricacies, subtleties, and complexities of his theological argument. The pastor takes the mystery out of daily discipleship.

2. Cockerill, *Hebrews*, 678.

3. Bruce, *Hebrews*, 368–69.

4. Wood, *Contending for the Faith*, 1–2.

Brotherly Love

The early church perceived "brotherly love" (*philadelphia*) as meeting one another's practical needs. Love was understood as ethical responsibility not necessarily emotional intimacy. The force of the analogy does not depend on whether you feel close to your siblings. You may be close or you may not be close. But if your needy biological brother or sister turns to you, you will try to meet his or her need without giving it a second thought. The pastor hopes the whole body of Christ will let themselves respond to the needs of one another in the family of faith in brotherly love.

Hospitality is another hallmark of Christian discipleship. When we open our homes to friends and strangers, set the table, put on a meal, and break bread together, we invite God's blessing. This pattern of hospitality is at the heart of the gospel. Food for the body and food for the soul belong together. Table fellowship fits into the New Testament narrative so unobtrusively that we can almost miss it. Jesus used simple hospitality and meal-time conversations to share the most profound truths of the gospel. Spirituality is often squeezed into a corner of life reserved for pious reflections and church services. But God intended spirituality to be at the center of our ordinary, everyday life together. Conversation around a simple meal may mean more to the Lord than all the hype we generate in busy churches. Opening our homes and our lives to friends and strangers holds real promise for spiritual growth. It is amazing how lunch together can build us up in Christ. Table fellowship in Christ is one of the best ways to experience the communion of the saints and to reach out to the lost. The Holy Spirit has assured us that there is a deep-level mystery involved in hospitality. We meet Christ in the midst of relating to others. "In as much as you have done it to the least of these, you have done it unto me" (Matt 25:40). The pastor's one-sentence admonition recalls Abraham's working lunch with none other than God himself (Gen 18). "Do not forget to show hospitality to strangers, for by so doing some people have shown hospitality to angels without knowing it" (Heb 13:2). Abraham is the epitome of the gracious host, humble, eager-hearted, and even extravagant. From beginning to end hospitality has always played a significant role in salvation history. The early church spread the gospel from house to house. The table was their pulpit (Acts 5:42; 20:20). If we follow their example we will add lunch to the liturgy.

One of the best kept secrets about hospitality is that those who offer it benefit more than those who receive it. We think of hospitality as giving to others, but what if hospitality is the Lord's way of bringing people into our lives who will give to us: the foreign student who enlarges our world, the homeless person who deepens our compassion, the missionary who causes us to pray more earnestly, the single mom who increases our family, and the neighbor whose next door-presence trains us in practical love? We may be like the reluctant widow at Zarephath, entertaining the prophet Elijah, or like the eager-hearted Lydia hosting the Apostle Paul. Hospitality was meant to be an opportunity, not an imposition.

The pastor develops the meaning of brotherly love to include caring for the persecuted church. The exhortation to "remember those in prison" calls for believers to extend tangible support for believers suffering for Christ. They are to be remembered "as if you were together with them in prison." We need to put ourselves in their shoes, in their prison cells, and respond accordingly. He then reiterates our responsibility by expanding the obligation to include "those who are mistreated" or "tortured." We are to support them and pray for them as if we ourselves were suffering (Heb 13:3). This deep empathy is a sign of our oneness in the body of Christ. According to the eighth Beatitude the unshakeable kingdom of heaven belongs to those who are persecuted for righteousness' sake (Matt 5:10). On this side of eternity their blessing comes at least in part from brothers and sisters in Christ who stand with them in their suffering. Jesus promised that "no one who has left home or brothers or sisters or mother or father or children or fields for me and the gospel will fail to receive a hundred times as much in this present age: homes, brothers, sisters, mothers, children, and fields—along with persecutions—and in the age to come eternal life" (Mark 10:29–30). The "condition of being despised and rejected, slandered and persecuted" is a normal mark of Christian discipleship.[5] The Apostle Paul put it simply when he said, "Everyone who wants to live a godly life in Christ Jesus will be persecuted" (2 Tim 3:12). Given the pervasive testimony of the New Testament it is important that we not distance ourselves from the persecuted body of Christ. The pastor exhorts us to embrace their suffering as our own.

The third quality of brotherly love focuses on the practice of sexual fidelity in marriage and sexual chastity outside of marriage. The Bible teaches the goodness of sexual desire and the badness of sexual lust.

5. Stott, *The Christian Counter-Culture*, 53.

Sexual intimacy is meant to be encouraged and protected in the personal, public, sacred commitment of marriage. Lust is a dehumanizing, depersonalizing drive to indulge the sexual appetite. In the broad sweep of church history Christians have run the gamut from sexual aversion to sexual immersion. The tragic history of Christian sexual renunciation meant that the church for centuries labored under a false and twisted interpretation of the Bible. Who can say how many Christian young people grew up believing that if they were to follow Christ wholeheartedly they had to disavow any desire for marriage and family? The church taught that marriage degraded the body, dulled the spirit, and divided the heart. Lifelong virginity symbolized the purity of a past when the human race was not yet polluted with sexual sin, and the hope of a future when there would be no sexual desire. Spiritual perfection was measured in degrees of sexual withdrawal.

Many Christians today find it difficult to imagine such life-denying sexual asceticism because we are immersed in a culture that is obsessed with sex. There is widespread passive approval of premarital sex, adulterous affairs, homosexual practice, pornography, and divorce. The selective nature of today's sexual sensitivity is peculiarly narrow. A man may be unfaithful to his wife with cultural approval, but discussing his infidelities at work could led to termination. Sexual activity among minors is accepted as a fact of life, but for an adult to have consensual sex with a minor is a felony. Homosexual practice is celebrated. Pedophilia is condemned. Abortion is a popular form of birth control amidst growing sensitivity about child abuse. Pornography and violence are big box office draws, but rape is a serious crime. As a culture, we have the good sense to know that some things are wrong, but it is a fragmented, selective sense of right and wrong.

Over and against this cultural confusion, the pastor lays out the biblical sexual ethic in a sentence. The simplicity of this positive exhortation, "Let marriage be honorably esteemed among all," is in sharp contrast to the pervasive experience of sexual immorality in both ancient and modern cultures. When it comes to sex, the people of God have always been resident aliens living in the wilderness. Unlike Lot, who was challenged to flee Sodom, we have no place to run to. Unlike Noah, who was rescued by a flood as well as from a flood, we are immersed in a lust-filled culture with no rescue in sight. Sex saturation is the order of the day. Lust, fornication, and adultery permeated first-century Rome and twenty-first-century New York. We live in 'burbs of Babylon and stroll the streets of

Corinth. We all live east of Eden in the company of Cain. The negative warning is as clear as it could be: "for God will judge the adulterer and all the sexually immoral" (Heb 13:4).

The fourth quality of brotherly love involves money and contentment. Money, sex, and power are huge issues for today's disciples, but our pastor manages to address them in the most concise and comprehensive fashion possible. He uses the imperative mood to express this issue with poetic brevity. "Let your way of life be free from the love of money." The Bible has much to say about the dangers of greed and worry, but the pastor only states the case; he doesn't make the case. He anticipates agreement and consensus, rather than debate and confrontation. James, on the other hand, rips into the problem of materialism with intensity. "Now listen, you rich people, weep and wail because of the misery that is coming on you. Your wealth has rotted, and moths have eaten your clothes. Your gold and silver are corroded" (Jas 5:1–3). James is determined to put the fear of the Lord in those who are tempted to find their self-worth in money and success. He is adamant that hoarded wealth, acquired at the expense of others, is a spiritual carcinogen. People who define themselves by their consumption will end up being consumed. James finds the world's prescription for profit guilty on three counts: "You have hoarded wealth in the last days . . . . You have lived on earth in luxury and self-indulgence. . . . You have condemned and murdered the innocent one, who was not opposing you" (James 5:3–6). James works out the implications of what it means to be free from the love of money. He challenges the body of Christ to be as honest about economic oppression and social injustice as the Bible is. He refuses to divorce spiritual matters from practical matters.

To be free from the love of money, in a world dominated by money and consumerism, requires supernatural spiritual discipline. Apart from the Spirit of Christ, it is impossible to remain free of envy and bitterness. This is why James calls for patience, not as a cop-out, but as an act of courage (Jas 5:7). This is why the Lord Jesus said, "Do not worry about your life, what you will eat or drink; or about your body, what you will wear. . . . But seek first his kingdom and his righteousness, and all these things will be given to you as well" (Matt 6:25, 33). And this is why the pastor calls for contentment. "Be content with the things which are available . . . ." His spiritual direction resonates with the Apostle Paul's advice to Timothy: "But godliness with contentment is great gain. For we brought nothing into the world, and we can take nothing out of it. But if we have food and clothing, we will be content with that. Those who want to get rich fall into temptation and a trap and into many foolish and harmful desires that plunge people into ruin and destruction. For the love of money is a root of all kinds of evil. Some people, eager for money, have wandered from the faith and pierced themselves with many griefs" (1 Tim 6:6–10).

To conclude, the pastor quotes Yahweh's promise of assurance, given by Moses to Joshua, "Never will I leave you; never will I forsake you" (Deut 31:6, see Deut 31:8; Josh 1:5). He then leads his hearers in a psalm of assurance, which affirms our confidence in Christ, a theme that runs throughout the sermon (Heb 3:6; 4:16; 10:19, 35). "The Lord is my helper; I will not be afraid. What can mere mortals do to me?" (Ps 118:6–7). If we have been crucified with Christ and we no longer live, but Christ lives in us, who can destroy us? We live by faith in the Son of God, who loved us and gave himself for us (Gal 2:20). Like the Apostle Paul, the pastor wants us convinced that nothing "will be able to separate us from the love of God that is in Christ Jesus our Lord" (Rom 8:39).

Congregational Life

The theme of "brotherly love" in the household of faith continues with a description of three dynamic, reciprocal relationships: first, between the people and their leaders (Heb 13:7, 17–18); second, between the church and her worship (Heb 13:8–11, 15); and third, between the body of Christ and God's mission in the world (Heb 13:12–13). This tight weave of interrelated themes has characterized the entire sermon and climaxes in the benediction (Heb 13:20–21). There is a chiastic structure to this concluding exhortation that centers on Jesus Christ who is critical to all three relationships. Leaders and people alike need to know that "Jesus Christ is the same yesterday and today and forever" (13:8). They know that the altar at the center of their worship is the crucified Lord Jesus Christ (13:10). And they know that since Jesus suffered outside the city gate. They must "go to him outside the camp, bearing the disgrace he bore" (13:12–13).

Jesus Christ

"Jesus Christ is the same yesterday and today and forever" (13:8)
"Jesus also suffered outside the city gate to make the people holy through his own blood" (13:12).
"Through Jesus . . . let us continually offer to God a sacrifice of praise . . . (13:15)

Leaders →	Worship →	Mission →	Worship/Mission →	Leaders
"Remember your leaders" //	"We have an altar" //	"Let us go outside the camp" //	"Offer a sacrifice of praise" //	"Submit to their authority."

The pastor offers a brief yet comprehensive take on leadership, worship, and mission. The depth and beauty of our life together is centered in the crucified Christ and invites our meditation. He begins by reminding the people to remember their leaders, those saints who have gone before (Heb 13:7). and those who are currently serving the body of Christ (Heb 13:17). They are to be remembered because they spoke the Word of God to them.[6] This implies that the primary role of their founding leaders was to preach and teach the word of God. The term for leaders (*hēgoumenoi*) was a secular term for people serving in a supervisory capacity. The church does not appear to be arranged and organized around ecclesiastical offices. A plurality of leaders was responsible for teaching and guiding the congregation, and little seems to have changed from its founding to its present. Their teaching is to be remembered; their way of life is to be considered; and their faith is to be imitated. "The whole course of their lives, from start to finish, now lies before their disciples and followers for review and imitation."[7] The exemplary faith of these leaders served as a working model of true discipleship for all to see and imitate and thus

6. Timothy Keller's message at the memorial service for John Stott at College Church, Wheaton, Illinois, highlighted five qualities worth remembering about the life and ministry of one of the Church's most powerful twentieth-century leaders. (1) We ought to be encouraged and convicted by John Stott's kingdom vision and (2) challenged by his ability to listen to the culture. (3) We ought to model our leadership after his irenic and charitable spirit and follow his Spirit-led innovations (expository preaching, the modern city center church, creative organizational impact, the pursuit of social justice, and an intellectually and socially engaged evangelicalism). (5) We ought to be empowered by John Stott's present glory in the presence of God. Truly, we are surrounded by such a great cloud of witnesses.

7. Bruce, *Hebrews*, 374

challenged the current generation of believers "to fix their eyes on Jesus" (Heb 12:2).[8]

Their legacy of faithfulness to the end was grounded in the stunning acclamation that "Jesus Christ is the same yesterday and today and forever" (Heb 13:8). In his eternal being Jesus is immutable and in his faithfulness unwavering. Richard Bauckham reasons, "we need not make a sharp distinction between immutability and faithfulness. . . . Jesus, in his participation in the unique divine identity, remains eternally 'the same,' that is, his identity is unchanged. He remains himself eternally and can therefore be trusted in the present and the future just as he was in the past."[9] The assertion applies to both the *being* and *becoming* of Jesus. His faithfulness is inexorable linked to his identity.

The pastor knows that our life together must be rooted in the finality of the gospel of Jesus Christ. As he said at the outset, "In the past God spoke to our ancestors through the prophets at many times and in various ways, but in these last days he has spoken to us by his Son . . ." (Heb 1:1–2). John Stott reminds us, "The gospel is a non-negotiable revelation from God and we have no liberty to sit in judgment on it, or to tamper with its substance."[10] True leaders long to be faithful to "the apostolic deposit as the essential deposit of faith" and relevant in its application.[11] "It is this search for a combination of truth and relevance which is exacting, yet nothing else can save us from an insensitive loyalty to formula and shibboleths on the one hand, and from a treasonable disloyalty to the revelation of God on the other."[12]

In the chiastic structure of his closing exhortation, the pastor returns to the theme of leadership. We take it up here before discussing worship and mission to round out his description of true leaders. He encourages believers to have "confidence" in their leaders and to "submit to their authority, because they keep watch over you as those who must give an account" (Heb 13:17). The submission he has in mind is not a capitulation to authoritarian power-brokers whose perceived purpose is to manage people and fix problems. It is rather the submission that is analogous to a child's submission to a loving parent or a patient's submission to a caring

8. O'Brien, *Hebrews*, 516.

9. Bauckham, "The Divinity of Jesus Christ in the Epistle of Hebrews," 36.

10. Stott, *Christian Mission*, 59.

11. Webber, *Common Roots*, 147.

12. Stott, *Christian Mission*, 43.

physician, or a client's trust in the counsel of a wise attorney, or a husband and wife's shared trust in a loving marriage. Submission and suffering are two critical aspects of Christian discipleship. The fact that they can be distorted and abused does not mean that they are not necessary in their true biblical practice.

The pastor's call for confidence in leaders and submission to their authority is based on the principle that godly leaders have our best interest in their hearts and minds. The pastor does not use the word *shepherd*, but the phrase "because they keep watch over you" reminds us of the shepherd or the watchman. Leaders are not distinguished by either their status or rank but by their conscientiousness and accountability. There is little difference between ordinary believers and leaders when it comes to obedience, holiness, devotion, and sacrifice. There are no elite saints. All the saints are the recipients of this pastoral letter and only here at the end are leaders acknowledged "as those who must give an account" (Heb 13:17).

The pastor shows his practical care when he encourages believers to submit to the authority of their leaders so that "their work will be a joy, not a burden." When leaders preach, teach, and live the Word of God; and when they show deep concern for people's spiritual welfare and holy living; and when they see themselves as accountable before God for the health and holiness of the body of Christ, then we need to do what we can to support their ministry and be faithful in fulfilling our own ministry. Pastor Ray Stedman notes "that the responsibility for making the operations of a church a joy, and not a burden, is placed on the congregation, not on their leaders."[13]

Hebrews proves that a theology of ministry is as much for the people of God as it is for the pastor. We are encouraged to support the priesthood of all believers and resist the clergy-laity divide. Pastoral leaders should be gifted by the Spirit, thoroughly trained and well-equipped for ministry. These leaders are set apart by a Spirit-led congregation to teach the Word of God and exercise spiritual authority in the household of faith. Faithful disciples also believe in every-member ministry, shared leadership, the distribution of the gifts of the Spirit among all believers, and the mutually received call to ministry. Every member of the household of faith is in some way a pastor, a missionary, a theologian, and a servant leader. In Christ, we are all called to take up a cross and follow

13. Stedman, *Hebrews*, 157.

Jesus. Leaders can exercise authority for the sake of the body of Christ without diminishing the ministry responsibilities of the congregation.

The central truth for both leadership and worship is this: "Jesus Christ is the same, yesterday and today and forever." The definitive revelation of Christ ends the ceremonial food laws of Judaism and the asceticism of Near Eastern spirituality. In Christ true spirituality is a matter of God's grace, rather than religious custom. "Food regulations of all kinds, whether positive or negative, are catalogued by our author among those external ordinances which Christianity has rendered null and void."[14] The Apostle Paul emphasized the same truth found here when he said, "For the kingdom of God is not a matter of eating and drinking, but of righteousness, peace and joy in the Holy Spirit, because anyone who serves Christ in this way is pleasing to God and receives human approval" (Rom 14:17–18). It must have been difficult for Christians converted from either Judaism or paganism to resist the "strange teachings" that promised a deeper spiritual life through religious rituals, ceremonial foods, and ascetic practices. The pastor may have had in mind "the tragic example of Esau, who bartered his birthright for a single meal (Heb 12:16)," but in any case he adamantly opposed any external religious customs or practices that promised to bolster the spiritual life.[15] His simple counsel was more radical than we can imagine: "It is good for our hearts to be strengthened by grace . . ." (Heb 13:9; see Eph 3:16–19).

The pastor's criticism of "strange teaching" regarding ceremonial foods is ironic because what the world finds strange is the absence of external religious customs, buildings, priestly orders, sacrifices, and vestments. People want religion to tell them when to sit, stand, and bow, more than they want to be challenged to live out the Sermon on the Mount. They want to admire Jesus more than follow Jesus. They want their prescribed sacred rituals and ceremonies, more than they want the visible righteousness of love instead of hate, fidelity instead of infidelity, and reconciliation instead of retaliation. External religious traditions, complete with tall steeples, stained glass, and ancient confessions, remain popular even though faith in the great invisibles has vanished. People who no longer believe in the atoning sacrifice of Christ long for the spiritual

14. Bruce, *Hebrews*, 377.
15. Hughes, *Hebrews*, 574.

ambiance of the Mass. As Kierkegaard said, "Everything goes on as usual, and yet there is no longer any one who believes in it."[16]

The absence of a literal, physical Jesus requires all disciples to learn how to follow Jesus without his physical presence. From the beginning the church has faced the danger of a "false literal." Given the absence of Jesus, we are given to substitutes that stand in the place of a physical Jesus. The literal concreteness of a pre-Easter Jesus can become transposed into the "false literal" experience of spiritual leaders who focus attention on themselves. It can be powerful personalities, but it can also be ecclesiastical bureaucracies, church buildings, cherished practices, and spiritual experiences, that stand in the place of Jesus. Traditional religious rituals, megachurch superstars, and down-home country pastors can substitute for the Spirit of the risen Christ. Instead of being dependent on the fruit and gifts of the Spirit of Christ we can all too easily give ourselves to "Christian" idols that stand in the place of a literal Jesus.

The pastor anticipated the courage required to worship Christ without the external religious features expected by both Jews and pagans. No wonder Christians were popularly ridiculed as atheists. They have no sacrifices, no priests, no altars, no sacred feasts. But to the charge, "You Christians have no altar," the pastor replies, "We have an altar from which those who minister at the tabernacle have no right to eat" (Heb 13:10).[17] The declaration, "We have an altar," sums up the central truth of the sermon, the truth that has resounded from the beginning to the end. This is the altar on which the Son "provided purification for sins" (Heb 1:3). He "suffered death" on this altar, "so that by the grace of God he might taste death for everyone" (Heb 2:9). Upon this altar he made "atonement for the sins of the people" (Heb 2:17). He "sacrificed for [our] sins once for all when he offered himself" on this altar (Heb 7:27). "We do have such a high priest," but before he sat down at the right hand of the throne of the Majesty in heaven, he "died as a ransom" to set us free from our sins (Heb 8:1; 9:15). "He has appeared once for all at the culmination of the ages to do away with sin by the sacrifice of himself" (Heb 9:26). This is the altar upon which "Christ was sacrificed once to take away the sins of many" (Heb 9:28). "For by one sacrifice he has made perfect forever those who

16. Bretall, ed., *A Kierkegaard Anthology*, 81.

17. Bruce, *Hebrews*, 379. The word *altar* is used by metonymy for "sacrifice."

are being made holy" (Heb 10:14). Yes! The pastor proclaims, "We have an altar!"[18]

God's altar-building instructions in Exodus point forward to Christ's sacrifice: "If you make an altar of stones for me, do not build it with dressed stones, for you will defile it if you use a tool on it. And do not go up to my altar on steps, lest your nakedness be exposed on it" (Exod 20:25–26). These instructions are an enduring guide for how the invisible God makes himself known.

The human response to a personal saving encounter with the living God was meant to be intuitively simple and inherently sacrificial. Yahweh refused to be reduced to an object that could be worshiped. God reveals himself as the living subject, present among his people personally, but not materially. The risen and ascended Christ remains incarnate with a particular face and body, seated on the throne of God from which he rules and reigns. He is not an object to be venerated but the subject in communion with his people. The altar, the physical setting for sacrificial worship, was not important—any mound of rock and dirt would do. The heart of the worshiper was not revealed in the design of the altar, but in the quality of the animal sacrifice. The perfect sacrifice was always created by God, not humans. The sacrificial lamb could never be an object of human pride.

The invisible God is iconoclastic. The warning against dressed stones and raised platforms applies to Western Christianity's propensity to build impressive buildings, celebrate high-profile personalities, glory in large anonymous audiences, deliver entertaining self-help sermons, and focus on one's own denomination or association to the exclusion of other believers. The visual, visceral impact of all of these things ends up placing an idol alongside the living God. Biblical iconoclasm rules out visual and emotional competition with the true focus of worship, human repentance, and divine mercy. Christ's once-and-for-all sacrifice for our

18. O'Brien, *Hebrews*, 521, writes, "There is little evidence that the term was used for the Eucharist until the second century, and it is surprising that there is no treatment of the Lord's Supper in this context, even to correct false views of the community meal." Hughes, *Hebrews*, 577, writes, "The term 'altar' is nowhere in the New Testament associated with the institution or the observance of the Lord's Supper, nor is it found as a synonym for the eucharistic table—indeed, it is perfectly plain that no altar was present when Christ inaugurated this sacrament in the upper room. And it is evident throughout this epistle that the author is not concerned to speak about the eucharist, though he might effectively have done so, had he wished." See also Bruce, *Hebrews*, 379.

sins is the reality that the unadorned altar anticipated throughout salvation history. George Herbert captures the sweep of salvation history in his poem *The Altar*, first published in 1633:

> A broken ALTAR, Lord thy servant rears,
> Made of a heart, and cemented with tears:
> Whose parts are as thy hand did frame;
> No workman's tool hath touched the same.
> A HEART alone
> Is such a stone,
> As nothing but
> Thy power doth cut.
> Wherefore each part
> Of my hard heart
> Meets in this frame,
> To praise thy Name:
> That, if I chance to hold my peace,
> These stones to praise thee may not cease.
> Oh let thy blessed SACRIFICE be mine,
> And sanctify this ALTAR to be thine.[19]

Like the unadorned altar in the wilderness Christ's sacrifice took place outside the camp. The pastor moves from worship to mission seamlessly. To be made holy through Christ's atoning sacrifice is to "go to him outside the camp, bearing the disgrace he bore." The way the sacrificial system was fulfilled in Christ becomes the model for the body of Christ's presence in the world.

> The high priest carries the blood of animals into the Most Holy Place as a sin offering, but the bodies are burned outside the camp. And so Jesus also suffered outside the city gate to make the people holy through his own blood. Let us, then, go to him outside the camp, bearing the disgrace he bore. For here we do not have an enduring city, but we are looking for the city that is to come (Heb 13:11–14).

Christ's bodily sacrifice is identified with the leftover bodily remains of the ancient atonement sacrifice. As prescribed by the Law the high priest entered the Most Holy Place and sprinkled the animal's blood on the atonement cover. Instructions were given for what to do with the

---

19. Herbert, *The Country Parson*, 139. George Herbert (1593–1633) served as an Anglican priest in rural England. Note the many implicit biblical references in his poem (Ps 51:17; Deut 27:2–6; 2 Cor 3:2–3; Ezek 36:25–27; Zech 7:12: Lk 19:40).

animal carcass. "The bull and the goat for the sin offerings, whose blood was brought into the Most Holy Place to make atonement, must be taken outside the camp; their hides, flesh, and intestines are to be burned up. The man who burns them must wash his clothes and bathe himself with water, afterward he may come into camp" (Lev 16:27–28).

Linking Christ's sacrifice "outside the gate" with the discarded refuse of the Levitical sacrifice must have been as shocking to second generation believers as Jesus' words, "Unless you eat the flesh of the Son of Man and drink his blood, you have no life in you" (John 6:53) were to his original disciples. Christian theology cannot get any more iconoclastic than that. It is not we who go to God, but God who comes to us. Jesus identifies "with the world in its unholiness," even as he continues to be condemned by the religious of all religions as a blasphemer and troublemaker (Mark 16:63–64; Matt 27:64–65).[20] Jesus is the outsider, standing aloof from any and all religious means to God, bringing salvation through his death and resurrection.

The example of Jesus who "suffered outside the camp" compels his followers to do likewise. "Let us, then, go to him outside the camp, bearing the disgrace he bore" (Heb 13:13). For the pastor's hearers this meant "departure from the old Jewish order of their upbringing." They were to leave behind the "first and purest" form of religion which had been designed by God as a provisional system that had fulfilled its purpose.[21] For Christ's followers today it means leaving behind "the religious establishment, whether of Judaism or of a distorted Christianity."[22] Society values visible religious practices and the need for "impressive buildings, rituals, altars, vestments, and the like," but Christ has upended the need for religious externals and focused on our inner personal relationship with himself. "God has never made anything more beautiful than a genuinely holy person whose inner commitment and fellowship with Christ is visibly evidenced by a loving spirit, a humble attitude, a forgiving heart and a moral walk."[23] The visibility of the gospel lies not in buildings and rituals but in Christ and his body. The Apostle John wrote, "No one has ever seen God, but the one and only Son, who is himself God and is in closest relationship with the Father, has made him known" (John 1:18).

20. Hughes, *Hebrews*, 579.
21. Ibid., 580.
22. Stedman, *Hebrews*, 154.
23. Ibid., 155.

The invisible God's visibility is revealed today in and through the body of believers marked by the love of Christ. "No one has ever seen God; but if we love one another, God lives in us and his love is made complete in us" (1 John 4:12). James agrees, "Religion that God our Father accepts as pure and faultless is this: to look after orphans and widows in their distress and to keep oneself from being polluted by the world" (Jas 1:27).

The only way to "go and make disciples of all nations" is for Christ's followers to "go outside the camp, bearing the disgrace he bore" (Matt 28:19; Heb 13:13). "This distinctive summons is equivalent to Jesus' call to discipleship, which involves taking up the cross, self-denial, shame, and disgrace (Matt 10:38; Mark 8:34; Luke 14:26–27).[24] We are motivated to take up our cross and follow him not to make the worldly wilderness our new home, but because we are "looking forward to the city with the foundations, whose architect and builder is God" (11:10). The church is not a sacred compound holding religious services to make people feel better about themselves and to soothe bad consciences. The church is a pilgrim people, a sojourning people, who know that they are resident aliens in their home cultures. In this world we do not have "an enduring city, but we are looking for the city that is to come" (Heb 13:14).

Our goal is not to simply identify with the poor and the oppressed or expose systemic evil, although this is a necessary and important part of Christian witness. Nor is it our job to harp on how bad the world is, even though the world is evil through and through. If our message is all rebuke and castigation, how will the world hear the good news of Jesus Christ and see the gospel lived out in the lives of Christ's faithful followers? Orlando Costas warns us not to misconstrue Christian solidarity with the outcast and the oppressed "as the ultimate goal" of Christ's mission. Costas reminds us that "the exhortation to move outside and participate in the suffering of the crucified Son of God is grounded on the vision of 'the city which is to come' (Heb 13:14)." The wilderness is not our permanent dwelling, but "service therein is a checkpoint on the way to the new Jerusalem."[25] Costas sees two dangers. On the one hand we don't want "to use the cause of evangelism to build ecclesiastical compounds that insulate Christians from the basic issues of life and impede them" from taking up their cross and following Jesus. On the other hand we don't want to "sell our missional birthright for the mess of pottage of

---

24. O'Brien, *Hebrews*, 524.

25. Costas, *Christ Outside the Gate*, 193.

a cheap social activism." Instead, Costas challenges, "let us be prophets of hope in a world of disillusionment and false dreams, pressing forward to the city of God—the world of true justice and real peace, of unfeigned love and authentic freedom."[26]

We move from the legacy of biblical leadership (Heb 13:7) to Christ-centered worship (13:8–12), to God's mission for us "outside the camp" (13:13), and then back again to worship (13:15), mission (13:16), and leadership (13:17). At every point Christ is the center of congregational life. He is the same yesterday and today and forever. He is the altar that makes us holy, the model for our mission, and the reason "we are looking for the city that is to come" (13:14). There is no trade-off between worship and mission; what is good for worship, is good for mission and what is good for mission is good for worship. First, the call to worship: "Through Jesus, therefore, let us continually offer to God a sacrifice of praise—the fruit of lips that openly profess his name" (13:15). Then, the call to mission: "And do not forget to do good and to share with others, for with such sacrifices God is pleased" (13:16).

Prayer and Postscript

The pastor has remained hidden behind his pulpit. His passion for Christ is revealed, but his ego has not been exposed. We have been drawn to Christ, not his personality. His persuasive and powerful case for perseverance has been based on the power of the word of God, not on his performance. He has not wowed us; he has inspired us to share in his "diligence to the end" (Heb 6:11). He has loved us as only a passionate and conscientious pastor can do, by delivering the pure and unadulterated word of God. He has driven home his partnership with us, his brothers and sisters in Christ, by inviting us to join him in the long obedience to the end. He does not want to win people to himself, he wants to win people to Christ. From beginning to end his sermon is a demonstration of how we should pay attention to "so great a salvation" (Heb 2:3). His hortatory subjunctive, "Let us . . . ," punctuates his proclamation at every strategic point.

But now he comes out from behind the pulpit as it were and asks for prayer. "Pray for us. We are sure that we have a clear conscience and desire to live honorably in every way. I particularly urge you to pray so

26. Ibid., 194.

that I may be restored to you soon" (Heb 13:18–19). The request is personal. The reference to "us" is a literary device deflecting attention away from any hint of self-centeredness, but it also reflects the pastor's keen sense of community. He is not alone in this gospel endeavor. He is always "together in Christ" with the "sons and daughters" of God. He asks for prayer, not because he senses any deficiency in fulfilling his pastoral responsibility, but because he wants to do more for God's kingdom work.

In fact, what he really wants more than anything is to be "restored" to them soon, clearly implying that "he was part of their congregational life."[27] He tries to make the most of his absence by sending a written version of the sermon he would have liked to have delivered in person. "Brothers and sisters, I urge (παρακαλῶ) you to bear with my word of exhortation (παρακλήσεως), for in fact I have written to you quite briefly" (Heb 13:22). The encouraging news about Timothy's release from prison makes him hopeful that he will come with Timothy to see them soon.[28] Until then, he sends greetings, along with believers from Italy, to "all your leaders and all the Lord's people" (Heb 13:24). "Grace be with you all" (Heb 13:25).

His personal prayer request opens the way for his congregational prayer and the benediction to follow is one of the most beautiful in the New Testament. F. F. Bruce identifies it as "a gathered-prayer" or collect consisting of six parts. First, the invocation, "Now may the God of peace;" second, the basis for the petition, "who through the blood of the eternal covenant brought back from the dead our Lord Jesus, that great Shepherd of the sheep;" third, the main petition, "equip you with everything good for doing his will;" fourth, a subsidiary petition, "and may he work in us what is pleasing to him;" fifth, the prayed out reminder that all of this is possible *"through Jesus Christ." It is only through, by and because* of Jesus Christ that God's will can be accomplished in his people.[29] Sixth, a doxology, "to whom be glory for ever and ever. Amen."[30]

In this prayer the pastor not only gathers and focuses the people, but he gathers up the truths of the sermon—all the exposition and all the

27. O'Brien, *Hebrews*, 532.

28. The consensus of scholars identifies this Timothy as the Apostle Paul's companion (Acts 16:1–2; 17:14–15; 18:5; 19:22; 20:4; 1 Cor 4:17; 16:10; Phil 2:19; 1 Thess 3:2, 6; 1 Tim 1:1–3; 2 Tim 1:1–2; 2 Cor 1:1; Phil 1:1; Col 1:1–2; 1 Thess 1:1; 2 Thess 1:1; Phlm 1).

29. Cockerill, *Hebrews*, 718.

30. Bruce, *Hebrews*, 386.

exhortation—and presents it before the Lord Jesus Christ for his blessing. Like the saints who have gone before, we hear in these brief and poignant phrases the salvation symphony. Each line lifts up a central truth. Like the Lord Jesus, the pastor has told us these things, so that in Christ we may have peace. He echoes Jesus' words to his disciples when he said, "In this world you will have trouble. But take heart! I have overcome the world" (John 16:33). This is the peace that only Christ can give, the God-given peace, that grounds the sermon's clarion call to all believers to remain confident and hopeful to the end. The "blood of the eternal covenant" captures in a phrase the supremacy of Christ over the Law, Aaron's priest-hood, the tabernacle, the sacrificial system, and the whole old order. The atoning work of Christ on the cross was forever vindicated and validated by the exaltation of Jesus, who "after he had provided purification for sins, he sat down at the right hand of the Majesty in heaven" (1:1). Even as God brought up Israel from Egypt, God brought up Jesus from the dead.[31] The resurrection of Jesus "plays a major role in Hebrews," albeit implicitly in the many allusions to "the power of [his] indestructible life" (Heb 7:16; see 5:7; 6:20; 7:8; 8:1; 10:12; 12:2).[32]

We have everything we need because the Lord is our Shepherd (Ps 23:1). He is the "great Shepherd of the sheep." He is "the good shepherd [who] lays down his life for the sheep" (John 10:11). In him the promises of Psalm 23 are fulfilled. He provides rest and provision for our lives: "He makes me lie down in green pastures, he leads me beside quiet waters, he refreshes my soul." He guides us in righteousness: "He guides me along the right paths for his name's sake." He comforts us in crisis: "Even though I walk through the deepest, darkest valley, I will fear no evil, for you are with me; your rod and staff they comfort me." His hospitality provides fellowship and security: "You prepare a table before me in the presence of my enemies." He calls us into significant work: "You anoint my head with oil; my cup overflows." His providence blesses us with his goodness: "Surely goodness and love will follow me all the days of my life." He is our everlasting security and joy in community and worship: "And I will dwell in the house of the Lord forever."

When we say, "the Lord is my shepherd, I shall not want," we ac-knowledge that our primary source of rest, guidance, comfort, fellow-ship, significance, goodness, and security comes from the Lord Jesus. The

31. Cockerill, *Hebrews*, 715.
32. Schreiner, *Hebrews*, 428.

pastor knows that pastors make poor substitutes for the risen Lord, but they make good shepherds if they keep challenging us to fix "our eyes on Jesus, the pioneer and perfecter of faith" (Heb 12:2). Their job is to guide us to the great Shepherd, because only he is able to equip us with everything good for doing his will, and work in us what is pleasing to him (Heb 13:21). The pastor knows that it is only "through Jesus Christ" that we can be empowered to draw near to God. Only he can inspire us to hold unswervingly to the hope we profess. Only he can spur us on to love and good deeds (Heb 10:24), and only he can embolden us "to go to him outside the camp, bearing the disgrace he bore" (Heb 13:13). The end of religion and faithfulness to the end is only possible through Jesus Christ, to whom be glory forever and ever. Amen.

Take Up Take Up Your Cross, the Savior Said [33]

Take up your cross, the Savior said, if you would my disciples be;
Take up your cross with willing heart, and humbly follow after me.
Take up your cross; let not its weight fill your weak spirit with alarm;
Christ's strength shall bear your spirit up and brace your heart and nerve your arm.
Take up your cross; heed not the shame, and let your foolish pride be still;
The Lord for you accepted death upon a cross on Calv'ry's hill.
Take up your cross, then, in Christ's strength, and calmly ev'ry danger brave:
It guides you to abundant life and leads to vic'try o'er the grave.

CHARLES WILLIAM EVEREST, 1833

33. McKim, ed., *The Presbyterian Hymnal*, 393.

Appendix

Practical Suggestions for the Household of Faith

Let us draw near to God. . . . Let us spur one another on to love and good deeds

1. Focus on the basics: teaching the Word, building relationships, engaging in worship, and learning to pray. Prioritize multi-generational worship and cross-cultural mission. In an effort to take God more seriously than budgets and buildings, build the leadership team on the foundation of prayer and Bible study.

2. Discover how God-centered worship is the most effective tool in evangelism, fellowship, disciple-making, and mission. Make worship the chief goal of God's mission in your congregation. Learn to pray the psalms and cultivate a comprehensive vision of life that proclaims Jesus is Lord. Use the psalms to focus devotional meditation, to guide the call to worship, and to give depth to corporate worship. Bring all those involved in directing the worship services together for monthly prayer and planning sessions.

3. Emphasize the importance of the sabbath principle for the rhythm and pattern of family and personal life. Reclaim Sunday from sport and shopping for the sake of spiritual growth, fellowship, and worship. This can be done positively through teaching and personal example, rather than dogmatically and legalistically. Do not fill Sunday with church meetings.

4. Nurture a congregation of worshipers by weaning people from a spectator mentality and a performance expectation. Move away

from entertaining, crowd-pleasing performances. Look at worship as an integrated whole, rather than component parts. Diminish the master-of-ceremonies role in favor of a liturgy that focuses on God through great hymns, songs of praise, prayer, preaching, and Holy Communion. Begin worship with a call to worship, include prayers of confession and intercession. Identify the Lord as the audience of your worship, not the religious consumer.

5. Restore to preaching its true purpose of guiding people in the whole counsel of God. Overcome the unwarranted distinction between preaching and teaching and edification and evangelism. The Bible is far more than a starting point for a series of illustrations and anecdotes. Preaching should be biblical teaching that moves, comforts, instructs, and challenges the body of believers. Authentic preaching will also be effective in answering questions and concerns of earnest seekers. Solid preaching that edifies and inspires believers is the best form of evangelism. Feeding a congregation a constant diet of entry-level evangelism neither builds up believers nor wins true converts.

6. Permit seekers and strangers easy access to information about the church. Designate key people, who are gifted in building relationships, to help befriend newcomers. Create a non-pressured approach to new people that will avoid both forced friendliness and uncaring anonymity. Personally invite visitors to a home fellowship group or a special gathering where they can meet the leadership team. Show people love, but do not chase them or cling to them.

7. Integrate the proclamation of the Word of God on Sunday morning with small-group ministries and youth programs. Not only is good preaching shaped by the Word of God from beginning to end, it also shapes the biblical community. The Bible ought to shape the leadership and administrative culture of the church. Real preaching enlivens the whole church to God's mission in the world.

8. Start early in training children to hear and interact with the Word of God. Move away from amusing young people and socializing adults. Encourage young people and adults to prepare for Sunday school and small group fellowships by working through a Bible study lesson. This will increase thoughtful participation and deepen the church's appreciation for the Word of God. Mentor parents to become their

children's primary spiritual directors. Pastoral care begins in the home.

9. Use the sacraments of the church, baptism and Holy Communion, in a theologically thoughtful way. Whether a particular church adheres to believer's baptism by immersion or covenantal infant baptism, the church has the opportunity and the responsibility of affirming the meaning and integrity of personal commitment to Christ. The sacraments should be preserved from a perfunctory administration. Leaders should meet with individuals and families who desire baptism and use this as an occasion to strengthen faith in Christ.

10. Educate people in a disciple-making process that begins early and extends through life. Show practical interest in how the Christian life is worked out in the home and at work. Special studies led by mature believers for Christians in business, retail sales, law, science, medicine, education, law enforcement, and the arts will help people think Christianly about their vocations.

11. Prepare high school students to understand their culture from a Christian worldview. Using the Word of God, interact with the events, philosophies, music, and personalities of the culture. Students should have at least a basic understanding of God and humanity, good and evil, pain and suffering, salvation and death. Carefully work through one of the Gospel accounts to develop a clear understanding of the life and purpose of Jesus.

12. Encourage mission trips. Begin close to home. These may include inner-city soup kitchens, nursing homes, hospitals, and daycare centers. Before students and adults go on African and Asian mission trips they ought to become involved in local ministries. There are many opportunities to minister in the name of Christ without going far from home.

13. Network with believers from other cultures and with missionaries. Develop a direct relationship with a church or churches in another culture. This may mean a close relationship with an inner-city church, where members of a suburban church teach tutorials and help meet physical needs, while members of the urban church teach Sunday school classes at the suburban church. Build genuine friendships across cultural and ethnic boundaries for the sake of the kingdom. This will change the way we pray and use the Lord's money.

14. Pray to the Holy Spirit for an openness and sensitivity to the dynamic of God's work in your church. Ask the Lord to lead you to people in need: single parents, widows, international students, young parents with disabled children, foster parents, and the unemployed. The unevangelized are everywhere, but it is often at the point of obvious need where people are most receptive to the gospel of Christ.

15. Expect the household of faith to evangelize through its counter-cultural distinctiveness, rather than through cultural accommodation. Remember, it is God's called-out, visible community, set apart to be salt and light in a dark world. Quietly refuse to accommodate by catering to the world's expectations. When the church gathers, it is for the purpose of glorifying and praising God. Weddings and funerals are not social services to the community; they are God-centered worship services. They can be done in integrity.

16. Reverse the trend that makes the pastor more a manager than a theologian, more an administrator that a spiritual director, more a master of ceremonies than a worship leader. Under the auspices of the leadership team, delegate administrative responsibilities to gifted, capable people. Develop a team ministry approach that relies on the spiritual gifts and commitments of mature believers. Encourage the priesthood of all believers while maintaining the authority of the pastoral team.

17. Offer training for prospective leaders based on the biblical rationale, description, and expectation of leadership in the household of faith. Develop a mentoring relationship between mature, gifted leaders and potential leaders. In all areas of church life, appoint leaders who are holy in character and spiritually wise. Constituency representation should not be a primary qualification for leadership in the household of faith.

18. Encourage membership in the body of Christ through a nurturing fellowship, rather than an informational program. Inclusion in the church is on the basis of a clear confession of faith in Christ and baptism. Membership classes stress personal commitment and responsibility to the church and its mission. Spiritual direction emphasizes the priesthood of all believers, every-member ministry, and the immense value of ministry outside the four walls of the church in the "secular" arena.

19. Practice preventative and corrective church discipline. Encourage nonthreatening conversations with church members about their walk with God, their growth in Christ, and their ministry responsibilities. Confront, rather than overlook, sinful behavior. Do this in a manner and spirit true to the counsel of the Word of God. Express a genuine concern for individual believers and the integrity of the household of faith, so that Christians will not be left in their sin and the witness of Christ will not be distorted.

20. Remember that the life of the church and the growth of the body are under God's sovereign care. It is our responsibility to actively participate in the divine patience—waiting, watching, working in the tradition and example of our Lord Jesus Christ. We make it our goal to do everything the Jesus way.

Bibliography

Allen, R. Michael, and Scott R. Swain. "In Defense of Proof-Texting." *Journal of the Evangelical Theological Society* 54.3 (September 2011) 589–606.

Aitken, Jonathan. *John Newton: From Disgrace To Amazing Grace*. Wheaton, IL: Crossway, 2007.

Attridge, H. W. *The Epistle to the Hebrews: A Commentary on the Epistle to the Hebrews*. Philadelphia: Fortress, 1989.

Augustine, "On Christian Doctrine," Book 4:6, *Nicene and Post-Nicene Fathers*, vol. 2, Edited by Philip Schaff. Peabody, MA: Hendrickson, 1995.

Baillie, Donald M. *God Was In Christ*. New York: Scribner, 1948.

Barna, George. *Revolution: Finding Vibrant Faith Beyond The Walls Of The Sanctuary*. Carol Stream, IL: Tyndale, 206.

Barth, Karl. *Dogmatics in Outline*. New York: Harper & Row, 1959.

———. *The Epistle To The Romans*. Translated by Edwyn C. Hoskyns. New York: Oxford University Press, 1968.

———. *Theology and Church: Shorter Writings 1920–1928*. Eugene, OR: Wipf and Stock, 2015.

Barth, Markus. "The Old Testament in Hebrews." In *Current Issues In New Testament Interpretation*, edited by William Klassen and Grayden F. Snyder, 53–78. New York: Harper & Brothers, 1962.

Bauckham, Richard. "The Divinity of Jesus Christ in the Epistle of Hebrews." In *The Epistle to the Hebrews and Christian Theology*, edited by Richard Bauckham and Daniel Driver, 15–36. Grand Rapids: Eerdmans, 2009.

Baxter, Richard. *The Reformed Pastor*. Edited by William Brown. Carlisle, PA: The Banner of Truth, 1656.

Blamires, Harry. *The Christian Mind*. London: SPCK, 1978.

Bloesch, Donald G. *Essentials of Evangelical Theology, vol 1: God, Authority, and Salvation*. San Francisco: Harper & Row, 1978.

Bonhoeffer, Dietrich. *A Testament To Freedom*. Edited by Geffrey Kelly and Burton Nelson. New York: Harper, 1995.

———. *Life Together*. Translated by John Doberstein. San Francisco: Harper, 1954.

———. *Spiritual Care*. Translated by Jay C. Rochelle. Minneapolis: Fortress, 1985.

———. *The Cost of Discipleship*. New York: Macmillan, 1963.

Borger, Joyce, Martin Tel, John D. Witvliet, eds. *Lift Up Your Hearts: Psalms, Hymns, and Spiritual Songs*. Grand Rapids: Faith Alive Christian Resources, 2013.

Brand, Paul, and Philip Yancey. "Blood: The Miracle of Life." *Christianity Today,* February 18 and March 4, 1983, 12–15, 38–42.

Bretall, Robert, ed. *A Kierkegaard Anthology.* Princeton, NJ: Princeton University Press, 1973.

Brooks, David. "The Ultimate Spoiler Alert." Commencement Address, Dartmouth College, June 14, 2015.

Brown, Brené. "8 Questions." Interviewed by Belinda Luscombe. *Time* (September 21, 2015) 88.

Brown, H. Jackson., Jr. *Life's Little Instruction Book.* Nashville, Tennessee: Rutledge Hill, 1991.

Brown, Raymond. *The Message of Hebrews.* Downers Grove, IL: IVP, 1982.

Bruce, F. F. *The Epistle to the Hebrews.* Grand Rapids: Eerdmans, 1990.

Buchanan, Mark. *Things Unseen.* Sisters, OR: Multnomah, 2002.

Calvin, John. *Institutes of the Christian Religion*, vol 2. Translated by Henry Beveridge. Grand Rapids: Eerdmans, 1979.

———. *The Epistle of Paul the Apostle to the Hebrews and the First and Second Epistles of Peter.* Grand Rapids: Eerdmans, 1994.

Carr, Nicholas. "Is Google Making Us Stupid?" *The Atlantic,* July/August 2008. http://www.theatlantic.com/doc/print/200807/google.

Carson, Donald. "Athen Revisited." In *Telling the Truth: Evangelizing Postmoderns.* Grand Rapids, MI: Zondervan, 2000. Accessed online at http://www.monergism.com/athens-revisited-exegetical-study-acts-17-da-carson.

Chapell, Bryan. *Christ-Centered Preaching: Redeeming the Expository Sermon.* Grand Rapids: Baker, 2005.

Cockerill, Gareth Lee. *The Epistle To The Hebrews.* Grand Rapids: Eerdmans, 2012.

Cole, Graham A. *The God Who Became Human: A Biblical Theology of the Incarnation.* Downers Grove, IL: InterVarsity, 2013.

Costas, Orlando E. *Christ Outside the Gate: Mission Beyond Christendom.* New York: Orbis, 1982.

Craigie, Peter C. *Psalms 1-50: Word Biblical Commentary*, vol. 19. Waco, TX: Word, 1983.

Creswell, Julie. "Investors Hope to Ride Swell of SoulCycle Fever in Coming I.P.O." *The New York Times,* August 20, 2015.

Deering, Edward. "The Reflections of Edward Deering on Hebrews." http://quod.lib.umich.edu/e/eebo/A20304.0001.001/1:3?rgn=div1;view=fulltext.

Denham, Michael Thomas. *Reverberating Word: The Concept and Role of Expository Worship at the National Presbyterian Church.* D. Min. dissertation, Beeson Divinity School, May 2015.

Denny, James. *The Death of Christ.* Edited by R. V. G. Tasker. Wheaton, IL: Tyndale, 1951.

Dickinson, Emily. *The Complete Poems of Emily Dickinson.* Edited by Thomas H. Johnson. New York: Little, Brown and Company. 1960.

Donne, John. *John Donne: Selected Poetry.* Edited by John Carey. Oxford: Oxford University Press, 1998.

Douthat, Ross. *Bad Religion: How We Became A Nation of Heretics.* New York: Free Press, 2012.

Dreyfus, Hubert, and Sean Dorrance Kelly. *All Things Shining: Reading the Western Classics to Find Meaning in a Secular Age.* New York: Free Press, 2011.

Dunn, James D. G. *Romans 1–8: Word Biblical Commentary*, vol. 38A. Waco, TX: Word, 1988.

Edwards, James R. *The Gospel According to Mark*. Grand Rapids: Eerdmans, 2001.

Edwards, Jonathan. *The Excellency of Christ*. http://www.ccel.org/edwards/sermons. excellency.html.

Eiseley, Loren. "The Cosmic Orphan." *Propedia, Encyclopedia Britannica*, 139–41. Chicago: Encyclopedia Britannica Inc., 1974.

Evans, Louis H., Jr. *Hebrews: The Communicator's Commentary*, vol. 10. Dallas: Word, 1985.

Forbis, Wesley L., ed. *The Baptist Hymnal*. Nashville: Convention, 1981.

Forsyth, P. T. *God: The Holy Father*. Blackwood, South Australia: New Creation, 1987.

———. *Positive Preaching and Modern Mind*. 2nd ed. London: Hodder and Stoughton, 1909.

———. *The Soul of Prayer*. 5th imp. London: Independent, 1966.

France, R. T. *The Gospel of Matthew*. Grand Rapids: Eerdmans, 2007.

Gagnon, Robert A. J. "The Bible and Homosexual Practice: Theology, Analogies, and Genes." *Theology Matters*, vol. 7, no. 6, November/December 2001, 1–13.

Gardiner, John Eliot. *Bach: Music in the Castle of Heaven*. New York: Knopf, 2013.

Gillquist, Peter. "A Marathon We Are Meant to Win." *Christianity Today* (October, 1981) 22–23.

Goetz, David. *Death by Suburb: How to Keep the Suburbs from Killing your Soul*. San Francisco: HarperCollins, 2006.

Goppelt, Leonhard. *A Commentary on 1 Peter*. Translated by J. E. Alsup. Grand Rapids: Eerdmans, 1993.

Greidanus, Sidney. *Preaching Christ from the Old Testament: A Contemporary Hermeneutical Method*. Grand Rapids: Eerdmans, 1999.

Grounds, Vernon. "Faith for Failure: A Meditation on Motivation for Ministry." *TSF Bulletin* (March–April, 1986) 4–5.

Guthrie, Donald. *Hebrews: Tyndale New Testament Commentaries*, vol. 15. Downers Grove: IVP, 1983.

Guthrie, George H. *Hebrews: The NIV Application Commentary*. Grand Rapids: Zondervan, 1998.

———. "Hebrews." *In Commentary on the New Testament Use of the Old Testament*, edited by G. K. Beale and D. A. Carson, 919–95. Grand Rapids: Baker, 2007.

Herbert, George. *The Country Parson, The Temple*. Edited by John Wall. New York: Paulist, 1981.

Hoekema, Anthony A. *The Four Major Cults*. Grand Rapids: Eerdmans, 1963.

Hughes, Philip Edgcumbe. *A Commentary On The Epistle To The Hebrews*. Grand Rapids: Eerdmans, 1977.

Huntemann, George. *The Other Bonhoeffer: An Evangelical Reassessment of Dietrich Bonhoeffer*. Grand Rapids: Baker, 1993.

Hunter, George. *Radical Outreach: The Recovery of Apostolic Ministry and Evangelism*. Nashville: Abingdon, 2003.

Hunter, James Davison. *To Change the World: The Irony, Tragedy, and Possibility of Christianity in the Late Modern World*. New York: Oxford University Press, 2010.

Jenkins, Philip. *The Lost History of Christianity*. New York: Harper-Collins, 2008.

Jobes, Karen H. *Letters to the Church*. Grand Rapids: Zondervan, 2011.

———. *1 Peter. Baker Exegetical Commentary on the New Testament.* Grand Rapids: Baker, 2005.

Johnson, Luke Timothy. *Hebrews: A Commentary.* Louisville: Westminster John Knox, 2006.

———. "Hebrews' Challenge to Christians: Christology and Discipleship." In *Preaching Hebrews,* edited by David Fleer and Dave Bland, 11–28. Abilene, TX: ACU Press, 2003.

Kapolyo Joe. "Matthew." *Africa Bible Commentary.* Edited by Tokunboh Adeyemo. Grand Rapids: Zondervan, 2006.

Keller, Timothy J. *Center Church: Doing Balanced, Gospel-Centered Ministry in Your City.* Grand Rapids: Zondervan, 2012.

———. *Preaching: Communicating Faith in an Age of Skepticism.* New York: Viking, 2015.

Kelly, J. N. D. *Early Christian Doctrine.* London: A. and C. Black, 1958.

Kierkegaard, Søren. *Attack Upon 'Christendom.'* Princeton, NJ: Princeton University Press, 1968.

———. *Parables of Kierkegaard.* Edited by Thomas C. Oden. Princeton, NJ: Princeton University Press, 1989.

———. *The Present Age, and Of the Difference Between a Genius and an Apostle.* Translated by Alexander Dru. New York: Harper Torchbooks, 1962.

———. *Training in Christianity.* Princeton, NJ: Princeton University Press, 1957.

Kinnier, Richard. *The Meaning of Life.* London: Palazzo Editions, 2010.

Kirkpatrick, A. F. *Commentary on the Psalms.* London: Cambridge University Press, 1947.

Lane, William L. *Hebrews: Word Biblical Commentary,* vols 1–2. Dallas: Word, 1991.

Lewis, C. S. *Miracles.* London: Fontana, 1972.

———. *The Problem of Pain.* New York: MacMillan, 1962.

———. *The Weight of Glory.* New York: Collier, 1965.

Litfin, Duane. *Conceiving The Christian College.* Grand Rapids: Eerdmans, 2004.

Long, Thomas G. *Hebrews: Interpretation: A Bible Commentary for Teaching and Preaching.* Louisville: Westminster John Knox, 2011.

Longenecker, Richard N. *The Christology of Early Jewish Christianity.* London: SCM, 1970.

Lovelace, Richard. "Evangelicalism: Recovering a Tradition of Spiritual Depth." *The Reformed Journal,* September 1990, 25–26.

Luther, Martin. "Third Christmas Sermon." In *The Complete Sermons of Martin Luther,* vol. 3, 166–93. Grand Rapids: Baker, 2000.

Marshall, Colin, and Tony Payne. *The Trellis and the Vine: The Ministry Mind-Shift That Changes Everything.* Kingsford, Australia: Matthias Media, 2009.

Massey, James Earl. *Preaching from Hebrews: Hermeneutical Insights & Homiletical Helps.* Anderson, IN: Warner, 2014.

McKim, LindaJo H., ed. *The Presbyterian Hymnal: Psalms, Hymns, and Spiritual Songs.* Louisville: Westminster John Knox, 1993.

Millar, Gary, and Phil Campbell. *Saving Eutychus: How to Preach God's Word and Keep People Awake.* Kingsford, Australia: Matthias Media, 2013.

Nicholi, Armand M., Jr. *The Question of God: C. S. Lewis and Sigmund Freud Debate God, Love, Sex, And The Meaning of Life.* New York: The Free Press, 2002.

Niebuhr, H. Richard. *The Kingdom of God in America.* New York: Harper, 1953.

O'Brien, Peter T. *The Letter To The Hebrews.* Grand Rapids: Eerdmans, 2010.

O'Connor, Flannery. "The Catholic Novelist in the South." In *Flannery O'Connor: Collected Works*, 853–64. New York: The Library of America, 1988.

Old, Hughes Oliphant. *The Reading and Preaching of the Scriptures: in the Worship of the Christian Church, vol. 2: The Patristic Age.* Grand Rapids: Eerdmans, 1998.

Pelikan, Jaroslav, and Hotchkiss, Valerie, eds. *Creeds and Confessions of Faith in the Christian Tradition,* vol. 1. New Haven, CT: Yale University Press, 2003.

Peterson, Eugene H. *Christ Plays in Ten Thousand Places.* Grand Rapids: Eerdmans, 2009.

———. *Earth & Altar: The Community of Prayer in a Self-Bound Society.* Downers Grove, IL: InterVarsity, 1985.

———. *Eat This Book: A Conversation in the Art of Spiritual Reading.* Grand Rapids: Eerdmans, 2009.

———. "Lashed to the mast." *Leadership.* Winter, 1996, 55–59.

———. *Leap Over A Wall: Earthly Spirituality for Everyday Christians.* San Francisco: Harper, 1997.

———. *The Message Remix.* Colorado Springs: NavPress, 2003.

———. *The Pastor: A Memoir.* New York: HarperCollins, 2011.

Roff, Lawrence, ed. *The Trinity Hymnal.* Philadelphia: Great Commission, 1990.

Rosner, B. S. "Biblical Theology." In *New Dictionary of Biblical Theology,* edited by T. Desmond Alexander, Brian S. Rosner, D. A. Carson, Graeme Goldsworthy, 3–11. Downers Grove, IL: InterVarsity, 2000.

Saucy, Robert L. *Minding the Heart: The Way of Spiritual Transformation.* Grand Rapids: Kregel, 2013.

Schreiner, Thomas R. *Commentary on Hebrews: Biblical Theology for Christian Proclamation.* Nashville: B&H, 2015.

Scotti, R. A. *Basilica: The Splendor and the Scandal: Building St. Peter's.* New York: Viking, 2006.

Seitz, Christopher R. *The Character of Christian Scripture: The Significance of a Two-Testament Bible.* Grand Rapids: Baker, 2011.

Shoeller, Martin. "Perfect Form." *The New Yorker,* August 21 and 28, 2000, 120–21.

Shorney, George, William G. Shorney, Jack Schraeder, David L. Weck, and Jane Holstein, eds. *Worship and Rejoice.* Carol Stream, IL: Hope, 2001.

Sire, James W. *Praying the Psalms of Jesus.* Downers Grove, IL: InterVarsity, 2007.

Smedes, Lewis. "A Man After God's Own Heart: David Hubbard." Fuller Magazine, 1996, 11.

Smith, Walter Chalmers. "Immortal, Invisible, God Only Wise." In *The Celebration Hymnal,* edited by Tom Fettke, 33. Waco, TX: Word/Integrity, 1997.

Stedman, Ray C. *Hebrews.* Downers Grove, IL: InterVarsity, 1992.

Stott, John. *Between Two Worlds: The Art of Preaching in the Twentieth Century.* Grand Rapids: Eerdmans, 1982.

———. *The Christian Counter-Culture: The Message of the Sermon on the Mount.* Downers Grove, IL: InterVarsity, 1978.

———. *Christian Mission in the Modern World.* Downers Grove, IL: InterVarsity, 1975.

———. *Romans: God's Good News for the World.* Downers Grove, IL: InterVarsity, 1995.

Taylor, Barbara Brown. *The Preaching Life.* Lanham, MD: Cowley, 1993.

Taylor, LaTonya. "The Church of O." *Christianity Today,* April 1, 2002, 44–45.

Tennent, Timothy C. "I Came, I Saw, I Loved: My Charge to the Asbury Theological Seminary Spring Graduating Class of 2015." http://timothytennent.

com/2015/06/03/i-came-i-saw-loved-my-charge-to-the-asbury-theological-seminary-spring-graduating-class-of-2015/.

———. "Gospel Clarity vs. 'The Fog.'" December 16, 2014. www.timothytennent.com.

———. *Invitation To World Missions: A Trinitarian Missiology for the Twenty-first Century*. Grand Rapids: Kregel, 2010.

Thielicke, Helmut. *The Evangelical Faith*. 3 vols. Grand Rapids: Eerdmans, 1977.

———. *The Trouble with the Church*. Translated by John W. Doberstein. Grand Rapids: Baker, 1965.

Todd, John M. *Luther: A Life*. New York: Crossroad, 1982.

Vanhoozer, Kevin J. *Faith Speaking Understanding: Performing the Drama of Doctrine*. Louisville: Westminster John Knox, 2014.

Walter, V. L. "Arianism." In *Evangelical Dictionary of Theology*, edited by Walter A. Elwell, 74–75. Grand Rapids: Baker, 1984.

Waters, Larry J., and Roy B. Zuck, eds. *Why O God?: Suffering and Disability in the Bible and Church*. Wheaton, IL: Crossway, 2011.

———. *The Spirit of the Disciplines*. San Francisco: Harper & Row, 1988.

Webber, Robert E. *Common Roots: A Call to Evangelical Maturity*. Grand Rapids: Zondervan, 1978.

Webster, Jeremiah. *Paradise in The Waste Land: T. S. Eliot*. Milwaukee: Wiseblood, 2013.

Wells, David F. *No Place For Truth*. Grand Rapids: Eerdmans, 1993.

White, R. E. O. "Salvation." In *Evangelical Dictionary of Theology*, edited by Walter Elwell, 967–69. Grand Rapids: Baker, 2010.

Wilberforce, William. *Real Christianity*. Edited by James M. Houston. Portland, OR: Multnomah.

Willard, Dallas. "Discipleship for Super-Christians Only?" *Christianity Today*, October 10, 1980, 24–25.

———. *The Spirit of the Disciplines: Understanding How God Changes Lives*. New York: HarperCollins, 1988.

Wilson, Edward O. *The Meaning of Human Existence*. New York: Liveright, 2014.

Wiman, Christian. *My Bright Abyss: Meditation of a Modern Believer*. New York: Farrar, Straus and Giroux, 2013.

Wood, Ralph C. *Contending for the Faith: The Church's Engagement with Culture*. Waco, TX: Baylor University Press, 2003.

Wright, Nicholas Thomas. *For All God's Worth: True Worship and the Call of the Church*. Grand Rapids: Eerdmans, 1997.

———. *Hebrews for Everyone*. Louisville: Westminster John Knox, 2004.

Zwingli, Huldrych. "Clarity and Certainty of the Word of God." In *Zwingli and Bullinger: The Library of Christian Classics*, vol. 24, edited by G. W. Bromiley, 49–95. Philadelphia: Westminster, 1953.